FORT PHIL KEARNY

An American Saga

Fort Phil Kearny

AN AMERICAN SAGA

DEE BROWN

UNIVERSITY OF NEBRASKA PRESS · LINCOLN

International Standard Book Number 0-8032-5730-9

First Bison Book edition: February 1971

*Bison Book edition reproduced from the 1962 edition published by
G. P. Putnam's Sons by arrangement with the author and the publisher.*

Manufactured in the United States of America

For L. L. B.

Contents

Illustrations follow page 128.

FORT PHIL KEARNY

An American Saga

I. April:

MOON WHEN THE GEESE LAY EGGS

My name is Henry B. Carrington: forty-three years of age, colonel Eighteenth U. S. Infantry, and now commanding post Fort McPherson, Nebraska, late commanding post Philip Kearny, Dakota Territory, and previously thereto commanding Mountain District, Department of the Platte, which command embraced the route from Fort Reno westward to Virginia City via the Big Horn and Yellowstone Rivers, and being the new route I occupied during the summer of 1866.[1]

SO began, on a spring day in 1867, Colonel Carrington's testimony before a commission convened at Fort McPherson to investigate the Fetterman Massacre of December 21, 1866. For several days Carrington defended his past actions, offering letters, records and reports relating to his command at Fort Phil Kearny, narrating a relentless procession of events which led to the violent deaths of three officers, seventy-six enlisted men and two civilians.

The Fetterman Massacre was the second battle in American history from which came no survivors, and was a nationally debated incident for ten years—until overshadowed by the Custer Massacre of 1876. Acting under orders from Colonel Carrington, Brevet-Colonel William Judd Fetterman led eighty men out of the gates of Fort Phil Kearny at 11:15 A.M. of that dark December day. Carrington's orders were explicit: relieve the wood train from Indian attack, but do not pursue the enemy beyond Lodge Trail Ridge.

At 11:45 A.M. Fetterman's command of forty-nine infantry-men and twenty-seven cavalrymen halted on the crest of Lodge Trail Ridge, with skirmishers out. The sky was bitter gray, thick-ening for snow, temperature dropping rapidly. A few minutes later Fetterman's rear guard disappeared from view of the fort, passing over the ridge, moving north. At 12 noon, almost as the bugler was sounding dinner call in the fort, sentinels at the gate heard firing from beyond Lodge Trail Ridge. Colonel Carring-ton was notified immediately. By the time the colonel had mounted the lookout tower above his headquarters, firing was continuous and rapid. Without further delay, Carrington or-dered Captain Tenodor Ten Eyck to move out to Fetterman's relief. At 12:45 P.M., Ten Eyck and seventy-six men reached the summit of a ridge overlooking Peno Creek. The valley was swarming with Indians, at least two thousand of them, probably more. One or two scattered shots rang out from the hill beyond; then there was no more firing, only the jubilant cries of Indians racing their ponies, some shouting derisively at Ten Eyck's troops, beckoning them to come down into the valley.

For several minutes Captain Ten Eyck could see no sign of Fetterman's command, neither the mounted nor dismounted men. Then as the Indians began withdrawing from the valley, an enlisted man cried: "There're the men down there, all dead!" [2]

Maintaining his position on high ground until the Indian forces had vanished northward, Ten Eyck then cautiously ad-vanced toward the battlefield. Near the Bozeman Road, dead men lay naked and mutilated, blood frozen in their wounds, in a circle about forty feet in diameter. They were mostly infantry-men. After loading the dead into his two ammunition wagons, Ten Eyck began a slow withdrawal to the fort, not reaching the gates until darkness was falling. The following morning, against the advice of his staff, Carrington led a second party out to the scene of battle and recovered the remaining bodies, mostly cavalrymen.

The full story of what happened in that brief hour of bloody carnage at high noon under the wintry sky of December 21, 1866, will never be known. During the years which followed, various Indian participants—Sioux, Cheyenne and Arapaho—told conflicting accounts of the battle. Yet the mystery is not so much what happened as why it happened. Why did Fetterman disobey Carrington's orders? Why did the cavalrymen leave the infantrymen to meet the full force of attack, and retire to high ground only to die a few minutes later as they had watched the infantrymen die? Why did the Indians retire from the field instead of attempting to annihilate Captain Ten Eyck's seventy-six men, a move which if successful would have left the fort vulnerable to immediate capture?

In the first place, why were Fetterman and his men there in that lonely, uncharted wilderness, 236 miles north of Fort Laramie, in a country which only one year earlier had been ceded by treaty to the tribes as inviolable Indian territory?

The commission investigating the Fetterman Massacre examined some of these questions directly, dwelling upon the necessity for three forts along the Bozeman Trail, debating whether or not the strength of Carrington's military force was sufficient, yet never more than hinting at reasons for opening this road through the Plains Indians' last unspoiled hunting ground.

The motivating factor of course was gold, which had been discovered in Montana in 1862, creating a rush to Virginia City through 1863 and 1864. During the Civil War, thousands of miners traveled to the diggings by two routes—either up the Missouri River by way of Fort Benton, or overland along the Platte Trail to Fort Hall and then doubling back into Montana Territory. These were roundabout routes, requiring weeks for passage. Public demand for a more direct route led two explorers in 1864 to mark out trails northward from Fort Laramie. Jim Bridger, aware of the Indians' determination to keep the white man out of their sacred Powder River country, avoided that area and led his party of trail blazers west of the Big Horn Mountains. John Bozeman, seeking an even more direct route, ran his wagons east of the Big Horns, straight through the heart of the hunting grounds.

Except for Indian resistance, Bozeman's route was by far the easier to travel, and by 1865 several parties of brave or foolhardy gold seekers risked their lives to make the crossing of what soon became known as the Montana Road.

In 1865, the Federal Government also became vitally interested in a direct route to the gold fields. After four years of Civil War, the United States Treasury was virtually bankrupt; gold was urgently needed to liquidate the accruing interest of the national debt. In hopes of encouraging more prospectors to make the journey to Montana, the government financed a survey for a direct route from Sioux City by way of the Niobrara River. Leader of this expedition of about one hundred men and 250 wagons was Colonel James A. Sawyer. The party included engineers and gold prospectors, and was escorted by two companies of former Confederate soldiers, who had sworn oaths of allegiance in exchange for release from military prisons.

Although Sawyer met with such strong Indian resistance that he was forced to abandon his original course, he finally reached Virginia City by following Bozeman's route much of the way. His official report, ordered printed by Congress in March 1866, received wide publicity and increased pressure from civilians to make the Montana Road safe for travel.[3] Recently discharged Civil War veterans were especially eager to journey west and seek their fortunes in the gold fields, but after surviving four years of war they were reluctant to fight their way there through tribes of hostile Indians.

In an effort to halt attacks upon travelers through the Powder River country, General Patrick E. Connor in the summer of 1865 led a three-pronged expedition northward into the Sioux country. Connor's orders to his officers were short and to the point: "You will not receive overtures of peace or submission from Indians, but will attack and kill every male Indian over twelve years of age." [4] Two of Connor's three columns suffered severely from Indian attacks; they lost many of their horses in night raids, and ran out of rations. The commander's own column managed to destroy one Arapaho village, and established a fort on the Powder that was first known as Fort Connor, later as Fort Reno.

But soon after Connor withdrew from the field, reports from Montana indicated that Indian resistance was more determined than ever along the overland route. "We thought it an impossibility to get through, and had to fight our way through," one correspondent wrote. "There is no place between Fort Reno and Virginia City where news can be sent. There will be no more travel on that road until the government takes care of the Indians. There is plenty of firewood, water and game, but the Indians won't let you use them." [5]

During the autumn of 1865, treaties were signed with several bands of Sioux, Cheyenne and Arapaho. Government representatives guaranteed tribal rights to territory lying between the Black Hills, the Big Horns and the Yellowstone—in exchange for the Indians' conceding white travelers safe passage through this Powder River country. The commissioners, however, overlooked the fact that almost all the treaty signers were peaceable Indians, chiefs who had already abandoned the warpath and were content to camp around the white man's forts and live off his handouts. White soldiers and warrior Indians alike referred to them contemptuously as "Laramie Loafers."

Under leadership of belligerent warriors such as Red Cloud, raids against white invaders of the Powder River country continued as before, and in the spring of 1866 the government sent a second treaty commission to Fort Laramie to offer new terms.

At the same time, in its slow, ponderous way the War Department was responding to pressures to police the Montana Road. The commander of the Department of the Missouri—which included the Powder River country—was Major-General John Pope, one of President Lincoln's unsuccessful commanders in the East. After disastrous defeat in the second battle of Bull Run, Pope had been sent west, and for three years had been battling Indians with little more success than he had had against Confederates. On March 10, 1866, Pope issued the following order:

> The 2nd Battalion, 18th U. S. Infantry, will constitute the garrison of Fort Reno on Powder River, and the two new posts on the route between that place and Virginia City in Mon-

tana. . . . At these posts the battalion will be distributed as follows: Four companies at Fort Reno and two companies at each of the other posts. The Colonel of the Regiment will take post at Fort Reno.[6]

The "colonel of the regiment" was Henry Beebe Carrington, and this order sealed the doom of the eighty-one men who died nine months later on Peno Creek. No more unlikely commander could have been selected for so dangerous a mission at that time or place than Colonel Carrington. In the spring of 1866, the United States Army was overstaffed to the point of absurdity with both permanent and breveted colonels and generals (literally hundreds of senior officers with three and four years of battle experience), many of them young men with West Point training. Yet Carrington had never heard a shot fired in combat; he had never commanded upon the field of action.

An ardent antislavery man practicing law in Ohio, he had organized the 18th Regiment with smooth efficiency during the first days after Fort Sumter, and was appointed colonel on May 14, 1861. His ability as a recruiter and organizer kept him in Ohio while his regiment moved south, and as the war wore on he was called to Indiana to establish prisoner-of-war camps, to deal with Copperheads and prosecute the leaders of the Northwest Conspiracy. Meanwhile the 18th Regiment, with other men acting in command, was winning an enviable record as a fighting unit. The 2nd Battalion came out of the Battle of Stone's River with half its officers and men dead or wounded. The junior officers who would serve later under Colonel Carrington at Fort Phil Kearny may have understood the reasons for his absence from the Civil War battlefields, but they never forgot that fact during the Wyoming ordeal of 1866.

Not until late in 1865, after all the battles were ended, did Colonel Carrington at last join his command. Determined to remain in military service, he shrewdly foresaw that future opportunities lay on the Indian frontier beyond the Mississippi. It was no mere chance that the 18th Infantry was the first regular regiment to reach the frontier; Carrington had been in a position during the war to make friends with men of considerable political influence in Washington. During the winter of

1865–66, eight companies of the 18th moved across the plains to occupy Fort Kearney,* Nebraska Territory, on the old Oregon Trail. Henry Carrington had finally achieved his dearest ambition, a military command in the field.

He was a small man physically (the Indians called him Little White Chief) with a dark beard and hair worn long, sensitive eyes set deep under a high forehead. Sickly as a youth, he had been unable to enter West Point. He went to Yale instead, where he was in ill health much of the time. Graduating in 1845, he took a position as teacher at Irving Institute, Tarrytown, New York.

The next year Carrington would have liked more than anything else to become a soldier in the war with Mexico, but instead he stayed in Tarrytown, meeting Washington Irving and serving for a time as that author's secretary. His brief acquaintanceship with Irving no doubt influenced his later ambition to become a writer. In 1847 he was back at Yale, teaching part-time and studying for a law degree.

A year later he made his big move—to Columbus, Ohio, where he began a successful legal career. He was fortunate in the choice of a law partner, William Dennison, who became Ohio's governor at the time of the Civil War. It was in Columbus that Carrington also met and married Margaret Irvin Sullivant, who would share with him the ordeal of Fort Phil Kearny.

This was the man, then, who largely through his own calculated actions had placed himself in position in the spring of 1866 to be chosen to lead the 2nd Battalion of the 18th Infantry into the heart of the most hostile Indian country of North America. Unfortunately neither he nor scarcely any other man of authority in the United States Government knew the real temper of the Plains Indians at that time.

In the years before 1850 the tribes had permitted settlers and

---

* Fort Kearney should not be confused with Fort Phil Kearny. Fort Kearney, Nebraska, established in 1849, was named for General Stephen W. Kearny. The second "e" in the name was used erroneously in so many official records that it became recognized as the standard spelling. Fort Phil Kearny, Dakota Territory (now Wyoming), was named for General Philip Kearny, Civil War hero, and was not established until the time of this narrative, 1866.

gold seekers to move across their lands with only an occasional raid. But when the invaders from the east built forts and chains of stations for overland stage routes, the Indians began to raid in earnest. To protect its westward-moving citizens, the government in 1851 invited leaders of the Sioux, Cheyenne, Arapaho, Crow, and other tribes to Fort Laramie for a peace conference. Treaties were signed giving the United States rights to maintain roads and forts across the plains, and reserving vast hunting areas for exclusive use of the various tribes.

Pressures upon these Indian lands continued, however, from white buffalo hunters and trappers, from gold seekers and settlers. In 1862 the Sioux in western Minnesota went to war with the settlers; in 1864 conflict in Colorado resulted in the massacre of the Cheyennes at Sand Creek. General Connor's invasion of the Powder River country followed in 1865. For fifteen years treaties had been made and broken; from south and east the Indians were being pressed continually toward the Rockies. Their hunting grounds grew smaller after every treaty, and now the last and best of these reserved areas was being invaded by miners and soldiers. In 1866 many of the Plains Indians' leaders had finally reached the conclusion that the white man's treaties were worthless; they were convinced that their way of life could endure only if they made a stand and fought for their lands.

On March 28, in complete disregard of the belligerent temper of the Indians, the Army ordered Carrington "to move immediately" to occupy Fort Reno and open two new forts along the Bozeman Trail. He was promised a year's supply of tools, rations, quartermaster stores, "the best horses and equipments and transportation in the district," and a water-power sawmill.[7] In late March, however, the 2nd Battalion at Fort Kearney carried only 220 men on its muster rolls, about one-fourth normal strength, and they were armed with obsolete muzzle-loading Springfields in poor condition. Carrington immediately queried his superiors concerning the whereabouts of promised recruits and arms, and asked for a departure delay until their arrival.

On April 13, he received orders establishing the Mountain District, with himself in command. The Mountain District en-

compassed the Powder River country; he would report directly
to General Philip St. George Cooke, commanding the Department of the Platte, a crusty fifty-seven-year-old campaigner with
almost forty years of frontier dragoon service behind him.

General Cooke's mood in 1866 certainly could not have inclined him toward friendship for ambitious "civilian" colonels.
After graduating high in his class from West Point in 1827,
Cooke had seen service in the Black Hawk War, the Mexican
War, won distinction in operations against the Apache and
Sioux, commanded cavalry in the Utah expedition of 1857–58,
and had moved up to the rank of colonel when the Civil War
began. Although a Virginian, Cooke announced immediately
that he would keep his "solemn oath to bear true allegiance to
the United States of America." His son, his nephew, and his
famed son-in-law, J. E. B. Stuart, all went with the Confederacy.[8]

Because of his long cavalry experience, Cooke's first Civil
War assignment was command of that arm of the service under
General George McClellan, even though certain high officials in
the War Department seemed to consider his loyalty suspect.
During McClellan's Peninsular Campaign of 1862, Cooke's
cavalry was made to look foolish by his own dashing son-in-law,
"Jeb" Stuart, and soon afterward he was relieved of command.
He spent the remainder of the war out of combat action, serving
on various boards, on recruiting duty, and as a functionary in
occupied territory. He came out of the war with only the rank
of brigadier-general; consequently when he took over command
of the Department of the Platte in 1866 he was an embittered
man.

At this time Carrington knew very little about Cooke; he
would learn a great deal about him as events unfolded. For the
moment he wasted no time in carrying out Cooke's order. "Immediately on receipt of the order establishing the Mountain
District," Carrington recorded, "I issued General Order No. 1,
assuming command, and made requisition for commissary and
quartermaster supplies for one year, upon the full basis of eight
hundred men, and fifty per cent additional for wastage and con-
tingencies." [9]

Carrington's zeal for his new assignment as well as his cautious stubbornness are revealed in this first general order. He was determined to hold out for full battalion strength, eight hundred men, before marching into the Indian stronghold.

High command decision, and communications transmitting them, moved slowly on the frontier. Carrington waited almost a month at Fort Kearney before he received official sanction on April 26 from General Cooke for delaying action on his "move immediately" order of March 28.

Carrington acknowledged Cooke's telegram with a long letter in which he proudly recorded all the steps he had taken to ready the battalion for marching. He had obtained two hundred excellent horses, almost enough to mount his entire present force; he had assembled fifty wagon teams, sets of tools for erecting forts, instruments for measuring distances and surveying routes. He had armed his regimental band "with Spencer carbines to make their services valuable every way." (Carrington must have sensed that he would be criticized for taking a 25-piece band into hostile Indian country, but he loved martial music, the pomp and ceremony of parade reviews, and considered his musicians among the least expendable units.) With his gift for never overlooking the most minute details, Carrington also reported purchase of a quantity of "potatoes and onions for seed and use," adding that he also had "other seeds, if practicable to use them this season."

He closed his letter with a suggestion that it would be "of value to my future operations if I reach Laramie in time for the meeting with the Indian tribes in council and thereby form acquaintance of many with whom I will have subsequent relations."[10] Those were the words of a lawyer preparing to meet his opposition; soon enough Carrington would learn to think like a soldier.

II. May:

PLANTING MOON

On the 16th of May Major-General Sherman reached
Fort Kearney, Nebraska, and upon full consultation with
him I matured my plans for the establishment of the new
posts and the occupation of the proposed new line to
Montana. Two days later, May 19, 1866, recruits having
arrived, I marched, reaching the vicinity of Fort Laramie
June 14, in nineteen marching days.[1]

SPRING was backward on the Great Plains that year, ice
lingering in the swales and fringing the running streams. At
Fort Kearney in early May the men arose to curse the monotonous frosty mornings. After a winter spent in barracks of rot-
ting cottonwood logs through which biting prairie winds
whistled and made them shiver in their bunks, the men were
ready for spring, ready for a change.

Quarters were only half large enough for the eight skeleton
companies of the 2nd Battalion. Officers' families shared cabins
designed for bachelors. Lieutenant William H. Bisbee, battalion adjutant, recorded that he, his wife and young son were
assigned one room and a small space under a hall stairway. "We
cooked, ate, and slept in this one room."

Bisbee's fellow tenant, who would play a tragic role in the
Fetterman Massacre, was the regimental quartermaster, Lieu-

tenant Frederick H. Brown, a reckless, happy-go-lucky bachelor. Brown's room, according to Bisbee, "was separated by a thin partition from mine. His chief joy was to pack the room full of Pawnee Indians, fill them with 'chow,' in return for which they gave gruesome and noisy exhibitions of scalping, war dances, and buffalo hunts." [2]

While the officers waited impatiently for the promised recruits and finals orders to march, they pored over new maps recently arrived from Washington and were surprised at how sparse was official knowledge of the Mountain District which they had been ordered to occupy. The maps told them almost nothing, and there were no guidebooks. They passed around tattered copies of Lewis and Clark's reports, and exchanged newspaper clippings, but they still could not learn whether the region was frigid or temperate, barren or covered with vegetation. All they knew was that it was precious to the Indians, and was the most direct route for emigration to Montana.

Occasionally the monotony of daily duties was relieved by arrival of Volunteer troops reporting from lonely western outposts to receive delayed discharges from Civil War service. Colonel Carrington wasted no time in mustering out these troops, especially if they were cavalrymen. He had been given authority to take over their horses, and every additional company passing through meant an increase in mounts, sorely needed for the march to Powder River.

Meanwhile the entire battalion was engaged in gathering and packing additional supplies. Mowing machines, shingle and brick machines, doors, window sash, locks, and nails began arriving from Fort Leavenworth. The officers' wives saw to it that rocking chairs and sewing chairs, churns and washing machines, and good supplies of canned fruit were posted on requisition lists. "Turkeys and chickens and one brace of swine," Mrs. Carrington recorded, "added a domestic cast to some of the establishments preparing for the journey." [3]

The colonel searched through his ranks for blacksmiths, wheelwrights, painters, harness makers and carpenters, and ordered these men to collect from the Fort Kearney storehouses all tools needed for their specialties. He tried to impress on every member of the expedition that no contingency should be overlooked; as soon as the column moved north of Fort Laramie it would be cut off from the States for several months.

By mid-May the weather had turned fine, and the regimental band under Bandmaster Samuel Curry was out drilling every day with new Spencer carbines, the envy of the regular infantry-men, who were still armed with old muzzle-loading Spring-fields. The Spencer was a breechloader with a seven-shot maga-zine, and each musician was supplied with an accompanying cartridge box containing tubes of seven cartridges which could be inserted into the carbine in one operation. The men were warned to guard these weapons carefully; any soldier who lost one would be charged thirty dollars, about two months' pay for a private.

At the same time, the infantrymen were learning how to ride the horses acquired from discharged Volunteer cavalrymen. "The men got upon the horses," Margaret Carrington noted, "and the majority actually made the first trip to water without being dismounted. Some men were embarrassed when the long Springfield rifle was put on the horse with them, but both man and horse soon learned how it was to be done." [4]

At last, on Sunday May 13, the 3rd Battalion of the 18th came marching in from Fort Leavenworth, with several hundred re-cruits for the regiment. Two days later, Captain J. L. Proctor arrived with another company of recruits, one of them being Private William Murphy who recalled later that upon arrival he was issued "two days rations, consisting chiefly of hardtack. Each hardtack was about four inches square and three-eighths of an inch thick. . . . A hungry man could have eaten the entire two rations at one meal and asked for more." [5] The half-famished arrivals were told simply that the quartermaster had run short.

What had happened was not unusual on the army frontier of 1866. The 3rd Battalion had expected the 2nd Battalion to be well stocked with rations in their cozy quarters at Fort Kearney, and had carried only enough supplies for the march from Leavenworth. At the same time the 2nd Battalion had hope-fully expected the 3rd Battalion to bring in fresh rations along with the recruits. The result, of course, was a temporary famine,

with several hundred men camped around Fort Kearney waiting for an overdue supply train.

Supplies arrived on the 16th, and accompanying the train
was an old hero to the men of the 18th Infantry, Lieutenant-
General William T. Sherman, then in command of all western
departments.

In contrast to the grim seriousness of his Civil War character,
Sherman seemed quite relaxed during his brief visit. Margaret
Carrington reported that he entered into the spirit and plans
for the expedition with his "usual energy and skill." Perhaps
because he was conscious of having made so much recent history, he suggested to her and the other officers' wives that they
keep daily journals of experiences in the new country so that
records might be available for posterity.[6]

At that time Sherman had had little experience with Plains
Indians; he foresaw no dangers for the women and children of
the party, but advised Carrington that he should avoid a contest of arms with the tribes if possible. He spent much of his
visit relaxing in the spring sunshine around Fort Kearney. Carrington's son, James, told afterward of a contest sponsored by
Sherman between him and some of the Pawnee boys. Sherman
wanted to see which of the youngsters could shoot an arrow the
highest. "My bow was boy's size," Jimmy Carrington recalled,
"but I won by lying on my back and putting both feet against
the bow to pull it."

Jimmy Carrington also remembered an exciting event which
occurred soon after Sherman departed. "Our house burned
down early in the morning, and I recall the terror of the scene,
the mad scramble to save a few things, but especially the rapid
popping of several big army revolvers that the fire set off." [7] His
mother mourned the loss of her best chairs and mattresses, all
packed and ready for the overland journey, but the Carringtons accepted the losses philosophically—"an incident very possible in army life"—and moved their few salvaged goods into an
army ambulance which would be their home during the long
march west.[8]

On May 18 recruits were assigned to the respective companies
of the 2nd Battalion. The Fort Kearney magazine was opened,

and ammunition which could be spared was drawn out and loaded into wagons. It was a meager supply, but Carrington had been assured that the deficit would be made up at Fort Laramie. With high spirits he announced that the regiment would march out for Laramie early on the following morning.

Saturday May 19 was a sunny spring day, the wide sky blue from horizon to horizon. More than a thousand men and 226 mule-drawn wagons moved out to stirring music from the regimental band, and by noon the column was beyond the adobe huts of Kearney City and strung along the Platte, a cloud of dust floating in its wake.

For the first time since the war the 2nd Battalion was at full strength, about seven hundred men, the majority being recruits in new blue uniforms which were darkened with sweat under the warm sun. The dismounted men of both battalions marched in advance, the wagon trains next, most of them driven by civilian teamsters employed by the quartermaster. Following the wagons was the cattle herd of about a thousand animals, with the mounted men serving as a rear guard.

Women and children rode in ambulances, and by midafternoon a few recruits, sore-footed from unaccustomed marching, were permitted to join these passengers. Each officer was responsible for the movement of his family and household goods. "My personal allowance," said Adjutant Bisbee, "embraced two six-mule teams, an ambulance, three saddle horses, cow, and chickens." Before the end of the day the expedition moved fourteen miles up the Platte, and someone had dubbed the long train "Carrington's Overland Circus." [9]

In addition to Adjutant Bisbee and Quartermaster Fred Brown, the 2nd Battalion's officers at that time included Captain Henry Haymond, battalion commander, Captains Nathaniel C. Kinney, Tenodor Ten Eyck, Joshua L. Proctor, and Thomas B. Burrowes, Lieutenants John I. Adair, Isaac D'Isay, Frederick Phisterer and Thaddeus Kirtland, the last being a cousin of Colonel Carrington. The battalion was well staffed with medical officers—Captain Samuel M. Horton, chief surgeon, and contract surgeons Mathews, McCleary and Buelon.

The second day out of Fort Kearney was a Sunday, and after

a brief religious service, they marched twenty miles to Plum Creek. At dawn Monday the "Overland Circus" was moving west again, the weather still good, recruits marching more briskly now that soreness was gone from their muscles. "My brother and I," James Carrington wrote afterward, "had been given a small Indian pony that we called 'Calico' and during the day we would take turns riding him, to get relief from the monotony and cramped quarters of the ambulance.* I can still remember passing prairie-dog villages where there were thousands of funny little rodents running around, or sitting up to bark at us and then ducking down into their holes. Never a day without a sight of leaping antelopes, an occasional sneaking coyote, big jack-rabbits, often herds of buffalo in the distance, and ever the monotonous expanse of sage-covered plain, blinding dust, the big skies stretching to the blue horizon, distant mountains, gorgeous sunsets, and in the heat of some days a shimmering mirage that looked like a great sea."[10]

While his young sons, Jimmy and Harry, were racing their calico pony alongside the wagon train, Colonel Carrington was rapidly becoming acquainted with three important civilian members of his party. They were Jack Stead, Henry Williams, and James Bridger. Stead was employed as official interpreter for the expedition; he had lived many years with the Pawnees, participating in their wars with the Sioux, who hated Stead and reputedly had placed a high price on his scalp. Henry Williams and Jim Bridger had served as scouts with General Patrick Connor during the Powder River expedition the previous year.

No white man knew more of the geography of the Big Horn and Powder River country than did "Old Gabe" Bridger. For forty years he had trapped, explored, and scouted in the area which was soon to become Wyoming Territory. He was a member of the party which opened the Oregon Trail; in 1843 he had defied the Indians by building a trading post known as Fort Bridger. In 1866 Bridger was approaching the end of his career —he was sixty-two—but Carrington would have been the first to admit that the grizzled frontiersman was the least expendable

---

* Calico was to become a casualty of the Fetterman Massacre.

member of his expedition. Bridger's pay was ten dollars a day, more than Carrington received, and more than twice the income of a junior officer, but he was a walking encyclopedia of Indian lore readily available to any man who needed him.

Carrington probably met Bridger early in 1866 at Fort Kearney. According to the *Kearney Herald,* he was there during the winter, en route to Washington "to tell the authorities how to manage the Indians." The *Herald* described him as being "fully six feet high, raw boned, blue eyes, auburn hair (now somewhat gray) is very active and communicative." [11] Lieutenant William Bisbee said he was "a plain farmer-like looking man dressed in the customary store clothes garments, low crowned soft felt hat, never affecting long hair or showy fringed buckskin suits, though he may on occasion have donned them as a convenience. His name of scout belied his calling in our expedition for we had no occasion to scout for Indians, they were always nearby." [12]

As the Overland Circus moved into hostile Indian country, Bridger and his assistant, Henry Williams, became more active, rising every morning before the bugler, preparing their own coffee, eating a few bites of pemmican, saddling their mounts. At reveille call, they would ride over to Carrington's tent, engage in brief conversation with the colonel, then canter out in advance of the column. Around sunset they would come riding back and report to Carrington. They always bedded down a short distance from the military camp, and except for Carrington and one or two other officers, few members of the battalion spoke with them or even saw them during the march. Bridger had little respect for what he called "paper-collared soldiers," inexperienced on the frontier.[13]

On May 24 the column marched into Fort McPherson—where less than a year later Carrington would be commanding under the shadow of an official inquiry. The fort was a dismal collection of shabby log-and-adobe quarters. Carrington had hoped to find additional rifle ammunition here, but there was none to spare. He ordered a detail to dismantle an idle steam sawmill which had been transferred to the expedition. The men loaded boiler and frame into spare wagons, and the train moved on, to camp for two days near O'Fallon's Bluffs.

On the 29th they reached Beauvais Ranche near the Old California Crossing. Westward travelers usually crossed the Platte at this point, but Carrington had been advised to proceed to Fort Sedgwick before attempting to ford his heavy wagon train. Late in the afternoon he received a visitor, a Cheyenne named Old Little Dog, who complained that some soldiers had entered his lodge nearby and stolen his rifle.

Carrington assured the Cheyenne that his rifle would be returned, and then to please his guest, ordered the regimental band to present a concert. Old Little Dog obviously enjoyed the music, especially admiring the bell chimes, and when the performance was ended and his rifle was returned to him, he thanked his host, leaped upon the bare back of his pony and galloped away. Carrington watched the Cheyenne until he vanished in the dusk, wondering if he had made a proper beginning in his first meeting with a representative of one of the tribes with which he must deal in the Powder River country.

Next day the train rumbled on westward, reaching Fort Sedgwick outside Julesburg, Colorado Territory, near sundown. After eleven days of marching they had put only two hundred miles between them and Fort Kearney. Laramie still lay more than a week's travel away, and the Powder River country was almost two hundred miles farther.

Carrington had allowed one day of his march schedule for fording the Platte at Julesburg. He was four days making the crossing. Melting snows upstream had flooded the river, and after conferring with his officers, he decided to float the wagons across on a large flatboat. He assigned the task of fitting out and caulking the boat to Captain Tenodor Ten Eyck, who had been a surveyor and lumberman before the war.

During the stay at Sedgwick, officers and men not on duty inspected the post. Few of them had ever before seen a fort constructed for defense against frontal Indian attack. A parapet and ditch guarded a rectangle of two-story adobes, each situated so that if one was attacked, the besiegers would be caught in a cross fire from the others. Another feature which impressed the visitors was a system of window barricades, pierced with loopholes and ready to be put into position at a moment's warning. All this was very sobering to recruits who had heard and read about Indian warfare, but as yet had not even seen a hostile Indian.

Meanwhile Ten Eyck and a detail of two hundred men made quick work of the flatboat, dragged it to the bank of the Platte, and laboriously set about stringing a cable across the currents and shoals of that treacherous stream. A twenty-mule team was then hitched to the cable, but the animals could not move the boat out of the sandy riverbank. Ten Eyck ordered the mules replaced by oxen, and the flatboat reluctantly became buoyant. Planking was laid out and wagons and teams moved aboard. Adjutant Bisbee, his wife and young son made the first crossing in the ambulance assigned to them.

But the capricious Platte was already falling again. By morning of the second day, sand bars were shining where currents had run a few hours earlier. "On trying the scow," Private William Murphy recorded, "we found it would not work owing to the quicksands and shallows. In places the water would be only two or three inches deep, while a few feet away there would be seven or eight feet of water." [14]

Captain Charles Norris, commanding a 2nd Cavalry company stationed at Fort Sedgwick, came down to the riverbank to commiserate with Carrington and his officers. "You'll have to push, cuss, and drive your train team by team across that mile of flat river," Norris advised.[15] Carrington ordered Ten Eyck to change his tactics, unload the wagons, replace them with false beds, and reload lightly. On Captain Norris' suggestion, a sizable collection of light and heavy timbers for prying and shoving was also assembled.

Realizing that the actual crossing would be delayed another day, Carrington decided to lighten the tension of waiting by arranging an evening entertainment. Soldiers not assigned to river-crossing operations erected several hospital tents into a single pavilion, and set up rows of campstools and chairs from the unloaded baggage wagons. Major James Van Voast, en route to Laramie to assume command of the post and the 18th Regiment's 1st Battalion, organized a program of music and comedy which he called the "Ironclad Minstrels." Amateur soldier actors blacked their faces, poked fun at their frontier environment, and sang to the accompaniment of the band's rollicking music which was complete with banjos and bones.

In a way, the evening's jollity was also a farewell party for officers of the 3rd Battalion, whose companies would take different routes west from Julesburg to forts in Colorado Territory and beyond on the old Oregon Trail. As he shook hands with these officers in front of his tent after the performance, Carrington must have wondered how he was going to accomplish his administrative duties as colonel of a regiment strung out across half the West—from headquarters in an isolated fort far north in the Powder River country.

One of the minor incidents occurring during the regiment's stay at Fort Sedgwick concerned a member of the band, Frank M. Fessenden. Although not yet twenty, Fessenden had brought his teen-age bride west with him, and all along the trail from Fort Kearney it had been obvious that young Mrs. Fessenden would soon become a mother. The Fessendens had been hopeful of reaching Fort Laramie, where the column would halt for a time, but the birth appeared so imminent at Fort Sedgwick that Surgeon Horton advised the expectant mother to travel no farther. "I was left behind the command with my wife," Fessenden wrote later. "A daughter was born to us here at Fort Sedgwick. She was a great favorite with Captain Fetterman who wanted to name her Sedgwick." [16]

Because of his youth and size—he stood only five feet, five inches high—Fessenden was a favorite of the regiment, a gray-eyed, brown-haired youngster from Twinsburg, Ohio, who upon enlistment noted his occupation as painter but soon ended up as a musician in the Army. When Carrington learned of the reason for Fessenden's temporary detachment from the regiment, he ordered a promotion in rank, dated back to the first of the month.

On June 2 and 3, Carrington's Overland Circus completed the formidable task of fording the Platte. "We finally crossed by having a long rope stretched from man to man," said Private Murphy, "strapping our guns and equipment to our backs and holding to the rope. Some of the men were up to their arm pits in water and some traveled nearly dry shod. We were ordered not to stop for anything, for if we did we would get stuck in the quicksand." [17] A few mules drowned, and in spite of all precautions some stores were damaged. Water melted the sugar, caked the flour, and swept away an occasional stray knapsack. But the Platte was crossed.

III. June:

MOON WHEN THE GREEN GRASS IS UP

On June 16, while encamped four miles east of Laramie, I was visited by Standing Elk, chief of the Brûlés (a band of the Sioux). He was thoroughly friendly—was entertained in my tent, and asked "Where I was going;" I told him; he answered me as follows: "There is a treaty being made at Laramie with the Sioux that are in the country where you are going. The fighting men in that country have not come to Laramie, and you will have to fight them. They will not give you the road unless you whip them." [1]

1.

EARLY on the morning of June 4, the last of Carrington's wagons was across the Platte, and the train camped that night on Lodgepole Creek. Next day they made eighteen miles, halting at Louis Ranche.

Along the trails of the West, crude stage stops had sprung up during the years between the California gold rush and the Civil War, most of them known as road *ranches*. Like many other wagon trains, Carrington's Traveling Circus took advantage of such amenities as were available at these stops, and often camped in the vicinity of a ranche. Margaret Carrington described Louis

Ranche as "quite a fort, and the out-houses and stables are advanced like bastions, so that enfilading fire can be had in all directions . . . a large yard surrounded by a stockade paling, with stabling, feed troughs, and hayricks, with here and there loopholes for the rifle . . . the wall of the upper stories and every angle of house or stable has its outlets for firing upon an approaching foe." She noted a wide selection of merchandise offered for sale: nutmegs, peppermint, navy tobacco, clay pipes, salaratus, baking powder, bologna, ready-made clothing, rows of canned fruits, black snake whips, tin cups, camp kettles, frying pans, wine, gin and whiskey.[2]

Next morning, Colonel Carrington and his officers said their farewells to the last companies of the 3rd Battalion, who were taking a route through Lodgepole Canyon on the first leg of a long journey to Camp Douglas, Utah. With their departure the train was shortened considerably; only the 2nd Battalion and recruits for the 1st Battalion remained. Carrington ordered a faster marching pace, over a smooth, hard-packed trail, but by noon the sun was scorching, and hourly rest stops had to be lengthened. The only trailside well marked on the map proved to be dry, and orders were passed to the men to conserve water in their canteens.

By midafternoon the thermometer in Mrs. Carrington's open ambulance indicated 101°, and a steadily rising wind tore at wagon covers. Clouds of gritty dust swirled across the treeless plain, driving into eyes, ears and noses. To add to the discomfort, swarms of buffalo gnats appeared out of nowhere, annoying the teams, stinging every exposed part of the human body. For protection, the men donned gloves and tied handkerchiefs over faces and necks. By late afternoon all vacant spaces in ambulances and wagons were filled with men suffering from lameness and heat exhaustion. Surgeon Horton and his assistants were kept busy trying to restore as many as possible to duty.

Yet in spite of everything the train traveled twenty-eight miles that day, rolling in to camp at Mud Springs where they found a group of log huts occupied by relief drivers for the Overland Mail. Off in the southwest the sky had turned a greenish gray, marked by jagged lightning flashes. No wood was available at

Mud Springs, and details were ordered out to gather buffalo chips. By the time coffee fires were started, a thunderstorm was upon them. Mules and horses jerked at their fastenings; tents ballooned, ripped up stakes, and flattened upon their occupants. The storm carried more wind than water and soon blew over, leaving little damage in its wake.

"Each day was much like another," Lieutenant Bisbee remembered. "The march at earliest dawn, the same adventures with rattlesnakes, the inopportune thunderstorms, routine of evening guard-mount and sound slumber." [3]

On the 7th an early halt was made near Court House Rock to take advantage of the plentiful supply of water in Pumpkin Creek. Several of the younger officers and wives, led by the adventurous regimental adjutant, Lieutenant Frederick Phisterer,* spent the last hours of the day climbing that curiously shaped bluff with its vast domed top and cupola which always reminded eastern travelers of their courthouses back home.

Most of the next day as they rolled westward through shimmering heat, they could see another famous landmark far ahead. When first sighted across the treeless plain it resembled the dead trunk of a gigantic tree, but as the train drew nearer, it took on the appearance of a chimney, tapering slightly to the top. That night they camped near this stratified clay mound known as Chimney Rock, and at dawn of the 9th were marching again, passing through Scotts Bluff down a gorge floored by drifting sands. The trail through Mitchell Pass narrowed in several places to the width of a single wagon.

Scotts Bluff, the Gibraltar of the Plains, was the most magnificent piece of scenery yet encountered by the travelers, the highest point in Nebraska Territory, embellished with terraced formations, fanciful towers and castles carved by water and wind. Here the expedition met with its first serious accident, involving the precious steam sawmill brought from Fort McPherson. "An eight-yoke bull-team," said William Murphy, "stampeded with two wagons loaded with parts and equipment

---

* Phisterer is best known today as the compiler of *Statistical Record of the Armies of the United States,* a standard source book for Civil War historians.

for a sawmill, and ran down a steep hill to the North Platte. I do not believe any of the steers were alive when they got to the bottom of the hill. This sawmill was intended for Fort Phil Kearny and arrived a month or six weeks later. This of course delayed us some in building the fort." [4]

At Camp Mitchell, west of the bluff, Carrington detached a company of the 1st Battalion under Captain Robert P. Hughes, assigned to replace Volunteer troops from Ohio and Missouri who had been there for many months. That night the train camped along the river west of the small fort.

Next day was a Sunday, and after holding morning religious services, the command rested. Mrs. Carrington recorded that Lieutenants Adair, Kirtland, D'Isay and the ebullient German, Frederick Phisterer, "helped to make something like true melody from the sweet Sabbath bell sent us by the Sabbath school of Rev. Mr. Dimock of Omaha before our departure from Kearney." [5]

Although Fort Laramie was only two days' march from Camp Mitchell, so many wagons were showing signs of wear from the long journey and the added rough jolting through Mitchell Pass, that Carrington decided to devote Monday, June 11, to emergency repairs, axle greasing, and reshoeing of some horses and mules. He also conferred with Jim Bridger. The trail between Scotts Bluff and Laramie was subject to occasional raids from hostile bands, but Bridger was confident that Indians would not attack so formidable a train. He expected, however, that they might attempt to raid livestock herds after dark.

Consequently, Carrington summoned his quartermaster, Lieutenant Fred Brown, and issued that day a special order:

> The troops and trains of this command will hereafter be camped and parked closely together, and in the following manner whenever the camping ground permits: All the trains will be parked, forming one closely locked square. If the wagons do not close together, the interval will be closed by means of ropes stretched from wagon to wagon, so that no animal may be able to escape. Headquarters will camp on one front of the square, the second battalion on the second, the mounted portion of the command on the third, and the quar-

termaster employees on the fourth front, and all outside of the square. In the fourth front a sufficiently large opening will be left to permit the public animals to be driven in in the evening, to stay there during the night. After sunset all animals must be within that square, and the quartermaster will be held responsible for the strict observance of this order. The second battalion will furnish the guard for its own and the fourth front; the mounted command will furnish the guard for its own and the front occupied by headquarters.[6]

Early Tuesday morning the column moved out, and by day's end was halfway to Fort Laramie. They camped on Cold Creek, a clear-water stream flowing into the North Platte. Sergeant John Barnes, a musician from Cincinnati, dropped a hook and line into the junction of creek and river and hooked a mountain pike. In a few minutes other soldiers joined him, making a seine from gunny sacks sewn together and weighted with mule shoes. Before sunset they had caught over a hundred fish. "Their hard white meat," Margaret Carrington recorded, "was excellent." [7]

It is not on record what her husband thought of the fishing party or the flavor of the catch, but for the past few days the colonel had noted with disapproval the casual attitude of his troops on the march and in camp, their habits of straggling, of riding out to shoot at wild game along the way, of carelessness after nightfall. Although Bridger had assured him that an Indian attack on the whole column was most unlikely, the scout had warned that any roving war party would strike without hesitation at small groups of men isolated by only a few hundred yards from the train.

With these thoughts in mind, Carrington decided to tighten security still further by issuing another special order. It was read that evening to all companies.

> I. Straggling for hunting or other purposes will at once be discontinued.
> II. Soldiers requiring rest or relief must avail themselves of the regular intervals of rest on the march, as established by battalion or detachment commanders.

III. Orderlies will remain with the officers for whom they are detailed, except when sent with orders.

IV. The mounted men attached to headquarters will march in front of headquarters train when not otherwise ordered, and all mounted men will carry their rifles by a uniform method and in readiness for use.

V. The regimental band will accompany the headquarters train, and will not stray from it unless by special permission of the regimental adjutant.

VI. No soldier will be permitted to visit ranches, or posts, or other sutlers than the one accompanying the command, or to leave the guard limits, except for wood and water, without permission of his battalion or detachment commander. Except in cases of trivial import, or such as only concern regimental headquarters or the mounted men of such, the permission above referred to must have the approval of the commanding officer of the Second Battalion Eighteenth U. S. Infantry.

VII. Wagon-masters, their assistants, teamsters, and all employees or attachés, connected with or accompanying this command will conform to these instructions, and such as they receive, pursuant thereto, from Captain F. Phisterer, acting assistant adjutant-general, and Lieut. F. H. Brown, chief quartermaster.

VIII. Order and silence after 9 o'clock P.M. will be observed by all within the command, whether soldiers or otherwise, and the chief quartermaster will so instruct wagon-masters and their assistants. The officer of the day, of the second battalion, will cause the arrest of all offenders against this paragraph.[8]

The column moved out early on the 13th for the last day's march to Fort Laramie, halting early in the afternoon by prearrangement about four miles east of the fort. Carrington wanted his camp close enough to Laramie to transact necessary military business, but far enough away to prevent any mingling of troops with the two thousand Indians who were there for the treaty ceremonies.

In accordance with his security orders, the train formed in a hollow square along the South Platte, and additional orders were read to the men:

The pending treaty between the United States and the Sioux Indians at Fort Laramie renders it the duty of every soldier to treat all Indians with kindness. Every Indian who is wronged will visit his vengeance upon *any* white man he may meet. As soldiers are sent to preserve the peace of the border and prevent warfare, as much as to fight well if warfare becomes indispensable, it will be considered a very gross offense for a soldier to wrong or insult an Indian. . . . Soldiers will attend to their own duties as soldiers and all intercourse with Indian lodges or individuals while at Laramie, or on the march from Laramie westward, will be through headquarters. Indian visitors will be kindly and patiently received, their chiefs only being admitted within the line, and such chiefs will be courteously conducted to headquarters for the transaction of their business.[9]

The ink was scarcely dry on this special order when Carrington received his first Indian visitor, a Brûlé chief. He was Standing Elk, a tall broad-faced man, with a single feather in his thick shoulder-length hair. The Brûlé was camped nearby, and his curiosity had been aroused by the arrival of the long military train.

With Jack Stead as interpreter, Carrington went through the necessary formalities of greeting, first presenting Standing Elk with tobacco, then smoking a pipe with him. The chief's first inquiry was blunt: "Where are you going?" Carrington replied frankly that he was taking his troops to the Powder River country to guard the Montana Road.

"There is a treaty being made in Laramie with the Sioux that are in the country where you are going," Standing Elk said. "The fighting men in that country have not come to Laramie and you will have to fight them."

Carrington replied that he hoped the presence of his troops would prevent a war rather than cause one. He said he was not going to the Powder River country to make war on the Sioux, but only to guard the road.

"They will not sell their hunting grounds to the white man for a road," Standing Elk declared. "They will not give you the road unless you whip them." The chief was quick to add

that he expected to sign the treaty and that Pegaleshka, who was
called Spotted Tail by the white men, also would sign the treaty.
The Brûlés wanted no war, he said. Those who talked of fighting were of the Miniconjou and Oglala bands, some of the
Bad Faces led by Red Cloud.[10]

With this sober warning of Standing Elk on his mind, Colonel
Carrington rode into Fort Laramie early the next morning. He
was accompanied by Major Van Voast and recruits for the 1st
Battalion, assigned to replace Volunteers at the post.

The fort lay between the Laramie and Platte rivers, a rectangle of thirty or forty log-and-adobe structures surrounding
a parade ground bare of sod. A flag flapped from a staff near a
corner of the rectangle, a spot of color against the somber landscape. Extending to right and left of the post along the river-
banks was a mile-long ribbon of Indian tepees, white cones
topped by blackened lodgepoles, smoke of cooking fires drifting
from smoke holes. Several hundred varicolored ponies were corralled here and there, finding scanty pasture in the sandy valley.
Small groups of Indians, a few mounted, moved aimlessly in
the open spaces.

As Carrington's party splashed over the Laramie River crossing, they could see strips of bright cloth flying from an Indian
burial platform a few hundred yards off to the north. They rode
on between horse corrals, passed a row of warehouses, and were
on the edge of the parade. Carrington noted then that there was
no stockade around Fort Laramie. No sentries challenged. Indians and civilians wandered about as freely as if they were on
the streets of a frontier town rather than in a military post.

At the southwest end of the parade a temporary platform with
wooden benches had been erected for treaty negotiations. In the
headquarters building beyond, Carrington and Van Voast met
with the post commander, Colonel Henry E. Maynadier. The
commandant was particularly pleased to greet Major Van Voast;
three companies of the 1st Battalion had arrived some days earlier from Colorado Territory, and now that the major was there
Maynadier would soon be free to relinquish command and arrange for the long-delayed discharges of his Civil War Volunteer
troops.

Along with other duties, Maynadier was serving as a member of the Peace Commission, and within the hour he was introducing Carrington to his associates, Thomas Wistar, E. B. Taylor, and Colonel Robert N. McLaren. A number of Brûlé and Oglala chiefs were also arriving for the day's harangues, most of them tall, well-formed men wearing buffalo-skin or red blanket robes, fringed leggings and beaded moccasins. They stood with arms folded over their broad chests, the vermilion paint on their stolid faces glistening in the sunlight.

"I was introduced to several chiefs," Carrington recalled later. "Without exception, every chief to whom I was then introduced as the 'White Chief going up to occupy Powder River, the Big Horn county, and the Yellowstone' treated me coldly." [11]

Commissioner Taylor, acting as chairman, was an ambitious Indian Bureau superintendent, dedicated to making a success of the treaty negotiations. He assured Carrington that everything was going well, that at least seven-eighths of the Brûlés and Oglalas were represented by leaders who would sign. Pegaleshka, or Spotted Tail, the influential leader of the Brûlés, had capitulated completely. It was his daughter, Fleet Foot, who lay on the platform in the post cemetery; on her deathbed she had asked to be baptized as a Christian and laid to rest there. Spotted Tail bowed to her wishes. After her death he slew her four favorite ponies and tied their tails to the four posts of the platform. He said that since his daughter had been adopted by the white man's Great Spirit he had no heart to fight the white man any more.

Carrington was encouraged by Taylor's remarks. He felt that if he could meet all the chiefs and some of the young warriors and talk with them face to face, he could convince them of his friendship. But such negotiations would require time, several days. Aware that Fort Laramie was in direct telegraphic communication with his headquarters at Omaha, he decided to request authority to remain at Fort Laramie until treaty negotiations were complete.

On the following morning, still confident of contributing personally to a treaty that would guarantee peace in the Powder River country, Carrington rode to the fort in company with his quartermaster, Lieutenant Brown, and several others of his regimental and headquarters staff. Mrs. Carrington and some of the other officers' wives, being eager to see the fort and visit the sutler's store, followed in an ambulance. A few wagons filled with infantrymen rolled in the rear. Carrington hoped to load these wagons with ammunition from the fort's magazine, and to mount the infantrymen on horses from the quartermaster's corrals. But this was to be a day of disappointments, even of personal danger, for Henry Beebe Carrington.

His first duty of the morning was to arrange for transfer of the ammunition. He had drawn up a requisition for 100,000 rounds which Omaha headquarters had assured him would be available. To his dismay, the post quartermaster informed him that Laramie would be placed in jeopardy if even a thousand rounds were removed. Carrington insisted on the thousand rounds.

The promised horses also were nonexistent. "I could not even find horses to make an exchange of twelve at that post," he testified later.

The only significant acquisitions for his expedition were twenty-six wagons loaded with provisions. Mules were available, but the drivers would have to be furnished from his command, removing half a company of men from combat readiness in case of sudden attack en route. A hasty inspection of the boxes and barrels also revealed that much of the food was inedible. The pilot bread, or hardtack, was so stale it had turned dark, and was so hard it could not be bitten, could scarcely be broken with a metal tool. "The flour drawn at Laramie," said Carrington, "was musty, caked, and very poor." [12] And nowhere on the post could be found utensils for baking it.

Meanwhile, Margaret Carrington and her "little coterie of ladies" were enjoying the sights in and around Bullock & Ward's sutler's store. They saw cups of rice, sugar and coffee emptied into the looped-up skirts or blankets of the squaws, they stared at a tall warrior grimacing delightedly as he sucked a long stick of peppermint candy. "Bright shawls, red squaw cloth, brilliant calicoes, and flashy ribbons passed over the same counter with knives and tobacco, brass nails and glass beads ... the debris of munched crackers lying loose under foot furnished both nutriment and employment for little bits of Indians too big to ride on mama's back, and too little to reach the good things on counter or shelves." [13]

The wives were received courteously by the traders, W. G. Bullock and Seth Ward, both of whom had lived in the Platte country for years. They assured their visitors that they had nothing to fear from Indians around the fort. Ward had been a trapper, but now wore fine clothes and a soft hat of the latest eastern fashion. A huge diamond glittered in his shirt front, and a large gold watch chain hung over his vest.

According to John Hunton, one of the clerks who "could talk Sioux, Cheyenne or English just as the case comes to hand," the Laramie sutler's store averaged one hundred dollars per day in cash trade, with additional credit sales. Because paper money was used to pay soldiers, greenbacks were standard medium of exchange, the wartime shinplasters—five, ten, twenty-five and fifty cent notes—being heavily discounted in that inflationary period.[14]

While his wife was absorbed in all the sights, sounds, and smells of the sutler's store, Colonel Carrington was meeting for the first time with some of the chiefs who had expressed opposition to opening the Montana Road. The chiefs, the commission members, and Carrington were seated around rough tables on the platform before post headquarters. On the parade in front of them, hundreds of warriors and squaws had gathered to watch and listen, some standing, some squatting, some sitting on extemporized benches under a blazing June sun.

Commissioner Taylor introduced Carrington and began a brief discourse upon the destination of the military train, and the purpose of the expedition. It was obvious from the beginning that the hostile chiefs already knew everything they wanted to know about the "Little White Chief." No doubt they had heard from Standing Elk full details of his conversation with Carrington the first evening the soldiers had camped outside Fort Laramie. As Carrington now rose to speak, the muttering grew in intensity, the Indians moving restlessly in their seats.

Carrington's interpreter quietly suggested that it might be wise to allow the chiefs to speak first.

Out of the long harangues which followed, it became clear that some of the chiefs considered the presence of Carrington and his soldiers proof that the United States Government was determined to occupy their hunting grounds even without consent by treaty. Two Oglala chiefs made no secret of their bitter opposition to construction of forts in the Powder River country—Red Cloud and Young-Man-Afraid-of-His-Horses.*

Young-Man-Afraid-of-His-Horses declared that if the soldiers went any farther into Sioux country, his people would fight. "In two moons the command would not have a hoof left," he boasted.[15]

In spite of the efforts of Commissioner Taylor and his associates, the covert hostility had now become open. Toward the end of that day's council, Red Cloud arose and made a dramatic speech. "Great Father sends us presents and wants new road," he shouted. "But White Chief goes with soldiers, to steal road before Indian says yes or no." [16]

Most of the Brûlés remained silent, but an approving chorus of *hun-huns* indicated that Red Cloud had followers on the platform. When the meeting began to grow disorderly, Commissioner Taylor ended it abruptly.

Margaret Carrington witnessed part of the affair while waiting in her ambulance beside post headquarters. "I could not hear what was said," she recorded, "but there was evidently some trouble which caused a sudden adjournment of the conference for the afternoon. Henry soon left the platform, walking rapidly towards his horse, which an orderly was lightly holding by the rein near the ambulance, and at his left were two Indians, one of them Red Cloud, who had his right hand upon a large knife at his side, and looking at Grey Eagle [Carrington's horse]. I thought the Indian was going to stab Henry in the back, and perhaps jump on Grey Eagle and ride off."

---

* A more exact translation of the latter: The-Mere-Sight-of-His-Horses-Inspires-Fear.

In her fright, Mrs. Carrington called her husband's name. He caught her warning and her indicative gesture, and slacking his step so the Indians would come within range, he drew his revolver belt to the front, keeping his hand upon it, then slowed his step, looking sidewise at the Indians and allowing them to pass. Whatever Red Cloud's original intention, he passed as stolidly as if Carrington were not even there, and walked with his companion across the parade and out of the fort.[17]

Carrington was depressed by this show of cold hostility; he felt that his presence at the council had made matters worse instead of better. And before he left the fort for camp, another disappointment was added to his day of frustrations. He received a telegram from Omaha in reply to his request for permission to remain at Fort Laramie until the peace treaty was signed. Headquarters not only denied his request but ordered him to resume march for Fort Reno no later than June 17. This was the crowning blow. Now he would have only one day in which to make his peace with Red Cloud and the other hostile leaders.

As Carrington prepared to start back to his camp, Colonel Maynadier attempted to reassure him concerning Red Cloud's actions. "Indians always have those tantrums," Maynadier said. "Red Cloud was no chief when he first came here, but as the old warriors said that he was at the head of the young men whom they call Bad Faces . . . the commission [appointed] him a chief as they did Spotted Tail . . . to make him our friend." [18]

After learning this, perhaps Carrington felt there was still a glimmer of hope that Red Cloud might yet be won over from war to peace. In the evening he talked with Jim Bridger about this and other matters, but Old Gabe was not sanguine about prospects. Instead the scout added one more burden to Carrington's bad day. He had seen kegs of gunpowder on Indian ponies around the river camps, and some of them were going north away from the fort. Carrington thought of the miserly thousand rounds of ammunition so grudgingly issued him that day, and was puzzled that even Bridger could not tell him who was responsible for the kegs of powder in the Indians' possession. After four years of Civil War experience, he was accustomed to military muddling, but now he was beginning to wonder if he was not taking his 2nd Battalion into a muddle more dangerous than he had bargained for.

If he had hoped for a better day on June 16, he was quickly disillusioned. The first tidings of morning concerned Red Cloud and his followers. During the night they had dismantled their tepees, loaded their travois, and vanished. Their trail led north toward the Powder River country.

When Carrington reached the fort, he found the peace commissioners arranging for a hasty conclusion to the council. Perhaps Commissioner Taylor feared that any further delay might be disastrous; other bands might follow Red Cloud's example and depart without signing a treaty.

As usual, the treaty signing was an elaborate ceremony. The chiefs were seated in a circle with the commissioners, and after long palavering, a fancifully carved redstone pipe was passed around, each Indian taking two or three slow puffs of smoke. They were all old men—Spotted Tail, Standing Elk, and the others—and it must have been clear to the knowledgeable white men present that these chiefs did not represent any of the belligerent young warriors in the north.

After signatures were duly affixed and witnessed, the commissioners distributed presents, and in a few hours "the friendly camps were ablaze with mounted Indians decked in yellow, red, and other brilliantly colored cheap fabrics flying in the winds." [19]

Private William Murphy of Company A, who had come into Laramie with a duty detail, said the Indians were also given beef steers to kill. "They ate them all but the hides, hoofs, and horns without washing. . . . We were shown samples of marksmanship with the bow and arrow. The young boys could hit a button, pencil or any small article at about thirty yards." [20]

All afternoon the fort was a festive whirlpool of colors, sounds, and smells. "Indians filled every available space, dressed, half dressed and undressed," said Lieutenant Bisbee, "all mingling with soldiers, teamsters, emigrants, speculators, half-breeds, squaw men, and interpreters . . . under the eaves of buildings, by doorsteps and porches were groups of Indians in assorted sizes, sexes and conditions, with the element of cleanliness just as critically wanting as usual among the aborigines." [21]

In his listing of human types frequenting the fort that day, Bisbee overlooked one bizarre newcomer who was engaged in an occupation then extremely novel to the frontier. He was Ridgway Glover, a photographer from Philadelphia, a well-to-do Quaker, with vague ambitions of recording the entire frontier in photographs. "I hope to make my talents for making negatives available to science," Glover wrote the editor of the *Philadelphia Photographer* from Fort Laramie. "I had much difficulty in making pictures of the Indians at first. . . . Some of the Indians think they will die in three days, if they get their pictures taken. At the ferry today I pointed the instrument at one of that opinion. The poor fellow fell on the sand, and rolled himself in his blanket. The most of them know better though, and some I have made understand the light comes from the sun, strikes them, and then goes into the machine. I explained it to one yesterday, by means of his looking-glass, and showed him an image on the ground glass. When he caught the idea, he brightened up, and was willing to stand for me. I make them Ferrotypes, and put brass around them, and they think they are *wash-ta-le-poka* (their superlative for good)."

Like all frontier photographers, Glover had his problems with wind, sand, and lack of clean water for washing negatives. "The water is muddy, and out of fifty negatives I have taken, I shall only publish prints from twenty-two. . . . The wind was blowing, and the sand flying. The negative is therefore not quite clean." In spite of difficulties he obtained stereoscopic views of Indian camps around Fort Laramie, and single and group photographs of Indians.

A blond-haired, energetic young man, Glover quickly became acquainted with Jim Bridger and Colonel Carrington, and when he learned of the proposed new forts on the Montana Road, immediately decided to visit the Powder River country. "I expect to travel, and trap this fall, and spend the winter in Virginia City, Montana, and to secure some winter Rocky Mountain scenery." Carrington's main column, however, was leaving too early to suit Glover's plans. The photographer decided to wait and travel north later with another wagon train.[22]

2.

Among last-minute duties at Fort Laramie, Colonel Carrington dispatched two reports to Omaha, stating in the first that he was still short of ammunition, and that the supply of hard bread obtainable at Laramie would last only four days. "I find myself greatly in need of officers, but must await the arrival of new appointments, or until others are relieved from recruiting service. I move tomorrow."

After he had sent this off, he decided he should be more explicit concerning his need for ammunition:

> I respectfully urge that the supplies of ammunition en route from Leavenworth, per order, be forwarded forthwith. The entire supply of .58 caliber at Laramie being only 1,000 rounds renders many troops almost powerless in case of delay of supplies and remoteness from base. All the commissioners agree that I go to occupy a region which the Indians will only surrender for a great equivalent; even my arrival has started among them many absurd rumors, but I apprehend no serious difficulty. Patience, forbearance, and common sense in dealing with the Sioux and Cheyennes will do much with all who really desire peace, but it is indispensable that ample supplies of ammunition come promptly.[23]

Carrington was still overconfident. But he had learned much during his three days at Fort Laramie.

When E. B. Taylor came out that evening to bid the colonel and his wife farewell, the commissioner was frank enough to say that Carrington should not place too much confidence in the treaty signing insofar as it would affect the expedition. Neither Carrington nor his wife were surprised or dismayed at this confirmation of their own feelings. As Margaret Carrington put it, "the ladies kept up a good heart, and as they could not well go back, concluded to go on, but agreed to limit their riding on horseback to the vicinity of the train." [24]

Being a religious man, Henry Carrington disliked marching

on Sunday, but at dawn of June 17, he put his column in motion, crossed Laramie River and headed northwest past the fort. Many of the Indians were also preparing to depart, leaving barren circles where their tepees had stood on the greening grass.

As the wagons creaked past the cemetery, all could plainly see the scaffold where Spotted Tail's daughter lay, the white tails of her ponies swaying in the morning breeze. Dwarf sunflowers, cactus and thistle blossoms brightened the slope, but off in the distance the hills were bare and bleak.

After leaving the fort, the Montana Road followed the North Platte. On the left was a perpendicular bluff, and in places the trail was so narrow that wagon hubs scraped against yellow clay walls upon which earlier travelers had carved their initials.

Carrington's command now consisted only of the 2nd Battalion. His eight companies, with regimental headquarters staff and band, totaled about seven hundred men, "splendidly furnished with everything except arms, ammunition, and horses." [25] Almost five hundred of these soldiers were new recruits, and to train and lead them Carrington had only twelve officers, including himself.

Whenever he gazed at the barren landscape across the Platte, Carrington was looking at the southern border of the Mountain District, a vast region of mountains and plains—unmapped, mysterious, ominous. Once they were across the river at Bridger's Ferry, he would be responsible for the peace and security of this domain. He believed that his force was sufficient to erect new forts, to build barracks, warehouses and stables, to make preparations for winter, to protect emigrants from small parties of thieving Indians. Yet he knew, inexperienced though he was in Indian fighting, that his seven hundred men could never sustain an aggressive campaign against the powerful Sioux and Cheyennes if the Indians chose war instead of peace. With the help of God, and by trusting in human forbearance and reason, he hoped to avoid such a war.

A few miles out of Laramie, Jim Bridger sighted the dust of a mounted party approaching from the west. The scout dropped back to notify Carrington; the train was halted and security precautions taken immediately. A few minutes later the horsemen came in peacefully, at a walk. They were Indians, Winnebagos, a thousand miles from their Wisconsin homeland.

For the past year this company of Winnebagos had been serving as soldiers at Fort Reno; the commandant there had discharged them a few days previously. When they learned that Carrington was marching to occupy the Powder River country, several begged to be allowed to return with him. At first, Carrington was inclined to add these Indians to his command, but Bridger was shaking his head. The Winnebagos, Bridger said, were the best of scouts, but they had been deadly enemies of the Sioux for many years, and some of the chiefs at Laramie had expressly demanded as a condition of the treaty that the Winnebagos must leave the country. To keep any one of them on, Old Gabe explained, would be construed by the Sioux as a hostile act.[26]

Carrington admitted he had not known of this. He thanked Bridger for his counsel and informed the Winnebagos diplomatically that he had no authority to employ them.

The column moved on, passed Nine-Mile Ranche, and halted a mile and a half beyond at a campsite along the North Platte. Dissatisfied because the train had covered only thirteen miles the first day, Carrington had the men bugled out at 3 A.M. and kept the wagons moving briskly until noon. On Bridger's advice, however, after a sixteen-mile march, he made an early halt on Little Bitter Cottonwood. A dangerous defile lay just ahead, the scout said, with no campsites in reach before sundown.

On the 19th they pushed forward eighteen more miles, passing the last telegraph station, Horseshoe Creek. None could have imagined on this bright June day that only six months later the operator there would flash to the world the first news of the Fetterman Massacre.

All afternoon the wagons rolled through a crooking gorge, with rock walls on either side rising to conical summits. Jim Bridger and his guides kept an alert watch for Indians, but there was no sign of hostiles anywhere. During one rest stop Adjutant Phisterer and Surgeon Horton led a party of wives into a side canyon in search of colorful stones and to try the echo effect of pistol shots. Bridger rode up and quietly warned them: "There's

Indians enough lyin' under wolfskins or skulkin' on them cliffs,
I warrant. They follow ye always. They've seen ye, every day,
and when ye don't see any of 'em about, is just the time to look
for their devilment." [27]

The camp that evening would be the last before they reached
the Platte and entered the Mountain District. Lieutenant Phisterer rode ahead with Bridger, selecting a velvety sward beside
the river, with a backdrop of cedars. When Carrington saw the
location, he was so pleased that he named it Camp Phisterer.
The dashing German was one of his and Mrs. Carrington's fa-
vorites. "He was most conspicuous in all that contributed to the
pleasure or progress of the march," she wrote in her journal.[28]

Before noon of the 20th, the train reached Bridger's Ferry.
This was familiar ground to Jim Bridger, who had bought and
improved the crossing ten years earlier. After collecting a small
fortune in tolls, the scout had grown reckless, sold out, and
moved on to less confining activities. A squaw man named Mills
was the current proprietor, and he was much excited over an Indian raid upon his livestock which had occurred only twenty-
four hours earlier.

Because his wife was a Sioux, Mills previously had been im-
mune from Indian depredations. After the raid he had sent
some of his employees, also Indians, in pursuit; they had returned after recovering part of the stock. The raiders, they said,
were Bad Faces of Red Cloud's band.

Jim Bridger advised Carrington that this was not a good sign.
If Red Cloud's followers had worked themselves up to raiding
stock from a squaw man, they could be expected to stampede
animals from the train at the first evidence of carelessness.

As two days were required to ferry his wagons across the
Platte, Carrington had considerable time to consult further with
his guides. In addition to Bridger and Williams, he had acquired
two others at Laramie: James J. Brannan and James P. Beckwourth. Brannan had served as scout with one of General Connor's columns the previous year, and knew the Tongue River
country above the Powder. Beckwourth, a mulatto, had several
Crow wives, and was considered a minor chief in the tribe. He
had been recommended to Carrington as a useful negotiator.

From his Crow friends, Beckwourth could obtain intelligence concerning the activities of hostile Sioux, Cheyenne and Arapaho bands in the north.

After discussions with his staff and guides, Carrington on June 21 drew up a new series of orders which he hoped would enhance security when march was resumed across the Mountain District to Fort Reno:

> The instructions heretofore given respecting the encampment of the command belonging to the Mountain District, Department Platte, derive special importance from the doubtful attitude of certain Indian tribes which lie in advance of the command and along and near its route. A careful and prompt conformity to orders will save the reorganization of a camp after it is once established. The following additional instructions are given:
>
> 1. No mules will be unharnessed or turned loose until the wagon-masters shall be so instructed by the chief quartermaster [Lieutenant Brown].
>
> 2. When the trains are parked the chief quartermaster will report at headquarters for orders or any additional instructions before the wagon-masters receive their instructions.
>
> 3. All wagon-masters will, accordingly, report to the chief quartermaster after trains are parked, and will, with all their assistants and subordinates, be held to strict obedience to orders received from or through this office.
>
> 4. Commanding officers of battalion or detachments will report daily, at 8 o'clock P.M., at the office of the acting assistant adjutant-general [Lieutenant Phisterer] for marching orders for the day following and during the march. Immediate report will be made of Indian signs or the appearance of Indians, indicative of doubtful or hostile intentions; also of any serious difficulties of the road, impeding or interrupting the march, or of any other substantial cause of delay, which will throw any portion of the command behind or break up the close order of march.
>
> 5. Assignments of commands to their respective locations in camp will be made from headquarters, and will be car-

ried into effect under the direction of the chief quartermaster, and those assignments will be daily made on survey of the ground selected, with view of the greatest compactness and efficiency in case of alarm, access to grass, water, etc.

6. As the only probable risk to be entertained on the march will be that of attempt to stampede or steal stock, the wagons will be corralled closely, so as to prevent any possible outbreak of animals, if alarmed, and no regard will be paid to night-feeding of animals, inconsistent with their perfect security; and wagon-masters, herdsmen, and drivers must observe the same regard to order, the same silence after tattoo, and the same rules as to leaving camp without due authority which govern the officers and soldiers of this command.

7. No discharge of firearms within or near the camp, or during the march, except the discharge of pieces by the guard, will be permitted, unless by due authority, and no firing will be permitted on the march, even upon Indians showing hostile intent, except under immediate orders of a commissioned officer; and not then without reference to headquarters, unless an attack be so sudden as to require instant repulse.

8. Bands of Indians met on the march desiring parley or conference will be referred to headquarters, or passed with simple recognition and common courtesy, and previous orders respecting intercourse or dealings between soldiers and Indians will be rigidly enforced.

9. Headquarters, with pioneer party, will as a general rule move in advance, then will follow the infantry command, then headquarters train, the train of the second battalion, and the present mounted rearguard thereof, then the supply trains, and in rear of all wagons and mounted command.

10. Unless otherwise at any time ordered, when the command halts for rest, trains will also halt, so as to preserve the entirety of the command and prevent inconvenience to the troops by the passing or sudden stopping of trains.

11. The camp of the infantry and the mounted detachment will conform in front to the line of wagons they cover, and in depth will as at general headquarters be restricted to

the space actually necessary to give a reasonable distinct-
ness of position to quarters for officers and companies.

12. The trains must be kept compactly closed up, and the
chief quartermaster is charged with the direct enforce-
ment of this instruction.

13. Immediately after coming in camp, the commanding officer of the mounted detachment [Lieutenant Adair] will
report to the field officer of the day six noncommissioned
officers and 42 privates for picket duty. These men are to
form a cordon or line of pickets beyond the grazing
ground, and will be returned to their camp by the senior
noncommissioned officer with them after all the animals
have been driven in and corralled. On the approach of
Indians, they will give the herders timely notice to collect
and drive in the stock and make report thereof to headquarters.

14. Every evening at 5 o'clock the commanding officer of the
second battalion [Captain Haymond] will cause one company officer and one company to report to the assistant
adjutant-general for outpost duty; the officer with this
company will perform the duties of a field officer of the
day and report to the colonel commanding for orders.
The company thus detailed will, previous to reporting,
be inspected by the adjutant of the second battalion
[Lieutenant Bisbee] and every man thereof should be supplied with 10 rounds of ammunition.[29]

While Carrington was composing this comprehensive set of
orders, his men were ferrying wagons and mules across the
Platte. Thanks to the ingenious system of cables and pulleys devised by Jim Bridger, round trips averaged only eleven minutes.
During the afternoon a detail of about one hundred lusty-lunged
men, armed with poles, forced the beef herd into the swift current and compelled the animals to swim across.

In early daylight of the 22nd, the last wagons were ferried
over, and the train rolled smoothly for sixteen miles along the
north bank of the river, camping opposite the mouth of La
Vinta Creek, where water, grass, and wood were in abundance.
"We had a picket line outside of the guards," Private Murphy
noted, in reference to Carrington's new orders.[30]

On the morning of the 23rd the column swung northward from the Platte, mules straining against traces to pull the heavily loaded wagons across several miles of red buttes, sand hills and rocky ridges. Once they were out of the valley the scenery was spectacular; the windings of the river could be seen far below, the level plain beyond extending into the horizon.

Near the Sage Creek crossing of the old Mormon Trail, they halted for nooning, and here discovered a sort of portable "ranche," an extemporized plank shed, offering merchandise to expected summer travelers over the Montana Road. The proprietors were Louis Gazzous and Henry Arrison, the former known to Jim Bridger and his fellow guides as "French Pete." Gazzous was married to a Sioux, and several of his half-breed children were playing happily over displays of canned fruit, liquor, tobacco, cutlery, and cheese.

Gazzous was a friendly sort, eager to gain the good will of the military, and when Surgeon Horton's wife expressed admiration for a young antelope the Frenchman was raising as a pet, he presented it to her as a gift.

Although the 24th was a Sunday, Carrington decided the urgency of his mission was too compelling to spare a day for rest. That night the train camped at the head of Sage Creek, and on Monday marched to the South Fork of the Cheyenne, where buffalo grass and timber were plentiful, and water was obtainable by digging into a sandy stream bed.

On the 26th, acting upon Jim Bridger's advice, the train cut away from the old Bozeman Trail and covered twenty miles in rapid time to Antelope Creek. Early the following morning, they had their first view of the Big Horns, bright under the blaze of the eastern sun. Margaret Carrington excitedly borrowed her husband's field glass for a closer look. Somewhere in the vicinity of that magnificent snow-crested range, still eighty miles away, the 2nd Battalion would build the first fort.

With their destination now in view, the infantrymen marched with lighter steps. "In half an hour," Mrs. Carrington wrote, "the air itself was invigorated by the currents from the snow banks; and even at that distance shawls became necessary, the ambulance side curtains were closed, and it seemed as if a November day was to succeed the summer's morning." [31]

Off to the right, the travelers soon sighted the four columns of Pumpkin Buttes, and by nightfall they were at the Dry Branch of Powder River. Fort Reno was now only a long day's march away. Thus far their enemies had been summer heat, dust, shortage of rations, and plain weariness of bone and muscle. The Indians as yet had made no demonstrations of hostility.

If the mood among the men was relaxation of tensions, there was certainly no relaxation of security precautions on this last camp before Reno. Bridger had assured Carrington that bands of Sioux were watching their every move; the scout had picked up Indian signs every day; at the first slacking of vigilance they would strike. On this last night, Carrington cautioned his officers to follow security orders to the letter. And because he was eager to reach Fort Reno early the next day, he also announced that march would be resumed as soon after midnight as the sky lightened.

By sunup the wagons were rolling again. For twelve miles the road followed the Dry Fork's bed, wagon wheels sometimes running in damp sand, sometimes in three or four inches of milky water. During the early morning they were confined to a narrow butte-locked basin, and Bridger and his fellow guides were doubly vigilant, riding far up on the powder-colored, cactus-studded ridges.

At last they swung northwest out of the Dry Fork, facing across a dusty gray plain broken by red-shaled hills. Even at midmorning the sun burned at their backs, but Carrington kept the column moving steadily. Shortly before noon the advance party topped a rise, and there was Powder River. Just beyond on a level bench above the stream lay Fort Reno.

With his headquarters party, Carrington led the way down through a mile of cottonwood bottomland, and at almost exactly 12 o'clock they were splashing across the shallow reddish stream. While Carrington rode on to report to the Reno commander, the first wagons were turning to form a corral just south of the fort.

Fort Reno was an open post, the building constructed of

cottonwood logs with earthen roofs, a high staked fence protecting warehouses and stables. The first view of its bareness was depressing, but Margaret Carrington recorded cheerfully that "so far, we are all right, and fast seeing the country." [32] Every member of the expedition knew that this fort, however unadorned it might be, was their last link with civilization, the jumping-off place before they entered the *terra incognita* which lay between them and the Montana gold settlements.

General Patrick Connor had ordered its construction during his unsuccessful campaign of the previous summer, and since the withdrawal of his columns, the post had been manned by Companies C and D of the 5th U. S. Volunteers and the company of Winnebago scouts met by the expedition on the first day out of Laramie. [33] The 5th U. S. Volunteers was one of those odd by-products of the late Civil War, the enlisted men being "galvanized Yankees," or former Confederate prisoners who had taken the oath of allegiance with a proviso that they would not be required to fight against the South but only against the Indians.*

The officer in command was Captain George M. Bailey, and he greeted Colonel Carrington almost as a deliverer. Bailey's men were in low spirits, irritable, some of them almost mutinous. The Civil War had been ended for a year, and they wanted to return home.

Carrington explained that he carried no orders for the discharge of the 5th U. S. Volunteers, but he did possess authority to appropriate all ordnance stores, rations, supplies and government livestock. In other words, Fort Reno was to be moved some miles to the northwest, probably near Tongue River where wood, water and grass were more abundant.

---

* A unique member of these galvanized Yankees at Fort Reno was Private Milo B. Tanner who was actually a Union soldier originally of the 121st New York Volunteers. Captured by the Confederates at Cold Harbor, he was sent to Andersonville prison. Tanner escaped from there in a stolen Confederate uniform and fell in with a Confederate patrol, only to be captured by Colonel Benjamin Grierson's Federal cavalry raiders. Unable to convince Grierson that he was truly a Union soldier, Tanner was sent to prison at Alton, Illinois, where the authorities also refused to believe his story. In desperation, he finally took the oath of allegiance and eventually found himself in a blue uniform again at Fort Reno.

The dilemma of what was to be done with the galvanized Yankees was resolved that afternoon by arrival of a mail courier from Fort Laramie. Among other messages for Carrington was a telegram from General Pope authorizing relief of the U. S. Volunteers and directing them to proceed to Fort McPherson for eventual discharge from service. John Ryan, a private in the 2nd Battalion, was present in the fort when the news was announced to the Volunteers. "They were certainly glad to be relieved," he said. "They had had no trouble with the Indians but had found the place far from being desirable as a permanent place of residence." [34]

Meanwhile, the 2nd Battalion proceeded to take over operation of the fort. Lieutenant Adair's mounted command camped at the base of the hill for ready access to the alkaline waters of the Powder, the wagon train and infantry companies formed their usual tight corral south of the fort, and regimental headquarters tents were erected near the fort's flagstaff. To establish proper military chain of command, Carrington ordered that Fort Reno would be garrisoned by Companies A, B, C, and H, under Captain Tenodor Ten Eyck, this command to be responsible for dismantling the old fort and establishing the new one.

As the busy day drew to a close, a sudden summer hailstorm swept down from the Big Horns. Private William Murphy, on herding detail, said the hailstones were as large as pullets' eggs. "We had had some trouble about an hour before in getting the stock to ford the Powder River, but they went back over it as though it were dry land. The animals that were picketed pulled their pins; the hobbled ones and even the stock the herders were riding all stampeded. The herders finally stopped their horses two or three miles from where they started." [35]

Not long after his arrival at Fort Reno, Colonel Carrington was surprised to discover the presence of three emigrant trains camped a few hundred yards beyond the post. These Montana-bound caravans had halted a few days earlier on the advice of Captain Bailey and were awaiting arrival of the soldiers before proceeding farther.

On the morning of the 29th, Carrington rode down to confer with the leaders. He was shocked by their lack of security pre-

cautions, by the slovenliness of their camps. "They were waiting for the protection it was understood would be furnished by
the troops ... these emigrants were impatient to proceed, but
so mixed with mule and ox trains that they had no concert of
purpose. They were naturally restless under the circumstances,
and could not agree among themselves."

Carrington realized at once that the movement of civilians
through his Mountain District was going to be a greater problem than he had believed. He informed the emigrants that
within twenty-four hours he would draw up a set of regulations
for civilian travelers to ensure their safety through the Indian
country. One of the train captains made light of the Indian
danger. "We'll never see an Indian," he said, "unless they come
to beg for sugar, flour, or tobacco." [36]

Carrington hoped the man was right, but warned all the
travelers to stay in camp until they received further orders from
him. On his way back to the fort, he noted a herd of horses and
mules grazing unguarded in a ravine. These animals, he
learned, were the property of Sutler A. C. Leighton, who
seemed confident the Indians would not disturb them.

That afternoon Carrington visited Leighton in his trailside
store just north of the fort. Perhaps the colonel wished to become better acquainted with the sutler, who had been authorized to supply stores for the three new forts. Carrington had
just entered Leighton's quarters when a soldier rushed in
shouting "Indians!" and excitedly informed the sutler that his
livestock was being raided. The men rushed to the door, and
off across the Powder they could see the herd stampeding up a
hill, followed by a party of Indians. Leighton was both aston-
ished and angry; he had never had any trouble with the Indians
before, he declared.

As soon as Carrington could reach his headquarters, he
ordered his bugler to sound the alarm, and a few minutes later
the mounted infantrymen were saddling up. In less than half
an hour after the Indian raid, Captain Haymond and Lieutenant Adair with ninety men were in pursuit. But the time lapse,
Carrington knew, had been too great. His men must learn to
react more quickly in future.

The afternoon wore on, watchers in the fort keeping an eye out for Haymond's pursuit party. There had been no sound of rifle fire, no trace of riders on the hills across the Powder.

Meanwhile, in preparation for moving the fort, Captain Ten Eyck's details were busily loading wagons with provisions from the warehouses. "The ware-rooms," said Private Murphy, "were built of cottonwood logs, chinked and daubed with mud. Some of the daubing had dropped out and snow had drifted in [during the previous winter]. The dirt roofs also leaked and added to the dirty mess. We loaded up some sacks of bacon. I do not know how old it was, but the fat had commenced to sluff off from the lean and it was from three to five inches thick. There was a lot of flour in the storerooms and the mice had tunneled through it and the bacon, evidently for some time." [37]

The day ended with the usual routines of retreat, roll call, mess, and guard mounting, but Haymond and Adair and their pursuit party were still missing. Carrington spent a bad night, was immensely relieved the next morning to see the column come riding in across the Powder, with no empty saddles. Captain Haymond reported that he had followed the raiders' trail into the Pumpkin Buttes, probably thirty miles, but had captured only one Indian pony abandoned so hastily that it still bore a pack. Haymond exhibited the contents—bags of brown sugar, coffee, navy tobacco, an army blanket, a stable frock, a folded length of bright calico. All Laramie treaty presents! The raiders no doubt had followed the train all the way north, waiting for an opportunity to take livestock. Sutler Leighton's herd had offered too tempting a target, too easy a reward for their patience. For Carrington, the incident was proof that his strict security precautions were necessary; the well-guarded military livestock had not even been threatened.

On the last day of June a decision was made, either by Carrington alone, or in council with his staff and civilian guides, not to abandon Fort Reno entirely. Possibly the presence of civilian wagon trains influenced the judgment; at any rate it was decided that at least one secure stopping place was needed on the long route between Bridger's Ferry and the future site of New Fort Reno—a place where travelers could halt to rest lame

stock and repair wagons. Carrington assigned one of his companies to garrison the station. Details from this company were
to be used for escorting mail, aiding travelers in distress, and
other emergency duties. For want of a better name, the place
would be called Reno Station.

It was also decided that the 2nd Battalion could not possibly
provide military escorts for the many emigrant trains expected
to be moving over the road during the summer. Yet the safe
passage of civilians was Carrington's immediate responsibility,
and recognizing this, he issued on June 30 a series of regulations governing the movement of civilian trains to Montana:

1. All trains, whether large or small, must stop at Reno Station, formerly Fort Reno, on Powder River, and report to
   the post commander.
2. Thirty armed men constitute a party which, upon selection
   of its commander or conductor, will be allowed to proceed.
   The reduction of this number will depend upon the general conduct of trains and the conditions and safety of the
   route, of which due notice will be given.
3. When a train shall have organized, the conductor will present to the post commander a list of the men accompanying
   the said train, upon which list, if satisfactory, he will en-
   dorse, "Permission given to pass to Fort Reno [soon to be
   named Fort Phil Kearny]." Upon arrival of a train at Fort
   Reno [Fort Phil Kearny], the conductor will report with
   his list, indorsed as above mentioned, to the post commander to receive the same indorsed approval as in the
   first instance to pass to the next post. This examination
   and approval must be had at each post, so that the last
   post commander on the Upper Yellowstone will have the
   evidence that the train has passed all posts.
4. The constant separation and scattering of trains pretending to act in concert must be stopped; and for the information of emigrants and well-disposed citizens the following
   reasons are given: viz:
      First, nearly all danger from Indians lies in the reckless-
   ness of travelers. A small party when separated, either
   sell whisky to or fire upon scattering Indians, or get in
   dispute with them, and somebody is hurt. An insult to

an Indian is resented by the Indians against the first white men they meet, and innocent travelers suffer.

Again, the new route is short and will be made perfectly secure. The cooperation of citizens is therefore essential for their own personal comfort as well as for the interests of the public at large; and if citizens ask, as they will of course rightly expect, the protection and aid from Government troops, they must themselves be equally diligent in avoiding difficulties with Indians, or among themselves, and the consideration paid to any complaint will be measured by the apparent good faith with which citizens regard the regulations for the management of the route.

5. When trains scatter and upon reporting at any post there shall be found a substantial variation from the list furnished, all of the remaining teams will be stopped until the residue of the train arrives, or is accounted for; and until this is done they will not be permitted to unite with other trains to complete numbers, which their insubordination or haste has lost or scattered.

6. The main object being perfect security to travel, all citizens are cautioned against any unnecessary dealings with Indians, against giving or selling ardent spirits, against personal quarrels with them, or any acts having a tendency to irritate them, or develop hostile acts or plans. A faithful and wise regard for these instructions will, with the aid of the Government troops, insure peace, which is all important and can be made certain.

7. A copy of these instructions will be properly and publicly posted at the office of each post or station commandant, and all conductors of trains will have their attention called thereto, with instructions to notify all who travel in their charge.[38]

IV. July:

MOON WHEN THE CHOKECHERRIES ARE RIPE

Whatever my own force I can not settle down and say
I have not the men; I must do all this, however arduous.
The work is my mission here and I must meet it.[1]

A MOST welcome visitor to Fort Reno on July 3 was Major Henry Almstedt, paymaster for the Department of the Platte. Although the men had received no pay for four months, almost any experienced frontier commander would have delayed payment until after the July 4 holiday. But perhaps Carrington did not realize how much contraband whiskey a flood of greenbacks combined with a holiday could attract even at so remote a post as Reno.

Independence Day was started in proper patriotic fashion by the firing of the fort's 12-pounder field howitzer. Paymaster Almstedt, being the only artillery officer present, supervised the loading and placed the portfire. A review and a few patriotic orations followed, and the men were free for the day.

According to Private Murphy there was some bootlegging but not much drunkenness. He described the punishment of one man who imbibed too freely that day: "At the guard tent four stakes were driven into the ground and the drunken soldier was stretched out full length and tied to them. This was called the 'Spread Eagle.' The sun was beating down on him when I saw him, and I thought he was dead. Flies were eating him up and were running in and out of his mouth, ears and nose. It was reported that he died, but in the army one can hear all kinds of reports." [2]

After reveille next morning all celebrants—regardless of the condition of their heads—resumed duties. Special details were assigned to remove wheels from wagons, grease axles, secure all nuts. Others inspected harness for flaws. The fort's six pieces of artillery were cleaned and prepared for movement; in addition to the 12-pounder field howitzer, there were five 12-pounder mountain howitzers.

Quartermaster Fred Brown kept the headquarters clerks busy invoicing supplies being transferred from warehouses to wagons, and it was already evident that available empty wagon beds could haul only about half the stocks.

As Carrington had definitely decided to keep Reno active, the depot stores which must be left behind presented no problem. Lieutenant Kirtland's Company B was ordered to remain at Reno, the post commander to be Captain Joshua Proctor, an aging officer with a full gray beard and a harassed though kindly face. Twenty-two horses were assigned so that Kirtland could mount about one-third of his men for necessary messenger and escort duties.

At four o'clock the morning of July 9, the seven remaining companies of the 2nd Battalion marched northward out of Fort Reno, exact destination unknown. The day before, a mail courier from Laramie had arrived, and the news from Omaha was not good; the Mountain District could expect no reinforcements before autumn at the earliest.

Carrington passed the word to his officers and established tentative assignments. Ten Eyck with three companies would command the new Fort Reno; regimental headquarters and the band would also occupy that post. Kinney with two companies would establish a post somewhere on the Big Horn River. Haymond with two companies would proceed to the Upper Yellowstone. It would be a long line, thinly held, but Carrington was determined to carry out his orders.

The day chosen for the march was the hottest of the summer

of 1866. The sun was blinding, the mercury reaching 113 in the shade by afternoon. Even the sagebrush seemed to shrivel under the baking heat. "Many of the soldiers had bad feet," said Private Murphy. "Add to this the fact that there was only one ambulance available for sick soldiers, as the women and children had all the others in use, and you have a picture of what it meant for a soldier to be sick." [3]

Except for water carried in canteens and barrels, there was none anywhere between Reno and Crazy Woman's Fork. Drivers were forbidden to use any for wetting wagon wheels which began to shrink, loosening the metal tires. Spares were used up rapidly.

And for the first time, they saw parties of Indians riding on the flanks, or watching from rises far ahead. Bridger and his guides parleyed with one small party of Sioux. These Indians said they were going across the Big Horns to fight the Shoshoni, but when Bridger reported to Carrington the scout expressed skepticism. He suggested the Sioux were counting soldiers, wagons and livestock—sizing up the strength of the train.

After twenty-six miles of heat, aching weariness, and wagon wheels falling apart, they reached Crazy Woman's Fork at dusk, finding sparse grass burned to a crisp and only a trickle of alkali water in the creek. From the guides, the soldiers heard two stories as to how the place received its name. One was that a squaw living alone there in a tepee had become demented and died; the other told of a party of whites attacked there, one man being killed and mutilated before the eyes of his wife, who became insane, wandered away, and disappeared forever. After what they had seen of Crazy Woman's Fork, the men could easily believe either story. It was not a good place to be.

Next morning the first order of business was a wagon inspection by Carrington and Brown. Almost half the wagons were unfit for another day's journey, and it was soon apparent that temporary repairs would not suffice. So much damage had been done to axles, spokes, and tires that smithies must be improvised. Details went to work immediately, cutting timber and digging charcoal pits. Every available wheelwright and blacksmith was drafted from both soldier and civilian contingents.

One ingenious workman devised a method of cutting gunny sacks in strips, soaking them in water, and tacking them to repaired wooden rims; when a heated tire was placed over one of these strips, it made a perfect seal.

After forty-eight hours of waiting for sufficient charcoal to be burned, Carrington grew restless. The best days of summer were passing, and he had three forts to build before winter. On the 12th, he ordered Captain Haymond to take command of the temporary camp at Crazy Woman's Fork. With Captain Ten Eyck and Companies A, C, and H, he would move on toward Tongue River.

Marching early to avoid the heat, the three companies by sunrise found themselves in a new and different country. "One narrow divide only is crossed, and the transition is like the quick turn of a kaleidoscope," wrote Margaret Carrington. The air was suddenly delightfully cool. Sagebrush and cactus disappeared, to be gradually replaced by green grass. Forests of evergreens showed dark against the slopes. By noon the first horses were plunging into Clear Fork, a swift mountain-fed stream "so clear that every pebble and fish is well defined." [4]

As they had been traveling steadily for nine hours, Carrington ordered his abbreviated train into camp. Tents were pitched along the banks of the rushing creek, and Mrs. Carrington told of how she, Mrs. Bisbee, and Mrs. Horton—the only women in the advance party—were sitting in camp chairs admiring the scenery when to their horror they discovered rattlesnakes coiled under their chairs. An orderly, hearing their screams, rushed to the rescue.

During late afternoon a small band of Indians visited the camp, cautiously escorted in by guides Bridger, Williams and Brannan. "We were peacefully inclined," Lieutenant Bisbee commented, "having nothing as yet to fight for, but suspicions grew strong that they were treacherous and we tied Gene (my son) by a trunk strap to the tent pole to prevent his straying away." [5]

Another of the small boys in camp, six-year-old Jimmy Carrington, afterward recalled these last nights of the long journey to the site of Fort Phil Kearny. "Nightly, we heard the weird and mournful howling of wolves, sometimes the deep rumble of a stampeded herd of buffalo, that fairly shook the earth. And all through the dark, at regular intervals, the reassuring calls of the sentinels on watch." [6]

Somewhat reluctantly next morning tents were struck and march resumed, the snow-covered Big Horns towering in the west, the land growing richer in timber and grass. Mounted Indians appeared suddenly on a high hill to the left, then vanished. After passing Rock Creek, Bridger's forward scouts came upon two small pieces of wooden cracker box posted by the roadside. Dismounting, they found messages scrawled on the boards, dated one week earlier. Indians had attacked two civilian trains there, driving off oxen and horses.

Bridger reported his discovery to Carrington. Soldiers were ordered to ready rifles, and flankers were sent farther out on the ridges. Hourly halts were suspended until they were clear of a long ravine. If the Indians had planned an attack, the bristling array of rifles must have discouraged them.

Before noon they were in more open country, with the glistening blue waters of Lake De Smet off to the east. With every passing mile, the luxuriance of plant growth increased. Stands of tall pines stretched for miles along the mountainsides, and grass was so heavy and thick in the bottomlands that a horse could not be trotted through it. For the first time they began to understand the fierce possessiveness of the Indians for this rich and beautiful country.

After a halt for nooning, they marched five or six miles and crossed Little Piney Creek. Carrington noted that on the left the ground rose gradually to a flat-topped grassy plateau. From where he sat his horse, the length and width of the rise seemed to be just about right for the dimensions of the headquarters fort he had planned back at Kearney. He pointed the location out to Bridger, indicating the expanse of timber a few miles beyond, and asked the scout's opinion. Old Gabe insisted that the colonel go on to Goose Creek or Tongue River before selecting a site.

The column moved on a short distance to Big Piney Creek, and Carrington ordered a halt. It was still early in the afternoon but he wanted to examine this location more closely. "The camp," according to Mrs. Carrington, "was organized with especial care. Greatly to the annoyance of the teamsters, the colonel had the corral formed three times until it was sufficiently compact and trim to suit." [7] Not until then did the meticulous commander select an escort for a seven-mile reconnaissance up Piney Fork toward the mountains "to determine whether the position was a judicious one for establishment of a post." [8]

"At last we had the prospect of finding a home," wrote his wife, "and Cloud Peak seemed to look down upon us with a cheerful face as the sunlight made his features glow and glisten." [9] During the next six months, that shining mountain would be her source of strength through hours of minor trials and fierce ordeals.

Carrington was up before dawn on the 14th, and at five o'clock rode off for a day's reconnaissance of the Goose Creek and Tongue River country. Captain Ten Eyck, Lieutenants Brown and Phisterer, Jim Brannan, Jack Stead, and twenty enlisted men accompanied him. Jim Bridger—the man who had been so insistent upon the superiority of the upper country—was conspicuous by his absence from the party. Just why Carrington left him behind is not clear; perhaps the colonel wanted to be free of Old Gabe's persuasive advice for a day, wanted to make the important decision of locating the new post entirely on his own responsibility.

The explorers rode for thirteen hours in a circuit of nearly seventy miles, sighting bear, buffalo, elk, deer, antelope, rabbits and sage hens. Wild raspberries, strawberries, gooseberries, currants, plums and cherries grew in profusion. Along Tongue River they found two brush tepees with signs of recent occupation, but did not see a single Indian all day. "I found less cottonwood on the streams, and that the pine region would be eighteen miles distant," Carrington later informed Omaha. "Neither in respect of grass, timber, water, or fuel, nor in any military sense, could I find any position even approximately equal to this [the ground between the Big and Little Pineys]." [10]

About six P.M., the reconnaissance party returned, to find the camp in a state of great excitement.

Everything had run smoothly in camp that morning until nine o'clock, at which time it was reported to Lieutenant Adair, officer-of-the-day, that nine men had deserted sometime during the night to head for the gold mines of Montana. Adair immediately sent a mounted detail in pursuit up the Bozeman Trail, but the party returned before noon, reporting they had been stopped about seven miles north by a band of Cheyennes who refused to permit them to go any farther. At the point where the Indians halted the detail, Louis (French Pete) Gazzous and Henry Arrison were camped with their traveling ranche, and were busily trading trinkets, and probably whiskey, for furs and buffalo robes.

Gazzous and Arrison had passed Fort Reno while the 2nd Battalion was there, and had added four civilians to their group, one a teamster who had left quartermaster employment to try his luck in Montana. The teamster's name was Joe Donaldson, and when the Cheyennes observed that he was well known to the soldiers, they ordered Donaldson to return to the military camp and deliver a message to Little White Chief, Carrington.

The message given to Donaldson by Chief Black Horse, through Gazzous as interpreter, was: "We wish to know does the White Chief want peace or war? Tell him to come to me with a black white man." Donaldson and the soldiers finally understood through questions and sign language that the "black white man" was the colonel's interpreter, swarthy Jack Stead.[11]

When the pursuit party returned to camp with Donaldson, Lieutenant Adair was at a loss as to what reply he should make to Black Horse. He feared the Cheyenne might take it as a hostile gesture if Donaldson was allowed to return without an answer. Donaldson indicated, however, that he had no intention of waiting around camp all day for the colonel to return, and Adair was forced to order him held in a guard tent.

During the afternoon a lone Cheyenne appeared outside Adair's picket lines, and in a few words of English made it known that he was a second messenger from Black Horse, sent to inquire about Donaldson. He asked that Donaldson be sent out, but Adair refused. The Cheyenne vanished, leaving a worried young officer-of-the-day and an excited camp behind him.

As soon as Carrington returned and learned of the situation, he lost no time in interviewing Donaldson and preparing a reply to Black Horse's message. The influence of Stead or Bridger is apparent in the style and wording of Carrington's letter, which ignored Black Horse's request for the colonel to come to him. Carrington also insisted on a delay of two days before the meeting, so that a show of military strength could be prepared for the visitors, if they came.

> HEADQUARTERS MOUNTAIN DISTRICT
> Piney Fork, July 14, 1866
>
> The GREAT CHIEF OF THE CHEYENNES:
>
> FRIEND: A young white man tells me that you wish to come and have a talk with me. I shall be happy to have you come and tell me what you wish. The Great Father at Washington wishes to be your friend, and so do I and all my soldiers.
>
> I tell all the white men that go on the road that if they hurt Indians or steal their ponies I will follow and catch them and punish them. I will not let white men do hurt to the Indians who wish peace.
>
> I wish the Indians would also find who stole mules and horses on Powder River and who stole mules and horses at Rock Creek two nights past.
>
> You may come and see me with two other chiefs and two of your big fighting men, when the sun is over head, after two sleeps.
>
> You may come and talk and no one shall hurt you, and when you wish to go you may go in peace and no one shall hurt you.
>
> I will tell all my chiefs and soldiers that you are my friends and they will obey.
>
> Your white friend
> HENRY B. CARRINGTON [12]

At twilight, Joe Donaldson and Jack Stead rode out of camp, bearing this first, and last, written communication from Carrington to the Indians.

Next day was Sunday, but it was not to be a day of rest. After brief religious services in the open, Carrington gave the order to lay out the new fort. During the night he had definitely decided to build the post on high ground between the two Pineys. Tongue River was not only too remote from pine timber, there was less grass and water, less advantage as to position. By running the stockade lengthwise of the site, water from Little Piney could easily be diverted and carried within the fort. Along both streams Carrington had noted an abundance of clay which would make a fine plaster for chinking and coating the buildings. And from the fort's interior the 12-pounder howitzers could command all nearby slopes and hills.

For years afterward—even into the twentieth century—Carrington was criticized for this choice of a fort site. It was said that soldiers within the fort could see nothing, but that their enemies could look down upon them and see everything. Actually the only restricted view was to the northeast, and this deficiency was overcome by placing a mounted picket on Pilot Hill, directly to the north across Big Piney. Private Murphy complained that "for some reason they picked out a location about seven miles from the timber and from five to eight miles from any hay bottom." [13] But Murphy, like the enlisted man of all armies, was a chronic grumbler, and if the fort had been in either a hay bottom or a forest, he would have continued to find fault. It is not on record that any of Carrington's officers objected to the site, nor did Jim Bridger, who had wanted to go on to Tongue River—probably because the hunting was better there.

During that Sunday morning, Carrington and Captain Ten Eyck staked out the future post's dimensions, following plans which they had drawn at Fort Kearney in the early spring. (They borrowed liberally from treatises on fortifications by Dennis Hart Mahan, professor of engineering at West Point.) The fort proper was to be a 400-foot square, with sixteen hundred feet of stockade enclosing barracks, officers' quarters, warehouses, administration buildings, sutler's store, hospital, magazine, battery, bandstand, and parade. To the southeast a quartermaster's yard 200x600 feet would extend to the waters of Little Piney. Here would be the stables, civilian teamsters' quarters, mechanics' sheds, woodyard and hay yard. The fort was planned to house one thousand men.

Its log stockade would be eight feet high with a continuous banquette about three feet above the ground. A flaring loophole was provided for every fourth log, and at diagonal corners of the square, enfilading blockhouses were designed with portholes for cannon. Carrington and Ten Eyck also worked out a detailed scheme for hewing the stockade logs to two smooth touching surfaces so that spikes would not be needed, the only tools required for construction being broadaxes, augers and chisels.*

They laid out the fort so that it fronted on the Bozeman Trail, with Big Piney and Pilot Hill just beyond. Little Piney was on the south, and to the west was an unnamed ridge which Carrington promptly called Sullivant Hills in honor of his wife's maiden name. To the northwest was Lodge Trail Ridge and beyond that Peno Creek. Carrington eyed this landscape with the delight of a discoverer, and proudly wrote to General Cooke in Omaha that he had occupied the very heart of the Indians' hunting grounds. "The mountains, five miles distant, are precipitous, but the gorges are full of pine, hemlock, balsam, fir, and spruce. This ridge is about 800 feet above the Piney bottoms, but behind, and stretching to the foot of the next or 'snow-capped' range is a sweep of prairie as rich in game as it is in grass and flowers. . . . In thirty days this post can be held by a small force against any force. . . ." [14]

After stakes were driven on that busy Sunday morning, the colonel assembled a train of wagons and ordered them driven repeatedly around the 400-foot square of the fort proper, until streets were beaten out of the high grass. When this was done, he brought up hay mowers to trim the inner parade into a lawn. Tents were pitched in exact mathematical lines along streets where buildings would rise; the 12-pounder howitzers were placed on the parade; signs were posted forbidding pedes-

---

* This system was later adopted by the British for construction of log defenses in South Africa and India.

trians to cross the freshly mown grass. Headquarters, adjutant, and guard tents were erected, sentinels and pickets posted. By noon, the camp looked as permanent as a tent camp can look, with a military precision about it that would have pleased the strictest of professional drillmasters.

The only diversion of the day was a grasshopper attack. The Carrington's Negro servant, George, rushed to inform Mrs. Carrington that it was snowing for sure, right out of the bright July sky. Instead, she found her tent was being eaten by giant grasshoppers. "They came in clouds like the drifting smoke of a prairie fire. . . . In vain were turkeys and chickens let loose against the destroyers; the whole camp hummed with the rustle of their wings as they filed themselves on the blades of grass and became familiar generally. A kind wind from the mountains came along in the afternoon, and they left as suddenly as they arrived."[15]

During the afternoon every soldier not on guard duty was assigned to a work detail—ditching, chopping, hewing or hauling. J. B. Gregory, a civilian engineer attached to the quartermaster, took a group of men down to the Little Piney and started assembling the horse-powered sawmill. The steam mill which had crashed into the Platte back at Scotts Bluff still had not caught up with the expedition, but was expected to arrive soon with one of the supply trains from Nebraska.

When sundown finally ended that first day of work on the new fort, three companies of weary men formed for hasty roll calls, fell out for supper, and rolled gratefully into blankets. The hard marches from Fort Kearney had toughened their muscles; now it seemed as if they would have to grow some new ones to build this fort fast enough to suit Colonel Carrington.

If the Indians had been forgotten in all the day's activities, the return of Jack Stead late that night was a reminder that they were still watching and waiting. Stead and the messenger, Joe Donaldson, had found Black Horse's camp thirty miles away on Tongue River. The Cheyennes had moved away from French Pete's camp, fearful of an attack from the soldiers. Stead informed Carrington that Black Horse accepted the colonel's invitation to visit the soldiers' camp. The Cheyennes would arrive "after two sleeps," which now would be sometime the following day.

During guard mount on the morning of July 16, the men were warned to be on the lookout for expected friendly Cheyennes. It was almost noon when the first few Indians appeared on the hills, waving white flags. Carrington sent Jack Stead out to assure them of a welcome, and about forty Cheyennes came riding in—eleven chiefs and subchiefs, several warriors, and a few squaws.

Preparations had already been made for an elaborate reception on the parade. Carrington and his officers donned shoulder scales, epaulets, and dress hats, hastily unpacked from trunks, and as soon as the Indians crossed Big Piney, Bandmaster Samuel Curry led the regimental band out on the parade where the musicians began performing a series of evolutions to the accompaniment of their brassiest martial tunes.

The Cheyennes also were dressed in their best—richly embroidered and beaded moccasins, fancy breechclouts, gay-feathered headdresses. Some wore large silver medallions, stamped with the heads of Presidents Jefferson, Madison or Jackson, over their naked chests. These trophies were highly prized, perhaps handed down from fathers who had visited Washington, or perhaps obtained in battle or trade. One tall chieftain carried a bright-colored umbrella over his head as his pony galloped briskly along.

To impress his guests, Carrington exhibited one of the howitzers, then ordered it fired at a distant hill. The Indians were startled by the loud noise of this "shooting wagon," were even more surprised when the spherical case shot exploded in the distance. "It shoots twice," said Chief Black Horse solemnly. "White Chief shoot once. Then White Chief's Great Spirit fires it once more, for his white children." [16]

A large hospital tent had been erected in front of Carrington's headquarters, and here the guests were assembled for a parley. Jim Bridger was present of course, sitting cross-legged facing the Cheyennes, listening attentively, saying nothing, leaving the business of conversation to Jack Stead, Carrington, and the chiefs. Black Horse was the Cheyenne leader, and with him was Two Moons, who in the next decade would make his name that of a mighty warrior, and another who was destined to become the greatest of all Cheyenne chiefs—Dull Knife. Ten years later Dull Knife would lead his people against Custer, and later still would lead them in an exodus from Indian Territory, a heroic flight which excited the admiration of even the men who hunted him down.

As the day was warm, the flies of both the hospital and headquarters tents were raised, and Mrs. Carrington, Mrs. Bisbee, and Mrs. Horton gathered in the latter to enjoy "a dress-circle view of the whole performance." After pipes were passed, Jack Stead arose and moved to the center of the tent. Although of English blood, Stead's hair and eyes were as dark as any of the Indians', his skin tanned to swarthiness. As a youth he had run away to sea, and after surviving a shipwreck near the mouth of the Columbia, he crossed the Rockies, took an Indian wife, learned the languages of the Plains tribes, and became skilled in hunting and fighting. "He was fond of big stories and much whiskey," said Margaret Carrington, "but a fair interpreter when mastered and held to duty." [17]

Now he was the first to break silence after the pipe smoking. "Black Horse wants talk," he said. [18]

The old chief rose and began the formalities of greeting. He and the other leaders present, he said, represented 176 Cheyenne lodges. They had recently quarreled with and broken away from another band of Cheyennes who wanted war. The other Cheyennes were willing to join the Sioux as allies to drive the white soldiers back to Powder River. But his own people wanted to make a strong treaty with the white men so that they might live out their lives in peace. "White man wants all," Black Horse said. "He will have it all."

After Black Horse finished his first harangue, the other chiefs spoke, and it soon became dramatically clear to Carrington that every move he had made since leaving Fort Reno had been observed and reported to Indian encampments throughout the area. He also realized for the first time that Red Cloud was his implacable enemy.

"They represented that on the day of my arrival," he said later, "Sioux Indians were encamped near them, and told them, 'I would be there that noon; that I had left half my white soldiers on the road at Crazy Woman's Fork; that I had sent men out from Fort Reno to chase Indians who had stolen mules, but the white soldiers did not catch them; that they (the Sioux) had a sun dance which was not over, and were insisting that they (the Cheyennes) must unite with them and not let the white soldiers go farther west; that if I would go back to Powder River (Fort Reno), a fort of last year, the white soldiers might stay there, but should build no more forts.' Responsive to my questions, they further stated 'that the band of Sioux referred to was led by Red Cloud, and numbered five hundred warriors; that they (the Cheyennes) were weak and could not fight the Sioux, and that if I would give them provisions they would make a lasting peace, to go wherever I told them, away from the Sioux and away from this road.'"[19]

In all the speeches the name of Makhpia-sha, or Red Cloud, was repeated again and again; there seemed no doubt in the minds of the Cheyennes that this tall, handsome Oglala—then in his middle forties—was the real leader of the hostiles. To the soldiers of the Mountain District he would soon become the symbol, the personification, of the enemy.

One piece of information concerning Red Cloud's activities was especially disturbing to Carrington. Red Cloud's warriors, said the Cheyennes, had gone toward Powder River to cut off further approach of travel. Being a theoretical military tactician, Carrington could understand the Sioux leader's reasoning: cut off the main body, isolate it, attack. The colonel was grateful for the warning. He must be prepared to meet a force led by a chief who knew how to fight a war.

The endless talk, slowed by translation, dragged on into late afternoon. But Carrington was patient. He knew that this was an opportunity to show his sincerity for peace; at the same time he was learning much which could be useful should hostilities become unavoidable. At one point he asked about the Crows. "This country is called Absaraka," he said, "the home of the

Crows. Why do the Sioux and Cheyennes claim land which belongs to the Crows?"

"We stole the hunting grounds of the Crows because they were the best," was the reply. "The white man is along the great waters, and we wanted more room. We fight the Crows because they will not take half and give us peace with the other half." [20]

Late in the day the arrival of Captain Haymond and his four companies from Crazy Woman's Fork provided a welcome interruption to the parley. Carrington excused himself and went to meet Haymond, who reported that repairs had been adequate to bring all wagons through. The four companies, Carrington decided, would camp between the forks of the Pineys. He informed Haymond to prepare for ten days' or two weeks' delay, at least until more junior officers reported for duty with the 2nd Battalion. In the meantime, Haymond's men could help with the building of this fort before moving north to erect others.

When Carrington returned to the council tent, he found the Cheyennes had become restless, perhaps suspicious because of the arrival of so many more soldiers in camp. Black Horse motioned toward the sun. It was going over, he said, and the Cheyenne chiefs must return to their camp. If they stayed too long in white soldiers' camp, the Sioux might attack in their absence. Then he made an unexpected offer: As soon as his young men returned from hunting he would give the Little White Chief one hundred warriors to go against the Sioux.

Carrington concealed his surprise. "I have men enough to fight the Sioux," he replied, "but if the Cheyennes keep good faith with the white men and have trouble with the Sioux, I will help them." As a gesture of his own good faith, Carrington then asked Lieutenant Phisterer to write a special "paper" for Black Horse:

TO MILITARY OFFICERS, SOLDIERS, AND EMIGRANTS:

Black Horse, a Cheyenne chief, having come in and shaken hands and agreed to a lasting peace with the whites and all travelers on the road, it is my direction that he be treated kindly, and in no way molested in hunting while he remains at peace.

When any Indian is seen who holds up this paper he must be treated kindly.

HENRY B. CARRINGTON
Colonel, 18th U. S. Infantry,
Commanding Mountain District [21]

Jack Stead translated, the Cheyenne leader expressed his thanks, and the other chiefs pressed forward immediately, requesting similar papers. While Phisterer wrote out copies, presents were distributed—twenty pounds of tobacco for the party, and one day's army rations for each visitor, including flour, bacon, sugar and coffee.

By the time the Cheyennes rode away, the sun was down, and the evening's guard mount was taking posts.

At five o'clock next morning, July 17, Red Cloud's war began. As reconstructed afterward, it was evident that several Indians had infiltrated Captain Haymond's picket lines. One brave leaped upon the bare back of Wagon Master Hill's bell mare and took off at a gallop, knowing from previous observation that the other animals would follow. "When the herd stampeded," said Private Murphy, "they ran across the Piney and we could scarcely see them for the cloud of dust they raised." [22]

At the first alarm, Haymond and his orderly flung saddles on their horses. After ordering his mounted detachment to follow as quickly as possible, Haymond took off in pursuit, accompanied only by his orderly. The trail of the Indians was easy to follow at first, with 175 stampeded animals, mostly mules, stirring up dust. Haymond held to high ground so that he could keep the course of the raiders in view until his men came up. But because of the suddenness of the raid, and the excited condition of the corralled riding horses, his mounted unit was slow in getting away, the men riding out in little groups of twos and fours instead of in proper formation. Consequently the pursuing force was strung out between the Pineys and Peno Creek.

This was exactly the opportunity the Sioux had been waiting for; small bands dropped back and began attacking the scattered pursuers. Haymond finally managed to rally his men, but when the Indians continued to press the attacks, he sent messengers galloping back to camp for reinforcements.

Colonel Carrington meanwhile had been waiting with angry impatience for some word from Haymond. On receiving Haymond's call for reinforcements, he dispatched fifty mounted men under Lieutenant Bisbee, and two companies of infantry. He also ordered work details in the fort to exchange tools for arms. Tarpaulins were removed from the howitzers, and the camp put in readiness for attack.

Back in the field, Captain Haymond was beginning to disengage his forces when the first elements of the relief party arrived. With Lieutenant Bisbee's fresh-mounted company, he resumed pursuit, later described by Bisbee as "a running fight for fifteen miles but the odds were against us and we lost the mules as Red Cloud had promised."[23]

They recovered only four animals, a poor exchange for their first casualties from Indian attack. Two men were dead, three wounded. "One man—John Donovan of my company," reported Private Murphy, "was wounded twice, once with a poisoned arrow and another a bullet wound."[24]

Falling back on the Bozeman Road, Haymond and Bisbee reluctantly turned about for camp. As the advance party rode down toward Peno Creek, they sighted the wagons of French Pete Gazzous's temporary trading post. It was obvious that something was wrong. Covers had been ripped from wagons, and plunder strewn all around. They found six dead white men, all mutilated.

"It was a terrible sight," said Private John Ryan. "The poor victims had been mutilated in the most horrible manner and it gave us all a most convincing lesson on what our fate would be should we fall into the hands of the Indians."[25]

Louis Gazzous had been killed by his wife's own tribesmen, and with him died his partner, Henry Arrison; the young teamster, Joe Donaldson; and three adventurers who had joined on for safe passage to Montana.

Bisbee reported briefly that signs indicated French Pete's "unlawful load of whiskey had led to his destruction, despite his squaw wife who was spared." The men found her with the five Gazzous children hidden in some bushes nearby.[26]

A few scattered beef cattle also were recovered; goods and

stores not destroyed by the Indians were reloaded into wagons; the mutilated bodies were buried. Haymond's party then returned to camp, the captain reporting to Carrington and presenting the Frenchman's squaw for interrogation.

The Gazzous woman talked freely. She told Carrington that the Cheyenne chiefs had stopped at her husband's camp the previous evening after leaving the soldier camp, and they had talked and traded for some hours. During this time, Red Cloud and a party of Sioux came up from Peno Valley. Red Cloud asked Black Horse what the white soldiers had said to him. Was the Little White Chief, Carrington, going to return to Powder River? Black Horse replied that the Little White Chief was not going back, but was going on north to build more forts. Red Cloud then asked: What did the Little White Chief give them for presents? "All we wanted to eat," Black Horse replied, and added that Carrington had promised presents for all the Indians in Tongue River valley whenever they went to Laramie and signed the treaty. "Let us take the white man's hand and what he gives us, rather than fight him longer and lose all," Black Horse had said.

Red Cloud retorted angrily: "White man lies and steals. My lodges were many, but now they are few. The white man wants all. The white man must fight, and the Indian will die where his fathers died." [27]

At this point, the Sioux unslung their bows and whipped Black Horse, Dull Knife, and the other Cheyennes over their backs and faces. After the Sioux left, Black Horse told French Pete that he was going with his people up to the mountains, and he advised the trader to go back to the white soldiers' camp or the Sioux would kill him.

Carrington of course was disturbed by the Gazzous woman's story. He thanked her for her co-operation, assured her that she and her children would be welcome to the protection of his camp, and then, as a lawyer might have been expected to do, he assigned an administrator, John Hugas—one of the civilian contractors in camp—to settle her husband's estate. Her ultimate fate is obscure. According to the laconic Private Murphy, "she was at the fort about two months and left one night." [28]

As soon as Carrington finished his interrogation, he sent Haymond an order to move his four companies closer to the fort site. He also gave the captain a mild dressing down for not reporting to headquarters before going in pursuit of Indians that morning. Privately he excused Haymond for his hasty action; after all, the captain had commanded the 2nd Battalion through its hardest fighting in the Civil War and had been cited for gallantry. Indian warfare was new and strange; none of them had really believed the Sioux would dare attack so large a force. But now they knew. Two soldiers were dead; three wounded. So ended the first day of Red Cloud's war.

The following week was deceptively peaceful around the Pineys. Work on the stockade continued without interruption except for daily military routines of reveille, roll call, guard mount, retreat, tattoo, and lights out. Wagons were unloaded, goods stored under canvas. A mail courier arrived from Laramie, bringing official communications relieving Captain Haymond and Lieutenant Phisterer from field duty and reassigning them to recruiting service in the States. Although commissioned replacements were en route to the Mountain District, Carrington was dismayed over the prospect of losing any officers, especially when they were as experienced as Haymond and Phisterer.

Food was also becoming a problem. Long hard hours in the open air gave the men voracious appetites which could not be satisfied by hardtack and half-spoiled meat. A few beef cattle from the herd brought overland were slain, but Carrington was determined to reserve most of this supply until winter. An occasional deer or antelope shot by men working in the timber also provided fresh meat, but there was never enough to fill demand. A few boxes of desiccated vegetables had been brought from Reno, and these were carefully rationed.

One of the enlisted men, Alson Ostrander, recorded his sergeant's description of the desiccated vegetables: "Somewhere back east there is a factory where they put 'em up. They take a heap of each kind of vegetable and slice 'em just as thin as possible and then they are thoroughly dried out. Then they mix them all together and put them under a tremendous hydraulic pressure until they are squeezed just like plug tobacco. They come in cakes about nine inches long, three inches wide, and nearly an inch thick. Then they are packed in air-tight caddies and when opened they look just like a big plug of tobacco, but when placed in boiling water, how they do swell! One of these plugs will make several gallons of good rich soup."[29]

At first the enlisted men used the same mess system as they had in the Civil War, four to eight men in each mess rotating duties of cooking, collecting fuel, and hauling water. To free more men for work details, however, informal company kitchens were encouraged, with regular cooks assigned. Private Murphy noted that "about July 20, Orderly-Sergeant Lang and I bought two fresh cows from an immigrant train. No one wanted to work in the kitchen, so I volunteered in order to be able to take care of the cows morning and evening. It was not known that I had any interest in the cows or it might have caused some trouble. We had a first class baker in the company who volunteered to do the baking. At that time the Government did not furnish cooks or bakers. They simply furnished the rations and the soldier could cook them himself or eat them raw if he saw fit. . . . We cooked soup, bacon and coffee and dished it out to the men in their cups and plates—we had no dining room. We boiled everything. I believe the bacon would have killed the men if it had not been thoroughly boiled . . . the bacon and flour I had seen at Reno was given to us. The flour had been hauled sixty-five miles and handled several times. The result was that the refuse left by the mice was well mixed with the flour and we found a number of dead mice in it also. As we could not get a sieve, we manufactured one out of burlap sack by pulling out some of the strings and nailed it on a wooden frame. We got most of the larger refuse out. The bacon where the fat had commenced to sluff off from the lean was yellow with age and bitter as quinine. Some of the worst we shaved off, but we could not spare too much. One reason why our rations were so scanty was that flour was worth $100 per sack and bacon, coffee and beans proportionately. The companies of those times had no quartermaster or commissary agents and two or three men would be detailed to go and get the rations. They were piled out in a heap and you could take them or leave them."[30]

By the weekend of the 22nd, a sufficient number of wagons had been unloaded and reconditioned to make up a return train to Reno to pick up stores left behind for lack of wagon space. Carrington gave the assignment to Captain Thomas Burrowes' G Company, with an added detachment of mounted men, and Jim Bridger as scout.

Sunday, the day of the wagon train's departure, was marked by a return of Indian raiding, not in force but in small parties. The Sioux were unable to break through Carrington's alert defenses, but succeeded in capturing four horses and four mules from a civilian train camped nearby.

At one o'clock in the morning of July 24, Carrington was awakened by his orderly. A courier had just arrived with an urgent message from Captain Burrowes. By the light of his tent lamp, the colonel read the penciled scrawl:

COL. CARRINGTON:

There is a train engaged 3 mi. from here. I can not send them any help. The Sioux are very numerous. Send a force at once.

CLEAR FORK, 7:15 P.M. [July 23]   T. B. BURROWES

On the reverse of this paper was the appeal for help Burrowes had received the previous evening:

COMMANDING OFFICER:

SIR: We have received the papers from you through Black Horse, and we would inform you that about 3 miles from this watering place, Mr. Kirkendall's train has been engaged all this afternoon. Troops should be sent immediately, as we are not in position to leave this bull outfit and they can not come in by no means.

Yours,

THOS. DILLON [31]

It was clear at once to Carrington that Red Cloud had not been merely boasting when he told Black Horse he would cut off further travel from Fort Reno. Three trains were under simultaneous attack—Burrowes', Dillon's and Kirkendall's. And

Black Horse and his Cheyennes were in the same area, complicating matters by presenting their letters of conduct signed by Carrington. The colonel wondered how many civilian wagon drivers, surrounded by Sioux, would stop to distinguish one tribesman from another.

Without delay, Carrington aroused Captain Nathaniel Kinney and ordered him to march Company D with one of the mountain howitzers to Clear Fork and relieve Burrowes.

What Carrington did not know on this dark night was that the main force of Sioux was engaged still farther south against a party of thirty-four, which included five long-overdue officer replacements for the 2nd Battalion. For twenty-four hours they had been the victims of an Indian surround, typical in most of its features of the classic surrounds which would become a part of the folklore of the West.

Their story began at Fort Sedgwick, where Musician Frank Fessenden had been left with his wife back in May. After Carrington's Traveling Circus moved on, the Fessendens became parents of the baby girl whom Captain Fetterman jestingly suggested should be named Sedgwick. Late in June they journeyed by army ambulance to Fort Laramie, and on July 13 left there with a small detachment under Lieutenant George Templeton en route to Fort Reno. In addition to Mrs. Fessenden, two other women were in the party, the wife of Lieutenant Alexander H. Wands, and her colored maid, Laura. The Wands also had a small child, a son named Bobby. In addition, three civilians accompanied the detachment, including the Philadelphia photographer, Ridgway Glover, and a former officer of Missouri Volunteers, Captain Marr.

"Our first camp after leaving Fort Laramie," Fessenden recorded, "a number of Indians came to our command. They appeared very friendly—so much so that it excited our curiosity. We soon discovered the reason. The squaws wanted to buy our baby, offering beads, furs and trinkets of all kinds in exchange. When we refused they acted very sullen, and told us plainly they would steal her if they got the chance."[32] For the remainder of the journey the Fessendens and the Wands guarded their children with special care.

After the detachment crossed the Platte at Bridger's Ferry, Ridgway Glover set up his camera and made a stereoscopic view of the river, but he was disappointed to find "very little scenery worth photographing." [33]

At Fort Reno they were joined by Chaplain David White and Assistant Surgeon C. M. Hines, who were under orders to report to Carrington. Captain Joshua Proctor, commanding at Reno, was reluctant to grant Templeton's party permission to proceed to the Pineys. Templeton had ten enlisted men, four lieutenants (Alexander Wands, James H. Bradley, Napoleon H. Daniels, Prescott M. Skinner), Chaplain White, Surgeon Hines, nine wagon drivers, and three civilians—or only twenty-nine armed men, including himself.

Proctor, however, recognized that all the officers and several of the men had long Civil War records, and he finally issued a permit to pass. Early in the morning of July 20, their five wagons and two ambulances rolled northward on the Bozeman Trail. As they had only four saddle horses, the officers took turns at riding.

One of the enlisted men, S. S. Peters, afterward wrote an account of the latter part of the journey. The first night camp, he said, was excessively warm, and coyotes howled unceasingly so that sleep was almost impossible. "Lieutenant Daniels, an Indianan, was especially restless and came over to where I was on guard and walked the beat with me. He said that he had a presentiment that something was going to happen to him very soon and he did not know how to account for it. All efforts to discourage him from entertaining the gloomy phantasy were unavailing, and he seemed determined to dwell upon it, and remained with me until the signal for calling in the guard was given and preparations were ordered made for the start before daylight."

They marched to Dry Creek without incident, hoping to find water there. They found not water, but in the dry basin of a pool they discovered the dead body of a white man, filled with arrows, scalped, and mutilated. "The fragment of a gray shirt still hanging about the shoulders of the dead man indicated that he was in all probability a soldier. He was evidently a courier."

After a hasty burial, they resumed march. "The finding of the dead body . . . had a very depressing effect on the entire command, and with the ascending sun the heat became intense. Our water supply, which was meagre at the best, had now given completely out and the animals began showing signs of severe suffering."[34]

As they approached Crazy Woman Creek around nine o'clock in the morning they could see the first thin fringe of cottonwoods five miles away, and beyond on a slope several dark moving objects. Lieutenant Daniels put his field glass on the objects and pronounced them to be buffalo. He persuaded Lieutenant Templeton that it would be a good idea for them to ride ahead, cross the creek somewhere above the buffalo and turn the herd in toward the road. By the time the wagons reached the valley, the buffalo should be within shooting distance of the entire party. Daniels took the lead, galloping away with Templeton close behind.

A few minutes later the train dropped down a hill toward the creek, and a belt of timber screened the two officers from view. Everyone was alert, readying rifles for the expected chase, forgetting thirst and heat in the excitement. For a hundred yards the trail ran through deep sand that slowed the pace of the mules; the drivers shouted, slapping their reins, eager to reach the creek.

"The entire detachment was in this dry bed urging the teams through the sand, when to our complete astonishment a volley of arrows and rifle-shots were poured into us. The shots were accompanied with a chorus of savage yells, and the timber land and brush above and about us was fairly alive with Indians."[35]

Miraculously no one was hurt in this first violent attack, and because rifles were held ready for the expected buffalo, fire was returned almost instantly. Led by Lieutenant Bradley, a dozen men jumped from the wagons and charged up a slope ahead of the lead team, driving the Sioux back toward the creek. Wagons and ambulances were brought up out of the sandy bed to higher ground. The first wagon was swung crossways, the second and fourth moving to the left, the third and fifth to the right, and then the two ambulances were swung crosswise to close the square, with leader and swing mules being turned inside for protection.

Even before this hasty corral was formed, the Sioux came whooping back, but another volley sent them scurrying. A moment later a riderless horse dashed out of the brush, its saddle twisted under, arrows sticking from neck and flanks. It was Lieutenant Daniels' mount. The premonition of doom he had revealed to Private Peters had come true. "A second later, Lieutenant Templeton appeared, riding up out of the dry bed of the creek, hatless, two or three arrows in his horse's withers and flanks, and an arrow in his own back. Templeton was bleeding profusely from a wound in the face, and his whole visage was one of extreme terror, and as soon as he reached the corral he reeled and partly fell from his horse. He was lifted from the saddle in a state of complete collapse." Before he lost consciousness, Templeton uttered four words: "Daniels! My God, Indians!"[36]

The wounded lieutenant was laid in one of the wagons for protection. Surgeon Hines removed the arrow as quickly as possible, but he could not remain to dress the wound. He was needed back on the line with a rifle. The Sioux were closing in, and two mules were already so badly wounded they had to be cut loose.

With Templeton out of action, Lieutenant Wands assumed command, and from his Civil War experience he realized that he was in an untenable position. The Sioux were sheltered by trees and brush and could pick off animals and soldiers one by one.

A half mile to the south was a high treeless knoll. Once corralled and dug in there, they could hold out at least until dark. But a withdrawal to a new position would be extremely dangerous. After a quick conference it was decided to bunch the wagons, two in front, the ambulances with the women and children next, and the other three wagons following as cover. Bradley, with seven men, established a rear guard, and Wands and Skinner with twelve men covered the flanks and advance.

As soon as the movement was begun, the Sioux guessed its purpose, and a party swarmed out of the creek bottom, attempting to reach the hill first.

"The advance guard held their ground like heroes," Private Peters recorded, "and fought every foot of the way. The teams were kept on the run and then came the charge of twelve men under Lieutenant Wands and Lieutenant Skinner up the hill for its possession. The Indians were poor shooters, and wounded only two men in the charge . . . then broke and ran from the hill. Captain Marr, who had a Henry rifle, a sixteen shooter, used it with wholesome effect on the running Indians, and stopped two of them permanently. They were gathered up, however, by a bunch of Indian horsemen and carried away. . . . In the meanwhile the rear guard was holding the Indians in check from the creek side, and the wagons and ambulances were safely brought to the hill. A corral was immediately made, with mules inside the corral. The ambulances were protected by the wagons. . . ."[37]

They dug a ring of rifle pits just outside the corral, and for the first time felt some sense of security. The scorching sun and lack of water seemed more unbearable than the constantly yelling Sioux, who now kept beyond rifle range.

The photographer, Ridgway Glover, meanwhile had been awaiting a good time and place to set up his Roettger camera. The Indians, he said, "looked very wild and savage-like while galloping around us; and I desired to make some instantaneous views."[38] Lieutenant Wands, however, forbade Glover to do so. Under the circumstances, Wands doubtless felt that if Glover meant to shoot Indians he should do so with a rifle rather than a camera. Thus was lost one of the rarest opportunities to photograph an Indian attack, although the slow-speed camera shutter of that period probably would have caught only a series of blurs as the Indians swept past on their ponies.

Not long after the establishment of the defensive position, a shower of arrows zipped in from the left without warning, wounding three men. One of the wounded was Chaplain White, more angered than injured. The arrows came again, seeming to fly out of the ground, but closer observation revealed their source as a narrow ravine, cutting its way down toward the creek. The Sioux had crept up this ditch unobserved until they were in arrow range.

White and an enlisted man named Fuller volunteered to clear out the ravine. Running crouched forward, the two men charged the position. White was armed with an old-fashioned pepperbox seven-shooter pistol, Fuller with a rifle. They dropped out of sight, and a moment later the watchers on the hill heard what sounded like a volley of rapid fire. Several Sioux leaped from the ravine, the men in the rifle pits opening fire upon them. Shortly afterward White and Fuller reappeared. "Got two of the devils!" the chaplain shouted. "Ravine clear down as far as the creek." [39] All seven charges in his pepperbox had gone off at once, killing one Indian and frightening the others into flight.

The afternoon wore on, the men in the pits suffering acutely from thirst. Every few minutes a party of mounted Sioux would circle the hill, yelling their eerie wolflike war cries. Occasionally two or three warriors would swing to the off sides of their ponies and make quick dashes close to the corral, firing with remarkable accuracy from under their ponies' necks. By midafternoon, over half the men in the detachment were wounded, some seriously.

In Frank Fessenden's account of this ordeal he told of seeing a Sioux "stationed on a little hill directing the fight by signals with a flag." [40] The most disturbing sight of the afternoon, however, was the sudden appearance down by the creek of a man dressed in army blues. When the figure began a savage dance, they realized it was a Sioux warrior dressed in Lieutenant Daniels' uniform.

Near sundown the piteous moaning of the wounded men for water led Lieutenant Wands to risk a dash for the creek. A small detail collected empty canteens and water buckets, and crawled one by one over into the ravine held by Chaplain White and Private Fuller. Then a diversionary party moved out of the rifle pits to cover the water detail concealed in the ditch.

Either the Sioux misunderstood the purpose of the action, or they could not resist the opportunity of rushing the weakened defenses of the corral. They ignored the diversionary party, and swarmed up to the rifle pits. With coolly spaced firing, however, the remaining riflemen—many of whom were already minor casualties—drove the chargers back. Before the Sioux could re-form, the water detail was back, the first canteens being passed in to Mrs. Wands and Mrs. Fessenden, who were attending the severely wounded cases. "The two ladies," said Private Peters, "were angels of mercy and tenderness and looked after the wounded most heroically and bravely."

Refreshed by water, some of the wounded returned to the pits just in time to help beat off two direct mounted charges. The Sioux—about 160 of them according to Fessenden—attacked fiercely, killing one sergeant and seriously wounding three more men. "Our condition was now becoming so desperate that a council of war was held. It was solemnly decided, that in case it came to the worst that we would mercifully kill all the wounded ... and then ourselves." Chaplain White, who had returned from the ravine for the conference, was reluctant to agree to this. He volunteered to try to cut his way out of the surround and ride back to Fort Reno for reinforcements. Private William Wallace immediately offered to join the chaplain in the attempt, and Wands and Marr offered their saddle horses.

"They were properly mounted and furnished with a revolver each, and heroically rode out from the corral amid the prayers and God speeds of the little band. They succeeded in reaching the dry creek bed before they were apparently discovered by the Indians. As they rode out of the creek bed up toward the hill, a body of Indians were seen to hurriedly ride out from the forks of the two creeks up the hill toward the two couriers. The ride was a magnificent one. White and Wallace saw the Indians coming and put spurs to their horses and soon reached the crest of the hill far in advance of their pursuers. A moment or two later, pursued and pursuers were lost to view in the gathering twilight, for the sun was already going down beyond the Big Horn Mountains to the west of us." [41]

As the long summer twilight deepened, the air turned cooler. The Sioux made no more attacks, but seemed to be gathering along the creek for a council of war of their own. Just before dark the men in the pits saw a dust cloud off to the northwest, and with dejected spirits watched its rapid approach. They were certain it marked the trail of reinforcements for the Sioux.

A few seconds later the Indians along the creek began dispersing, small groups moving away in different directions. Daylight was almost gone now, the mounted Indians vanishing into the dark smudge of cottonwoods.

One of the riflemen cried out, pointing to a low ridge beyond the leftward ravine. A silhouette of an approaching horseman was black against the paling sky. Before the lone rider reached the ravine, Lieutenant Wands called an order to halt.

The horseman reined up, shouting that he was a friend.

"What's your name?"

"Jim Bridger." [42]

And so it was. The men cheered Old Gabe as he let his horse pick its way around the ravine and up to the corral. He told them that Captain Burrowes and two companies of the 2nd Battalion were coming down the road a mile or so back. The action at Crazy Woman's Fork was ended.

Next morning they found Lieutenant Daniels' body near the road. Frank Fessenden, a member of the search party, said it had been pierced by three bullets and "there were twenty-two arrows sticking in it." [43] Daniels' scalp and fingers were gone, and he had been "barbarously tortured with a stake inserted from below." [44] The men also found a dead Sioux in a ditch nearby; in the Indian's possessions were the lieutenant's shirt and scalp.

On the advice of Bridger and Captain Burrowes, Lieutenant Wands decided to turn back to Fort Reno with the wagon train. The return march had scarcely begun when they met a detachment of mounted infantry led by Lieutenant Kirtland from Reno. With the horsemen were Chaplain White and Private Wallace, safe but weary from their long night ride.

In the last week of July, the Wands party returned with Burrowes' wagon train to the Pineys, where the young officers at last reported for duty with the 2nd Battalion. Carrington welcomed them warmly, assigned them to companies, and they were soon engaged in the major work at hand—the building of the fort.

Ridgway Glover was delighted with the fort and the scenery around it, although he was disappointed over a failure to obtain photographs of some visiting Cheyennes. "My collodion was too hot, and my bath too full of alcohol," he wrote the editor of the *Philadelphia Photographer,* "to get any pictures of them, though I tried hard." He added that the military camp was "hemmed in by yelling savages who are surprising and killing some one every day. I expect to get some good pictures here, and hope that before Christmas you will see how these mountains look in July." [45]

Frank Fessenden reported to Bandmaster Samuel Curry and was assigned a double tent for his wife and child. In addition to morning and evening band duties, Fessenden assisted with construction work. The stockade around the 400-foot square of the main fort was almost completed now, and foundations were being laid for quartermaster storehouses. "Colonel Carrington," wrote Fessenden, "was a very busy man, and took great interest in the building of the fort. He was always out early in the morning and saw that everyone was in charge of their special departments, doing their duty." [46]

During the first ten days of construction, Carrington had been pondering over a name for his new fort. Officially it was Fort Reno, but he had already notified Omaha that he was retaining the original Fort Reno. Some of his junior officers suggested that it be called Fort Carrington, but he knew that recent Army policy disapproved use of names of living officers for forts. The problem was solved when Adjutant Phisterer opened the mailbag brought back from Reno by Captain Burrowes. Among the dispatches was an order from the Department of the Platte:

> The 2nd Battalion, 18th U. S. Infantry, will take post as follows:
>
> Two companies at Fort Reno, on Powder River; four companies about 80 miles nearly north of Reno, on the new route to Virginia City, Montana. . . . This post will be known as Fort Philip Kearny.[47]

And so on July 27, Carrington issued a general order proclaiming the new post as Fort Philip Kearny, in honor of the heroic one-armed general killed in action at Chantilly in 1862. To veterans of the Grand Army of the Republic, however, General Kearny was *Phil* Kearny, and in popular usage the post would be Fort Phil Kearny.

On July 29 a contract wagon train arrived with the long-overdue steam sawmill which had been badly damaged at Scotts Bluff when the eight-yoke bull team hauling it had stampeded down a steep hill into the North Platte. Carrington ordered Engineer Gregory to put the steam mill into operation immediately. He also notified Quartermaster Fred Brown to establish a timber cutters' camp on Piney Island and to make preparations for daily log train movements from the cuttings to the fort.

The steam sawmill was a Lane & Bodley, manufactured at Cincinnati, and was set up to slab large logs on two sides so that each would have a touching surface of at least four inches. It was equipped with a steam whistle which soon proved useful for sounding Indian alarms. (When the mill was renovated in 1940, the cast flange was found to have been mended in several places with strips of wrought iron; one of the bearings from the saw shaft had been crudely babbitted, and several holes had been cut through the frame with cold chisels. Some of these repairs may have been made after the accident at Scotts Bluff; others probably by J. B. Gregory. But in spite of its condition, the mill sawed thousands of feet of timber for construction of Fort Phil Kearny.)

Piney Island, the source of timber six miles west of the fort, was not a real island but was a thick stand of tall pines surrounded by North and South Piney and Spring creeks.* Frank Fessenden, who was occasionally assigned to timber-cutting duties, said there were two separate loggers' camps. "We built two blockhouses, one at each cutting, we having what was known as the 'upper' and 'lower' cuttings. Detachments of men went out and cut timber each day. Every morning twenty wagons were sent out for this purpose. About half a mile before reaching the timber, the road forked at an angle of about 45 degrees, one

---

* It is the present site of Story, Wyoming.

road running to each cutting. Here we found trees that were 90 feet to first limb and straight as an arrow." [48]

Operation of logging and hauling work was Quartermaster Brown's responsibility, and he used both military and civilian personnel. He must have been at constant odds with company, battalion and regimental adjutants in efforts to secure adequate details of men. To add to his burdens, wild grass in the nearby bottomlands was ripening for mowing, and he had to find additional men to operate mowing machines and rakes.

During this busy period the weather was fine, the air dry and winy, temperatures sometimes reaching ninety during the afternoons but dropping to sixty after dark. Only six men reported on sick call during the month of July, and these were minor surgical cases, results of accidents.

The clear nights were beautiful with a sky full of huge glittering stars, and sometimes a moon bathed the snow-clad Big Horns in a magical silver. By moonlight the limitless expanse of hills and mountains seemed empty, the silence broken by the deep roar of Big Piney. Late in the month, wolves began gathering after dark around the slaughter yard near Little Piney, howling and snarling over the offal there, ending the peaceful nights. For a time sentries were permitted to fire at the wolves, but the firing broke more sleep than the animals' howls, and Carrington forbade the practice, ordering poison put out to kill them. The unseen but watchful Indians noted this change, and one night a Sioux warrior donned a wolfskin, crept near the stockade, and shot a sentry from the banquette. A man was dead; another lesson in frontier warfare had been learned.

By the 29th of July, Carrington had completed interviewing leaders (Dillon and Kirkendall) of civilian trains which had been attacked by the Sioux at the same time Lieutenant Wands' party was under siege at Crazy Woman's Fork. The colonel was much disturbed by reported treacherous actions of the Sioux. In two instances the Indians had approached trains, expressing friendship, and then after shaking hands and accepting presents of tobacco, had shot their benefactors in the backs.

There was no longer any doubt in Carrington's mind that Red Cloud had opened aggressive operations in his rear, threatening communications with the outside world. At the same time, General Cooke in Omaha had already made clear that no reinforcements could be expected before autumn. The arrival of Alex Wands and the other three lieutenants had been a timely gain, but the post was still so short of officers that two lieutenants were alternating as officer-of-the-day.

On the 29th, Carrington decided his situation was grave enough to warrant a direct appeal to The Adjutant General in Washington. After protesting the transfers of Captain Haymond and Lieutenant Phisterer to recruiting duties, he added: "I have to give sergeants important duties, having for a line of one hundred miles active Indian hostilities. Lieutenant Daniels, en route to join me with escort of fifteen men, was scalped and horribly mutilated. I have lost three men, killed and wounded, besides Lieutenant Daniels. I need officers and either Indian auxiliaries or men of my regiment to build my posts, prepare for winter, and clear out the Indians. I can resist all attacks and do much active fighting, but I have a long line to watch and cover. The Indians are aggressive to stop the new route." [49]

The next day he also composed a long report for General Cooke:

> Character of Indian affairs hostile. The treaty does not yet benefit this route. . . . My ammunition has not arrived; neither has my Leavenworth supply train. Working parties keep arms in constant readiness for use: and with this dispatch I send an escort to look for advices and guard emigrants and supplies.
>
> My infantry make poor riders, and, as I can only fight Indians successfully on foot, my horses suffer in pursuit and in fight.
>
> I am equal to any attack they may make, but have to build quarters and prepare for winter, escort trains, and guaranty the whole road from the Platte to Virginia City with eight companies of infantry. I have to economize ammunition, and yet, from Kearney out, I picked up all I could get. I send two officers on recruiting service, under peremptory orders from Washington, leaving me crippled and obliged to trust too much to non-commissioned officers . . . there is at Laramie and elsewhere a false security, which results in emigrant trains

scattering between posts, and involving danger to themselves and others.

. . . It is a critical period with the road, and many more outrages will injure it. Still, if emigrants will properly arm and keep together, having due warning, I have confidence in the route.

. . . My eight companies of eighty effective men each, with quarters to build, and 560 of them new recruits . . . do not give me a fixed adequate command for the present emergency. My own supply trains are to be guarded, trains are to be escorted, a courier line is to be maintained. Whatever my own force I can not settle down and say I have not the men; I must do all this, however arduous. The work is my mission here and I must meet it. But . . . when I am my own engineer, draughtsman, and visit my pickets and guards nightly, with scarcely a day or night without attempts to steal stock or surprise pickets, you will see that much is being done, while I ought to have all my officers and some cavalry or Indian auxiliaries at each post.[50]

On the 31st, the harassed colonel wound up his paper work for the month of July by ordering F Company to join B Company at Reno—in compliance with Cooke's order to retain that fort as a two-company post. At the same time he brought Fort Phil Kearny's strength to four companies by transferring E and H to the permanent garrison. As Companies A and C were already assigned to Phil Kearny, this left D and G to make the march north to the Big Horn River to build the third post on the Montana Road.

V. August:

MOON WHEN THE GEESE
SHED THEIR FEATHERS

*From the middle or latter part of August, Indians ap-
peared more frequently about Fort Philip Kearny, and
from that time I assumed the condition of affairs to be
decided, unequivocal hostility on the part of the Indian
tribes about me. On the 29th August I made reports to
the department commander of the condition of affairs.*[1]

AUGUST was to be a month of accelerated activities as
Fort Phil Kearny's stockade was completed and warehouses and
quarters began to take form around the green close-clipped
parade. From sunrise to sundown, every day including Sundays,
there was a continuous humming of sawmills, pounding of hammers and ripping of handsaws, as the post grew log by log.
Military routines were cut to a minimum; the men were transformed into blacksmiths, painters, harness makers, teamsters,
wheelwrights, carpenters. In Quartermaster Brown's storage
tents, details began unpacking quantities of nails, doors, sash,
glass, and stoves.

On the first day of the month Captain Ten Eyck, command-
ing post, also assumed command of the 2nd Battalion, replacing
Captain Haymond. In his official record of events for August,
Ten Eyck wrote: "Stockade around garrison completed early in

this month and the entire force of the garrison was employed, officers and men laboring incessantly on the public buildings necessary for the preservation of the stores, and our company quarters. Our steam sawmill was put in operation during the month." [2]

The shortage of officers led to a combination of duties for all. Lieutenant Bisbee commanded E Company and also served as post adjutant and 2nd Battalion adjutant. Lieutenant John Adair commanded C Company and also performed the duties of regimental adjutant and acting adjutant general for the Mountain District.

As Phil Kearny was simultaneously headquarters for a district, regiment, battalion, and post, the paper work even in that day was immense. Before the month was scarcely begun, Colonel Carrington transferred four enlisted men into the combined headquarters tent for various duties—Private Dominic St. Geiger, Archibald Sample, Horace Van Kirk, and Thomas Maddeon. Sample eventually became the colonel's orderly, and played an important role in the Fetterman Massacre. Maddeon was an excellent gunsmith, but he preferred action in the field rather than the duties of regimental armorer. He would die in the Massacre.

The first day of August saw the departure of two of Carrington's most experienced officers, Captain Haymond and Lieutenant Phisterer. The entire staff turned out to bid them farewell as they departed for Laramie with the mail escort.

Very early on the third day, Captains Nathaniel C. Kinney and Thomas Burrowes had their respective companies, D and G, ready for the march north to open a new post on the Big Horn River. Carrington spared them a few horses for scouting and dispatch duties, and also one of the mountain howitzers. As ranking captain, Kinney would be in command. The new post by orders from Washington was to be called Fort C. F. Smith, in honor of the Mexican War hero, and was to be located some ninety miles northwest of Fort Phil Kearny.

Carrington ordered Jim Bridger to act as chief guide, but insisted that Old Gabe return to Phil Kearny as soon as the new fort was located. The colonel also sent Jim Beckwourth along to assist Bridger in gathering information from Crow tribes in the north. As Beckwourth was married to several Crow squaws and claimed to be a tribal chief, Carrington hoped to learn through him the Crows' "disposition toward the whites and the occupation of the route, and to induce them, if possible to communicate with Red Cloud quietly, and learn the disposition of himself and the Sioux of the Tongue River valley." [3] Military intelligence work against an Indian enemy, the colonel had discovered, was exceedingly difficult. He did not know what his enemy was doing, and it troubled him.

The two companies moved out with a line of wagons belonging to civilian trains which had been camped for several days along the Pineys, awaiting this well-armed escort. "Jim Bridger was our pilot," one of the wagon drivers recalled afterward. "He was a quiet familiar figure about the camp. . . . He would ride ahead across the untraveled country and return to the train at noon, or sometimes not until nightfall, when we had made camp. He rode a quiet, old flea-bitten, gray mare, with a musket across his saddle in front of him and wore an old-fashioned blue army overcoat and an ordinary slouch hat. He was very quiet in camp and I never saw him ride as fast as a slow trot." [4]

August saw the high tide of 1866 emigration over the Montana Road, with wagons trains rolling past Phil Kearny almost every day. Several drivers had tragic stories to tell of surprise Indian attacks along the route. In terse military language the post records reveal what was happening: "Train under H. Merriam as captain left Phil Kearny for Montana. Lost two men killed by Indians between Forts Laramie and Phil Kearny, viz. Geo. M. Moore of Georgetown, Ill. and P. G. Carr of Charlestown, Ill." [5] On the same day, August 6, another train was listed as having lost fifteen men killed and five wounded between Laramie and Phil Kearny.

The sturdy stockade of Phil Kearny was always a welcome sight for these harassed travelers. "Stopped below the fort," George W. Fox recorded in his diary for August 8. "I was up to the parade ground. They were mounting guard. They have a good band, 30 members. The music sounded well; something like civilization. . . . A captain [Ten Eyck probably] went down and saw the men and guns and we were permitted to go on. Had to have 60 armed men. The fort is just building; the garrison is in tents. . . . We left the fort at 11, crossed 2nd Piney fork, 50 ft. wide, 2 ft. deep, swift and rocky." [6]

As George Fox indicated, the post band which "sounded something like civilization" never failed to surprise and delight travelers passing through this wild country. The band was also highly prized by the fort's occupants. "We had the fine music of our splendid band . . . which played at guard-mounting in the morning and at dress-parade at sunset, while their afternoon drills and evening entertainments were in strange contrast with the solemn conditions that were constantly suggestive of war and sacrifice of life." [7]

Rumors had been flying about all year that as an economy move the Army would abolish regimental bands, and reports from The Adjutant General's office now began to confirm this drastic action. No direct orders had been received from Washington, but in fearful anticipation of losing the 18th Regimental Band, an anonymous correspondent signing himself "Dacotah" addressed an urgent letter about this time to the *Army and Navy Journal*:

> Concerning the subject of Army bands, we can but consider it small economy to deprive the regiments of their bands. . . . What soldier is there who does not take the greatest pains with his musket, put an extra polish to his plates and bootees, knowing he will march to "Dress parade" to the sound of music . . . it adds to the pleasures of the soldiers, it gives them amusement and enjoyment, when otherwise they might look to the card-table or whisky-bottle for excitement, and it gives them an *esprit de corps* and a life to the command that it never felt without it. [8]

If put to a choice, the men and women of Fort Phil Kearny undoubtedly would have voted for a cut in rations over elimination of their beloved band. The noncombatants, confined as they were to the stockade, regulated their lives around its performances.

As there was yet no floored building for holding party dances, recreation was at a premium, and when the band was not making music on the parade, the post's single croquet set was in constant use by women and children on the smooth green turf.

At least eleven married couples lived within the stockade: the Carringtons, Bisbees, Hortons, Wands, and Currys on officers' row, and six others among the enlisted men and civilian employees. Frank Fessenden afterward recalled that there were eleven children, six girls and five boys. Adding a domestic cast to this assemblage were two colored servants: the Carringtons' faithful George, and Mrs. Wands' maid, Laura.

The post's only pets were Mrs. Horton's spotted fawn, given her by the ill-fated Louis Gazzous, and Jimmy Carrington's pony, Calico. Both were destined for violent ends, the fawn from drinking paint, Calico from Indian arrows in the Fetterman Massacre.

Early in August—before the first attacks were made on the timber trains—Colonel Carrington granted permission for a picnic to be held at Piney Island. This would be the last opportunity for women and children to leave the eight-foot walls of their stockade. The food was a delightful treat, dainties being furnished by Judge Jefferson T. Kinney, who had recently arrived at the fort and purchased the sutlership. (Kinney was a former Utah territorial judge, dismissed by President Lincoln during the war. Because of clashing temperaments and differing political viewpoints, he and Carrington soon grew to dislike each other. After the Fetterman Massacre, Kinney's criticism of Carrington did much to undermine the colonel's reputation.)

"Choice elk steaks, furnished by the timber choppers, and suitable accessories, supplied a delightful meal, and no Indian disturbed the pleasure," wrote Margaret Carrington. "The bill of fare was not printed, but canned lobster, cove oysters, and salmon were a very fair first course; and associated with the game, were jellies, pineapples, tomatoes, sweet corn, peas, pickles, and such creature comforts, while puddings, pies, and domestic cake, from doughnuts and gingerbread up to plum cake and jelly cake, with coffee, and Madame Cliquot for those who wished it, and pipes and cigars for the gentlemen, enabled everybody to satisfy desires." [9] After the simple rations of the fort, Judge Kinney's catering seemed more like a banquet than a picnic.

Only a day or so following this outing, the Sioux made their first strike at a timber train. Along the road about four miles southwest of the fort, a war party sent a shower of arrows into a loaded train. One of the civilian drivers panicked, cut his mules loose, mounted one and headed for the fort. Rifle fire from the train's guard meanwhile had alerted Captain Ten Eyck, and he sent out a mounted platoon from Company H under Corporal George Phillips. The corporal proved to be a good Indian fighter; he recovered the mules, killed one Indian, wounded another. Ten Eyck recorded the incident in his usual terse style: "A party of troops had an engagement with Indians four miles from post. Indians attempted to stampede mules from teams coming from timber. One Indian killed and one mortally wounded." [10] Corporal Phillips had got his first Indian. Four months later the score would be evened when the Indians killed George Phillips in the Fetterman Massacre.

Although Carrington was pleased with the work of Corporal Phillips, he was determined to secure his wood trains against further attacks. Uninterrupted movement of timber from Piney Island was vital to construction of the fort. Wagons and mules must be protected, drivers taught to defend themselves with a minimum of guard forces.

"The system adopted in the management of my wood train," he explained afterward, "guaranteed protection whenever there was due conformity to orders. The train, varying from twenty-four to forty wagons, went in two parallel lines, about three hundred feet apart, after leaving the mill-gate until they reached the pinery, with mounted pickets on either flank, especially on the crest of Sullivant Hills with orders, upon an Indian alarm, for the front wagons to turn in, left and right, and halt; and all other wagons to move on the trot or run; the mules to pass within each wagon in advance, thus making an instant corral." [11]

As an added security measure, a permanent lookout was established on Pilot Hill, just across Little Piney east of the fort. From this point observers could obtain unobstructed views of the country for several miles in all directions. A simple system of flag signals was devised for communicating with a watch within the fort:

> Flag out of sight: "All quiet."
> Flag raised and still: "Attention."
> Flag waved, three times from vertical to right: "Small party on Reno road."
> Flag waved three times from vertical to left: "Small party on Big Horn road."
> Flag waved five times from vertical to right: "Large party on Reno road."
> Flag waved five times from vertical to left: "Large party on Big Horn road."
> Flag waved three times from right to left: "Indians."
> Flag waved around the head: "Train attacked."
> Flag raised and carried in a vertical position around the picket defense: "The attack." [12]

The Sioux, however, refused to relax their pressure. As if in amused defiance, they began using flags themselves, and on sunny days from every hill there seemed to be a continuous flashing of their mirror signals. On the 13th they made a quick dash at another wood train, which happened to be guarded by Corporal Phillips' platoon, and this time Phillips' first sergeant, Alexander Smith, had to rush to the corporal's rescue. Alex Smith claimed two dead Indians that day, but his life also was destined for forfeit in the Massacre.

This constant vigilance kept timber moving from Piney Island into the fort in a steady stream, the tall trees furnishing 30-inch boards without knots or blemishes. Many of the planks coming off Engineer Gregory's saws would fit into a wall so neatly that no chinking was necessary. By mid-August, shingles were needed for roofing buildings, and these were rived from bolts sawed by hand. Determined to beat the cold autumn weather which would soon be upon them, Quartermaster Brown organized a series of all-night shingle bees, but even these efforts could not supply demand, and earthen roofs had to be used on several structures.

Meanwhile the hostile Indians seemed to have shifted their main efforts back to the Reno road. On the 12th they raided a civilian train camped for a Sunday rest near Powder River, driving off cattle and horses. Lieutenant Kirtland led his mounted detachment in pursuit, recapturing some of the cattle but none of the horses. On the 14th two civilians were killed within four miles of Reno, and three days later the Indians boldly entered that fort's corral, driving off seventeen mules and seven of Kirtland's precious cavalry mounts. None was recovered.

During this breathing spell at Fort Phil Kearny, three civilians who were to play important parts in the Fetterman Massacre arrived at the post. They were James Wheatley, Isaac Fisher, and John "Portugee" Phillips. When they were offered quartermaster employment by Lieutenant Brown, they decided that as the season was growing late they would defer their mining ventures until the next year and remain at the fort for the winter. Wheatley had brought his beautiful nineteen-year-old wife and two young sons from Nebraska, and post records for August show that he asked for permission to erect a building just outside the stockade for keeping a civilian mess. The building was constructed shortly afterward alongside the Bozeman Trail, with ready access to the main gate of the stockade, and no doubt young Mrs. Wheatley served as cook in this family business venture.

On August 22, the first mail in three weeks came through from Laramie, and there was welcome news indeed in a telegram which had been dispatched August 11 by General Cooke: "Two companies of 2nd Cavalry have been ordered to assist in the protection of the road. You are authorized to enlist not to exceed fifty Indian scouts. Pay and allowance of cavalry soldiers. Let them use their ponies if you can't do better. Be very cautious. Don't undertake unnecessary risky detachments." [13] A second telegram dated August 9 stated briefly that "reinforcements have left St. Louis. Colonel Carrington must use his judgment about establishing Fort C. F. Smith at present." [14]

Also in the mailbag was a surprise letter from Fort Reno:

August 20, 1866

Col. H. B. Carrington,
   Commanding Mountain District:

DEAR COLONEL: I am on my way through the district as assistant inspector-general of the department, and will be at your post as soon as cavalry escort ordered to join me reaches here in about one week.

The mail going up will carry from General Cooke authority for you to suspend establishing the extreme west post (C. F. Smith) if you think from the condition of Indian affairs it is expedient. He telegraphed me at Laramie to consult with you about it, and since coming within the theater of Indian troubles I am of the opinion that there is no sufficient reason for longer delaying the establishment of that post, but, on the contrary, it should be established without further delay.

I think there is no danger on the route to parties well organized and that do not straggle, but that the greatest caution will be necessary both on the route and at the posts till the Indians are thrashed.

                              W. B. HAZEN
                              Bvt. Brig. General,
                              Asst. Inspector,
                              Dept. of the Platte [15]

Carrington no doubt was pleased that the general agreed with his plan to open Fort C. F. Smith, but he must have reflected on the slowness of communications which inhibited co-ordinated planning, and the fact that during the forthcoming week construction must be delayed somewhat in order to put Fort Phil Kearny into spit-and-polish condition for the visit of the veteran Indian fighter and West Pointer, General William Babcock Hazen.

In the mail also were the first personal letters any of the men had received since leaving Fort Kearney, Nebraska, in May. Many letters had gone through error to the 1st Battalion in Utah and had been forwarded from there. A few scattered newspapers from New York were ten weeks old, but were welcomed nonetheless. The frontier soldier's forum for complaints, the letters column of the *Army and Navy Journal,* not long afterward contained this significant contribution from an anonymous correspondent of the 2nd Battalion: "The common report is that Ben Holladay * throws out all papers as worthless. However true this may be, I know that *very* few papers reach these outposts. I think there should be some remedy, as without a regular mail, and deprived of our newspapers, we will be unable to keep posted in the affairs of the outside world." [16]

General Hazen arrived on the 27th, escorted by a mounted detachment of Lieutenant Kirtland's Reno company rather than by the expected 2nd Cavalry company from Laramie. The general could not explain the cavalry's delay, but he was an optimistic man and assured Carrington that the two companies of cavalry should be reporting any day, and that a regiment of infantry could be expected from St. Louis in a matter of weeks. (No cavalry reached Fort Phil Kearny to join the permanent garrison until November, and then only one company. The infantry regiment never arrived.)

Hazen spent three days inspecting the fort and pinery, expressed his satisfaction over Carrington's progress, and was most complimentary about the solid eight-foot stockade. "The best stockade I have seen," he said, "excepting one in British America built by Hudson Bay Company." [17]

On the 29th Hazen announced that he would be departing the following day to inspect Fort C. F. Smith, and would require an escort troop. Had Carrington been able to foresee the future he might not have been so generous, but as he had been assured of the arrival of two companies of cavalry, he ordered the best horseman among his lieutenants, James Bradley, † to collect twenty-six picked men of the mounted infantry. The colonel also assigned one of his two remaining scouts, James J. Brannan, to act as guide for the general's escort. (Carrington of course could not foresee that the promised cavalry would be delayed until November and that Hazen would retain Bradley's escort for almost two months at a time when Fort Phil Kearny was critically short of officers and mounted men.)

---

* Holladay operated the Overland Mail system through the West.

† Ten years later in 1876, Lieutenant Bradley was in command of the company of mounted scouts which discovered Custer's dead at Little Big Horn. He was killed in action during the Nez Percé War of 1877.

On this same day, photographer Ridgway Glover wrote the editor of the *Philadelphia Photographer* that he was "waiting for the medical supply train to come up, to get some chemicals, being at present in a 'stick'; but though unable to make negatives, I have been enjoying the climate and scenery, both being delightful." [18] Glover had made several views, the nature of which he did not disclose. He was not destined to live until the medical supplies arrived in October.

As soon as General Hazen departed, work on the fort returned to normal. The weather had been good all month, the clear nights growing perceptibly cooler as August drew to a close. The Sioux held off attacks on the heavily guarded wood trains, but from the middle or latter part of August, as Carrington reported afterward, "Indians appeared more frequently about Fort Philip Kearny, and from that time I assumed the condition of affairs to be decided, unequivocal hostility on the part of Indian tribes about me. . . . I had at first little drill on parade, except at roll call, but I had willing, obedient soldiers. Drunkenness was rare; the post was orderly and quiet at all times. My men went from guard duty to hard work, and from hard work to guard duty without a murmur. Often they could not have two consecutive nights in bed, and were always subject to instant call." [19]

Muster rolls of the fort for August 31 showed 345 officers and men present for duty, 43 absent.

VI. September:

DRYING GRASS MOON

The foregoing furnishes an outline of the main hostile demonstrations in September resulting in loss of stock or life; but, as will appear from my official correspondence, there were other and almost constant hostile demonstrations of some kind requiring of the garrison that every detail sent out for whatever purpose should exercise constant watchfulness and be kept well in hand.[1]

ON the first day of September snow fell on the Big Horns only four miles from Fort Phil Kearny. In the hayfields along Goose Creek and out toward Lake De Smet, the high grass had turned a golden yellow. Reacting to these signs of approaching autumn, Lieutenant Fred Brown kept his quartermaster crews working long hours. Great mounds of hay for stock were heaped in the quartermaster yard; billets and bark slabs for winter fuel were stacked high in an improvised woodyard.

On the 4th a long-overdue freight train escorted by a detachment of the 2nd Cavalry arrived at the fort in four sections, fifty-three wagons in all, loaded with commissary and military stores brought overland from Nebraska by contractor A. Caldwell. The sacks and barrels of hams, beef, bacon, flour, coffee, sugar, hardtack and soap ensured adequate rations for weeks ahead, but Quartermaster Brown was deeply disappointed that not one bag of corn or oats was in the shipment. Horses and mules under his care were losing weight daily from their monotonous diet of hay.

For lack of ready tents and storehouse space, unloading was delayed four days, and on the morning of the 8th, during a blinding storm of wind and rain, a corralled herd broke loose from contractor Caldwell's train. The wagoners pursued, but a band of Sioux in the vicinity made off with twenty of the stampeded horses and mules. Later in the day—as if this easy booty had aroused their zeal for raiding—the Indians made a daring strike at one of the fort's herds. Carrington's alert pickets headed them off, however, and Lieutenants Brown and Adair gave the raiders a fast chase into the hills.

On that same day the industrious Lieutenant Brown sat on a board of survey with Lieutenant Wands, "to examine and report upon the quality and condition of certain military stores and supplies arrived at this post." As was usual in long overland shipments, there were shortages in Caldwell's bills of lading. The hams and bacon had shrunk; soap and coffee were short; 210 sacks of flour and 238 boxes of P. Bread (pilot bread or hardtack) were missing.

After hours of questioning drivers and members of the train's cavalry escort, Brown and Wands finally adjusted matters satisfactorily. They were inclined to be lenient because Caldwell had been delayed four days for unloading and then had lost livestock to the Sioux. Meat shrinkages were blamed on "drying out in a dry season" and "oil and grease absorbed into sacks." Sergeant William H. Brooks, in charge of the 2nd Cavalry detachment, presented a written receipt explaining shortages of soap and coffee: "On the road between Laramie and Fort Reno, the Sgt. in charge of the escort run short of provisions and got an order from Captain Shanks commanding a post on the road [Bridger's Ferry] and on this order took from this train 17½ lbs. roasted coffee and 10 lbs. of soap." The missing flour and P. Bread had been erroneously unloaded at Fort Reno "owing to changes in names of military posts in this District since this [Fort Phil Kearny] has been started." [2]

Two days later, the 10th, the Sioux returned with a band of Arapaho allies, eager for more horses. In the deceptive faint light of early dawn, they swept down the hills and cut out forty-two mules from a grazing herd belonging to A. C. Leighton, who had just brought up several wagons of supplies for the sutler's store. Lieutenant Adair pursued for twenty miles, but caught no Indians, recovered no stock.* His horses, starving for grain, were no match for the fleet Indian ponies.

While Adair was still out, the Indians, in a gesture almost of contempt for the soldiers' ability to pursue, raided again—this time one of the fort's herds only a mile from the stockade—and swept away thirty-three horses and seventy-eight mules. "They were pursued promptly," Carrington reported, "but night and broken-down horses rendered pursuit hopeless." [3]

This was a most serious loss of riding and draft stock, and no doubt led the colonel to make an immediate decision concerning recruitment of a company of Indian scouts which had been authorized by General Cooke on August 11. Carrington would have liked Jim Bridger's counsel on this matter. Back in June the scout had warned against re-enlisting Winnebagos for fear it would antagonize the Sioux. But the Sioux had already demonstrated their inflexible hostility, and Carrington decided he must act before Bridger returned from Fort C. F. Smith.

"I have the honor," he wrote General Cooke that evening, "to send by bearer, Mr. W. B. C. Smith, who desires to organize a band of Winnebago scouts, the following report, as he goes by stage and may anticipate a mail. He is a good man for the work, if it has not been earlier attempted. . . . I sent twenty-five of my best mounted men with Gen. Hazen—have no corn, and with all pains to keep up my stock can not pursue successfully until I have more cavalry . . . if the single company of Indians, which were sent down for muster out on my way here, had been with me I could have punished the Indians and regained much stock. . . ." [4]

---

* Leighton put in a bill for his lost mules to the War Department, valuing them at $250 each. Twenty-four years later, 1890, he received a check for the loss.

The day ended sadly for the garrison of Fort Phil Kearny. Bandmaster Samuel Curry, who had been ill only a few days, died of an ailment diagnosed by Surgeon Horton as typhoid pneumonia. "The night he died," Frank Fessenden recalled, "I well remember how the wolves howled and made the night hideous, and we could hear them scratch at the stockade posts." Next morning the band under a new leader, Peter Damme, marched with muffled drums to the cemetery at the base of Pilot Hill. "When we buried the body we had to dig very deep, place heavy planks over the box, and then haul heavy stones and fill the grave to prevent the wolves from digging the body out." Bandmaster Curry was the first occupant of the post's rapidly growing graveyard to die of natural causes.[5]

After a three-day respite, the Sioux and Arapaho unleashed a well-co-ordinated double thrust at the fort's beef herd and upon a camp of about eighty civilian hay cutters along Goose Creek. The attacks came late in the day, and it was after midnight before a messenger brought the alarm to Fort Phil Kearny.

John Bratt, a bullwhacker who arrived at the fort early in September, had hired out to the hay contractor, Leviticus Carter, for sixty dollars per month, and was present during the fighting at the hay camp. He reported:

> One afternoon the Indians had made several attacks on us. They killed three of our men and wounded some others, captured nearly all our mowing and rake teams and had us all corralled on a high hill where we spent the evening and greater part of the night in digging rifle pits and defending ourselves and the stock we had left.
>
> Mr. Carter was with us and paid our old stuttering blacksmith, Jose, five hundred dollars to go to the fort to get relief. ... Mr. Carter knew Jose and he knew he would execute the order or die in the attempt. ... We estimated that more than one thousand Indians had us surrounded, and judging from the many signal fires being built around us other Indians were being told to come and help finish us. ... It must have been about nine o'clock in the evening when Jose mounted the best horse we had in camp and started for the fort. A few stars were out but the night was rather dark. Thin clouds of smoke from

the prairie fire the Indians had started in the afternoon hung over our camp. . . . Jose, armed with two revolvers and a sharp butcher knife on his belt, had been gone some ten minutes . . . when to our surprise he came at breakneck speed into camp followed by a bunch of Indians, some of whom we tumbled off their horses before they escaped. Mr. Carter and others were soon at Jose's side asking him what he proposed to do next when Jose answered, "I most believe I will try it another way," and in less than ten minutes he disappeared in the darkness in an opposite direction. . . .

Just about the peep of day we saw the Indians scattering to right and left of a large body of mounted men . . . with old Jose in the lead." [6]

It was Jose, the blacksmith, who taking a circuitous route had finally reached Fort Phil Kearny about one o'clock in the morning of the 13th and awakened Colonel Carrington. "Six mowing machines had been broken with hatchets, hay heaped upon them and fired," Carrington reported later. "I sent Lieutenant Adair with forty men to relieve them, in wagons. Six miles out, a small body of Indians rode toward the train; prompt deployment of the men sent them galloping to the hills. Lieutenant Adair reports from two hundred to three hundred Indians on the hills following his course." [7]

A most damaging blow in this double action was suffered by the fort's beef herd which had been grazing nearby under a guard of a sergeant and ten men. The Indians shrewdly maneuvered a buffalo herd into the area, drove them among the cattle, and stampeded the combined animals. At least two hundred beef cattle, sorely needed for the post's meat supply, were irrecoverably lost.

That morning Carrington scarcely had time to promise contractor Carter a stronger military guard for his hay cutters and to offer assistance in the prompt repair of mowing machines, before the Indians struck again. They stampeded a convalescent herd of horses and mules just outside the stockade, wounding two privates on picket duty, one taking an arrow in his hip, the other a bullet in his side. Captain Ten Eyck and Lieutenants Brown, Bisbee and Wands led mounted parties out in various directions, but all returned without success, blaming failure to overtake the scattering raiders on the poor condition of their horses. After this night and day of staggering losses, Carrington decided he must tighten defensive measures against the hostiles, and issued a new special order:

1. Owing to recent depredation of Indians near Fort Philip Kearny, Dak., the post commander [Ten Eyck] will issue such regulation and at once provide such additional escorts for wood trains, guard for stock and hay and the steam saw-mills as the chief quartermaster [Brown] may deem essential. He will also give

2. Instructions, so that upon Indian alarm no troops leave the post without an officer or under the antecedent direction of an officer, and the garrison will be so organized that it may at all times be available and disposable for exterior duty or interior defense.

3. One relief of the guard will promptly support any picket threatened at night, and the detail on posts should be visited hourly by a non-commissioned officer of the guard between the hours of posting successive reliefs.

4. Stringent regulations are enjoined to prevent camp rumors and false reports, and any picket or soldier bringing reports of Indian sign or hostilities must be required to report to the post commander or officer of the day or to the nearest commissioned officer in cases of urgent import.

5. Owing to the non-arrival of corn for the post and the present reduced condition of the public stock, the quartermaster is authorized, upon the approval of the post commander, to purchase sufficient corn for moderate issues, to last until a supply already due, shall arrive, but the issue will be governed by the condition of the stock, and will only be issued to horses unless the same in half ration shall be necessary for such mules as are daily in use and can not graze or be furnished with hay.

6. Reports will be made of all Indian depredations, with the results, in order that a proper summary may be sent to department headquarters.

7. Soldiers while on duty in the timber or elsewhere are forbidden to waste ammunition in hunting, every hour of

their time being indispensable in preparing for their own comfort and the well-being of the garrison during the approaching winter.[8]

The next day another casualty was added to the morning report. Private Allando Gilchrist, unreported for four days, was listed as "missing, presumed killed by Indians" when "a portion of his clothes were found bloody, without his body." [9]

Two days later, Sunday the 16th, a train of twelve wagons was sent out to the hay flats near Lake De Smet. A rifleman sat beside each driver, and six mounted infantrymen covered flanks, rear, and forward positions. After the wagons were loaded, Private Peter Johnson moved out on point position and carelessly allowed his horse to take him three or four hundred yards ahead of the slow-moving train. As Johnson approached a ravine, an Indian dashed suddenly between him and the wagons. "Johnson would have been all right had he returned to the hay detail," said Private John Ryan, one of the guards, "but he must have become confused, as he started toward the fort with the evident intention of trying to outride the Indian. The savage, however, mounted on a fast pony, rapidly gained on him, when Johnson apparently lost his head completely, jumped off his horse, threw his gun away, and made for a washout east of the road. Being still armed with a six-shooter, he could have defended himself, but he did not, and the Indian had no trouble capturing him."

According to Ryan there was nothing the others could do to help Johnson. The hills surrounding them had suddenly become alive with Indians, and any attempt to leave the protection of the wagons might have sacrificed the entire party. Another problem was shortage of ammunition (Carrington still had received none since leaving Laramie) . "The guards had but three rounds of ammunition to the man and the teamsters were practically unarmed." [10] After the hay train reached the fort and reported the incident, Lieutenant Brown led a large detachment out to the scene, but no trace was ever found of Peter Johnson's body.

On this same Sunday one of the fort's civilians, Ridgway Glover, was also spending his last day on earth. "He had a camera outfit," said Frank Fessenden, "and was taking views for his paper. While taking pictures he would go around alone on the mountains, and sometimes would not be seen for five or six days at a time. He made his headquarters with the woodchoppers. He had long yellow hair, and I had often told him that the Indians would delight to clip that hair for him some day. He said he was safe, as the Indians would take him for a Mormon."

For some reason on this Sunday, Glover decided to leave the timber camps and go to the fort. When the photographer was told that the wood train detail had been given a Sunday holiday, he announced that he intended to walk in alone. "The woodchoppers tried to get him to remain and wait for the wood train Monday. He left one cutting and said he would go to the other, which he did. The men at this cutting also warned him of the danger, and almost certain death, if he attempted to go on to the fort alone. He told these choppers that he would return to the other cutting—which he did not do, as he was on his way to the fort alone, when he met the certain fate which overtook every man caught alone away from the garrison. Glover had escaped so many times that he apparently thought he was Indian proof." [11]

They found his naked body next morning less than two miles from the stockade. He had been scalped, his back cleft with a hatchet. Lieutenant Bisbee, commanding the detail which discovered Glover, said he was "lying face down across the roadway, a sign that he had not been brave." [12] An ambulance was attached to Bisbee's detail, the driver being the same Private Ryan who had witnessed the capture of Peter Johnson the previous day.

"We were something over a mile from the fort," Ryan recalled,[13] "and I could look across the Big Piney to the north and the Little Piney to the south and see Indians who were watching our every movement, and I did not relish the idea of going back unsupported by the soldiers, and I asked the officer [Bisbee] if he did not think the body would be all right where it was for a while, and we could get it on our return. He was obdurate, however, and said, 'Young man, if you don't obey my orders it will go hard with you.' I told him it would go hard with me also if the Indians caught me, but I had to go back just the same." *

The reason for Lieutenant Bisbee's impatience was that he was in command of a follow-up party to a large mounted detachment under Lieutenant Brown, who as usual was pursuing Indians. Early that morning a large force of hostiles had appeared out of the valley at the junction of the Pineys, galloping upon what was left of the fort's beef herd. The pickets being short of ammunition withheld fire until the raiders surprised them by using revolvers for the first time in an attack. Forty-eight head of cattle were cut loose, but this time Fred Brown was ready for immediate pursuit and was successful in recapturing all the stock. In his report of this action, Colonel Carrington said that he witnessed the swift attack and was fearful that all the pickets would be killed before a rescue party could reach them. "I loaded and fired a 12-pound field howitzer, having no one else experienced, bursting the first shell in the Indians' midst. This drove them back to the creek. A second shell dismounted one Indian, and all crossed to the hills." [14]

This day, the 17th of September, was to be a busy Monday at Fort Phil Kearny. Lieutenant Brown had scarcely returned with the recaptured beef cattle when a contract commissary train arrived with sixty thousand rounds of Springfield rifle ammunition. The contractor was also willing to sell a few bushels of corn, badly needed for reconditioning mounts. At about the same time a mail escort arrived, with a baggage wagon and an ambulance, aboard which were two contract surgeons, a young lieutenant, and his wife.

The lieutenant was George Washington Grummond, and he and his wife, Frances, who was pregnant, were the post's most romantic couple. Grummond had served through the Civil War as officer of a Michigan Volunteer Infantry regiment. He met

---

* One of the unsolved mysteries of Fort Phil Kearny is what happened to the photographs made there by Ridgway Glover. Twenty-two of his Laramie negatives were sent to Wenderoth, Taylor & Brown in Philadelphia. His Fort Phil Kearny negatives or prints, if ever discovered, would furnish the only photographic record ever made of scenes and personnel in and around that vanished Wyoming post.

Frances in Tennessee and married her after the war's end. Determined to pursue a military career, he applied for a regular commission, and as his war record was brilliant (he held a brevet rank of lieutenant-colonel) he was assigned to the 2nd Battalion as a second lieutenant.

In recording her arrival at Fort Phil Kearny, Frances Grummond told of seeing the picket on Pilot Hill signaling the approach of the mail party on the east road. "We moved toward the stockade," she wrote, "but just before entering a halt was made, and I looked eagerly for the occasion of the delay. It almost took my breath away for a strange feeling of apprehension came over me. We had halted to give passage to a wagon, escorted by a guard from the wood train. . . . In the wagon was the scalped and naked body of one of their comrades. . . . My whole being seemed to be absorbed in the one desire—an agonized but unuttered cry, 'Let me get within the gate!' . . . That strange feeling of apprehension never left me, enhanced as it was by my delicate condition. . . ." [15]

Frances Grummond's fears were not without prescience. Her husband was one of the three officers who would die in the Fetterman Massacre.

In the mail for Carrington was a letter from General Sherman, written at Fort Laramie where the general had visited near the end of August on a tour of western defense posts. "I shall instruct General Cooke to reinforce his force at this post," Sherman wrote, "so that expeditions in sufficient strength can go out to punish the Indians. We want to avoid a general Indian war, as long as possible, until we get the new army further advanced in recruiting. The Indians seem to oppose the opening of the new road, but that must stimulate us to its prosecution, and you may rest assured that you will be supported all that is possible. . . . We must try and distinguish friendly from hostile and kill the latter, but if you or any other commanding officer strike a blow I will approve, for it seems impossible to tell the true from the false." [16]

Carrington did not share Sherman's philosophy of ruthless extermination, but agreed with his hope of avoiding a general war as long as possible, and was grateful for any support from a general who was second in command to Ulysses Grant.

The mail also contained a petulant message from General Cooke complaining about women and children being captured on the Montana Road, reports of which he had read in newspapers. As Carrington had seen no recent newspapers and had heard of no such incidents, he was puzzled as to what Cooke meant. An even more annoying letter, dated August 15, had been sent directly from The Adjutant General's office in Washington. The A. G. complained that no returns of the post for June 1866 had been received—the reason for which should have been obvious had the Washington officials checked the date of the fort's establishment, July 14.

Toward the close of this busy day a party of about forty miners arrived from the north. They had been unsuccessful in finding gold in Montana, and had decided to prospect the Big Horn country, but on the trail down from Virginia City hostile Indians had given them a bad time. Two men had been killed only the previous day near Tongue River.

Their leader, William Bailey, reported to Carrington, requesting permission to camp near the fort for protection for themselves and their horses. When the colonel learned that Bailey had been a scout and prospector in the West for seventeen years and that his followers were all of the same rugged mold—crack shots, well armed and well mounted—he suggested that the miners would be more than welcome to spend the winter, and would be given quartermaster employment if they wished it. The miners put the offer to a vote and accepted. By nightfall they had pitched their tents in front of the fort, just across Big Piney under a slope rising to the north, and Carrington had gained for the post the equal of a company of trained cavalrymen.

Accompanying Bailey's party was a messenger from Fort C. F. Smith, with news of Jim Bridger. Old Gabe reported that he had talked with several Crows, who had informed him that at least five hundred lodges of Sioux were along the Tongue, all hostile, some armed with rifles. Bridger also had heard from the Crows of renegade white men among the Arapaho, squaw men and miners probably, who had allied themselves with the hostiles to drive other white men out of the gold country.

Carrington worked late that night over his lantern-lit writing table, while the season's first snow whirled across the fort's parade. The mail escort for Laramie was scheduled to leave at dawn, and the colonel had much to report to General Cooke:

> Mail has arrived. I send directly back. Lt.-Gen. Sherman wrote me from Laramie to endeavor to keep you more frequently advised. I am doing all I can with my broken down and famished horses, not having received a pound of corn yet.... No women or children have been captured or injured by Indians in this district since I entered it.... While more troops are needed I can say (and I am in the very heart of the hostile district) that most of the newspaper reports are gross exaggerations. I gather and furnish you, as requested, all the bad news, neither coloring nor disguising facts.

He went on to tell of Bridger's report, of the purchase of a few bushels of corn from a contractor, of the welcome arrival of sixty thousand rounds of Springfield ammunition. "I ought to have, if possible, a hundred thousand more, and from Laramie more ammunition for my 12-pounder field howitzer and mountain howitzers.... Red Cloud is known to command the parties now immediately engaged ... they are determined to burn the country, cut off supplies, and hamper every movement." [17]

Next morning when Frances Grummond awoke after her first night of unsound sleep in Fort Phil Kearny, she found that snow had drifted into her tent, "covered my face, and there melting trickled down my cheeks until if I had shed tears they would have been indistinguishable ... pillows, bedding, and even the stove and the ground within the tent were also covered." [18]

Almost a foot of feathery snow had fallen on the fort, but the sun was out bright and warm, and by afternoon most of it had melted. The Indians kept to their lodges this day, and Captain Ten Eyck chose the peaceful interlude for a post arms inspection. His report to Carrington was blunt: "Many Springfield rifles unserviceable. Some men not armed at all, because of thefts by deserters and others. Want pistols and carbines, as rifles no good for mounted men."[19]

With most of the snow gone by Wednesday (the 19th) the hostiles came back just after breakfast, as Peter Damme was marching the regimental band out on parade. Their objective was the open camp of Bailey's miners across the Piney. Frances Grummond watched the incident from inside the stockade; it was her first experience of hostile Indian attack and she described it vividly.

"Quite a large body of Indians suddenly appeared at the summit of the hill in full warpaint, brandishing their spears, giving loud yells and lifting their blankets high in the air as they moved down slowly in an attempted charge upon the miners' camp. Between one and two hundred Indians were scattered along the crest of that hill, but hardly three minutes had elapsed after they first came in view before the smoke and crack of the miners' rifles, out from the cottonwood brush that lined the bank of the creek, had emptied half a dozen warriors' seats and brought down three times as many ponies, while the cheers of the miners and their perfect confidence in defending their camp were enlivened by the music of the 18th Band which Colonel Carrington had play on the parade ground, while the whole garrison was under arms ready for a fight, and three howitzers were ready to open their fire in case of need. A small detachment had been sent to support the miners. . . ."[20]

Colonel Carrington, having grown accustomed to these monotonous raids, reported the same incident much more succinctly. "A large force attacked the miners encamped across Big Piney. . . . A shell from the fort scattered them; no stock was lost; miners pursued several hours in view."[21]

The next day's report was equally brief: "Indians attacked citizen train lying in angle of two Pineys, repulsed by aid from fort, losing one red man killed and another wounded."[22]

But on the 21st he was sufficiently concerned by another heavy attack upon Levi Carter's hay mowers to order the party to cease operations. Melting snow and rain showers had almost halted cutting already, and the colonel sent one of his new officers, Lieutenant Winfield Scott Matson, out with forty men to assist in bringing in all hay and equipment.

That Carrington was more alarmed over continuous Indian raids than his sparse reports indicate is revealed in a special order issued that same day:

> The fastenings of all gates must be finished this day; the locks for large gates will be similar, and the district commander, post commander, officer of the day, and quartermaster will alone have keys. Keys for the wicket gates will be with the same officers.
>
> Upon a general alarm or appearance of Indians in force or near the gates, the same will be closed, and no soldier or civilian will leave the fort without orders.
>
> No large gate will be opened, except the quartermaster gate, unless it shall be necessary for wagons. Stock must invariably pass in and out of that gate.
>
> The west or officers' gate will not be opened without permission, even for wagons, unless for timber wagons or ambulances, or mounted men.
>
> Upon a general alarm the employees in the sutlers' department will form at the store and wait for orders and assignment to some part of the interior defense, but will not be expected to act without the fort unless voluntarily, and then after sanction is given, and under strict military control.
>
> All soldiers, however detailed or attached, or in whatever capacity serving, will, upon a general alarm, take arms and be subject to immediate disposal with their companies or at the headquarters or department with which serving.
>
> All horses of mounted men will be saddled at reveille.
>
> It is also expressly enjoined that in no case shall there be needless running in haste upon an alarm. Shouting, tale-bearing, and gross perversion of facts by excited men does more mischief than Indians. And the duty of guards being to advise of danger, soldiers who have information must report to the proper officer, and not to comrades.
>
> At the sounding of assembly the troops of the garrison not on daily duty will form in front of their respective quarters.
>
> The general alarm referred to in foregoing paragraph will be indicated by the sounding of the assembly, followed by three quick shots from the guard-house, which latter will be

the distinction between the general alarm and the simple alarm for turning out the troops of the garrison.

This order will be placed upon a bulletin-board for early and general information.

Officers and non-commissioned officers are charged with its execution, and the soldiers of the 18th Infantry are especially called upon to vindicate and maintain, as they ever have, the record of their regiment.

This will require much hard work, much guard duty, and much patience, but they will have an honorable field to occupy in this country, and both Indian outrages and approaching winter stimulate them to work, and work with zeal and tireless industry.

Their colonel will with his officers share all, and no idling or indifference can, under these circumstances, have any quarters in the breast of a true soldier.[23]

Since early August the women of the fort had been virtual prisoners within the 400-foot-square stockade. From now on the same situation would apply to soldiers and civilian employees. In reference to these regulations Frank Fessenden said that "orders were given that none of our men should ever go out of the fort alone. . . . The chaplain bought a cow for which he paid $75. He told me if I would milk her I could have all the milk that was left after he was served. I remember how I used to arm myself and go out hunting after that cow. I presume the Indians also wanted her for they eventually got her anyhow. Orders finally became so strict that I did not dare go outside the stockade."[24]

Meanwhile, Lieutenant Matson's detachment and the hay-field workers were having a difficult time withdrawing machinery and wagons from the Goose Creek flats. A force of three hundred Sioux and Arapaho forced them to corral five miles from the fort, pinning them down until Carrington sent out a mounted relief Saturday morning. During the fluid action of the Indians' withdrawal, Matson was suddenly confronted by a horseman on the road, a white man dressed like an Indian, the fingers missing from one of his hands. He identified himself as Captain Bob North, but Matson, remembering rumors of white men fighting with the Arapahos, was suspicious. A few minutes later Matson's advance scouts reported that a contractor's train returning from Fort C. F. Smith had also been attacked on the road. The contractor, Grull, and two of his drivers had been killed. During the ensuing excitement, the mysterious "Captain North" disappeared.

The mystery of Captain North may or may not have been solved the next day. In the gray dawn of Sunday, under cover of a rainstorm, a raiding party struck at a civilian cattle herd. They dashed among the grazing animals, yelling and waving blankets and buffalo hides, stampeding almost a hundred. This time there was no delay in pursuing. In accordance with Carrington's order of the 21st, horses had been saddled at reveille, and before the raiders could head away, a small detachment under Lieutenant Brown dashed out the east gate of the quartermaster's corral. Fifteen miners joined Brown's galloping pursuit force, and after a ten-mile chase they overtook the Indians. For a few minutes the Indians tried hard to keep their stolen cattle, but Brown dismounted his men and went into quick skirmish formation.

The hostiles grouped for a charge, and as they thundered down upon the soldiers, the men were startled to recognize the leader as a white man. Two or three times the Indians charged, each time led by the white man swearing in English, but in each attack they were driven back, several warriors dropping from their ponies. In the last charge, the white leader went down; an Indian swept him up and carried him off the field, apparently dead.

Was he the same man Lieutenant Matson had met Saturday on the road, the mysterious Captain Bob North, the renegade mountain man with four missing fingers?

In his official report Colonel Carrington assumed he was. "Lieutenant Brown and a few men charged the Indians with revolvers, killing five Indians and one white man, I think Bob North, who led them in every case, and wounding sixteen." [25] (If the renegade was North, he survived only to die three years later in Kansas by hanging.)

Carrington also considered this fight his first real victory over the hostiles:

> One of our party was wounded slightly with an arrow, which grazed the temple, and six of our horses were wounded by revolvers and rifle shots. All were brought from the field. One chief carried from the field by his men wore an elaborate feather head-dress and proper ornament of the same kind upon his person. They retired to a high hill silently, and without their usual bravado. They felt the blow. Every head of stock was rescued and brought back to the fort. It has inspired my men with new courage. . . . One week's feeding on corn has given new life also to my horses. . . .

Carrington's claim that the hostiles "felt the blow" in the wounding or death of at least two leaders is supported by the fact that they made no demonstrations around the fort during the next three days.

This breathing spell gave Carrington an opportunity to collect his thoughts and compose two leisurely letters to General Cooke, discussing the flora and fauna, the climate and minerals, of the surrounding country.

> Coal abounds in exhaustless supply. I have recently opened a vein of cannel-coal, that will weld iron within fifty feet of the quartermaster's corral, east of the fort. . . . Late in the season as it is now, while the cottonwood is yellow from frost, the hills and slopes bear innumerable patches of green shrubs, marking the work of the last lingering snows of spring and the abounding springs which are everywhere found. . . . The pine timber has furnished novel results: the trees of one mountain have been girdled by fire apparently two years since. The boards from these take the plane and polish equal to No. 1 merchantable seasoned pine lumber. The pitch has dried out, the grain is close, and the material is sound. Shingles that are rived from it furnish bolts three feet in diameter and of the best quality. . . .
> Altitude of the post I find to be 5,790 feet by barometer. . . . The mountain range nearest rises abruptly from 850 to 900 feet more. . . . It has rained at the post when snow was falling within two miles . . . and again we have had snow when on the creek, 160 feet below, there was rain.

He also discussed the progress of the fort's construction and the morale of his men:

> I have changed company buildings to 84 feet in length, kitchen in rear. This will allow four buildings each side, and these four will be roofed this week. A large commissary building with plank floor and good roof will be equally advanced.
> Everything moves well; the men cheerfully come off guard and go to work and respond to alarm instantly and eagerly by night and day. Sickness is almost unknown. Sometimes one, and often none, at sick-call. Antiscorbutics arrived in good time, as scurvy began to appear. I trust fresh potatoes will be sent us on my April requisition. I shall have a cellar ready.[26]

By that last week of September, Carrington had perfected the defenses of his fort to a point where the Indians respected its immediate power of retaliation, and no longer dared approach the stockade. Wagon trains, strongly guarded by escorts of seventy-five to one hundred men, were also seldom attacked. Two vulnerable points remained, however—Pilot Hill where mounted pickets rotated duty in fours, and the timber cuttings where the men, because of the nature of their work, were sometimes separated individually by several yards from their comrades.

On the 27th, Red Cloud's hostiles moved against both these weak positions. It was a sunny morning, with snow still lingering under the tall trees on Piney Island. The crack of axes and shouts of the cutters rang clear in the crisp air. Private Patrick Smith and two companions had worked their way upslope about half a mile from the nearest pine-log blockhouse; a dozen or more men were less than a hundred yards below them trimming fallen trunks in a partial clearing. Without warning nearly a hundred Indians dashed between the three men and the main party, and the latter immediately exchanged axes for rifles. Within a few minutes the cutters withdrew to the safety of their blockhouse. Shortly afterward two of the isolated men came in safely, after eluding the Indians by dashing into a thick part of the forest. They assumed that Private Smith was dead.

Private Smith had been shot down by arrows and hastily scalped, the Indians leaving him to die. Recovering consciousness, he began crawling the half mile toward the blockhouse. He was too weak to withdraw the arrows deeply imbedded in his body, but managed to break off the shafts so that he could crawl unimpeded through the thickets.

When he appeared, scalped and bleeding, before the blockhouse, his comrades lifted him into a bunk and sent an emergency detail hurrying to the fort for a surgeon.

In the meantime the same band of Indians which scalped Private Smith had moved east from the cuttings, crossed Little Piney, and was making a dash toward Pilot Hill where four pickets were on duty.

Margaret Carrington, who witnessed this incident, said "the sudden repeated shriek of the steamwhistle at the farther mill, and the equally hasty signal of the pickets, gave the alarm that Indians were again close by. We could all see fifteen Indians between the fort and the mountain, galloping . . . directly for Pilot Hill, with the plain purpose of capturing and scalping the picket under the very eyes of the garrison."

Lieutenants Brown and Adair by this time were out the gate and in hot pursuit with a party of twenty mounted men. "Private Rover (who is of a good Chicago family, and enlisted under the false name of Rover) was in charge of the picket.* He had been signally brave in several tight places before. On this occasion he dismounted his three men, turned his horses loose toward the fort with a good urgency, and slowly fell off the northern slope, with arms at a 'ready' to join the supporting party. The horses came down the steep grade toward the fort on a run, passing through the Indians, who dared not stop them and could only give them a few arrows as they passed."[27]

Lieutenant Brown, who seemed to consider Indian chasing a part of his regular quartermaster duties, pursued this band until almost dark. As he was on the point of breaking off pursuit, Brown saw the hostiles suddenly stop and parley with another party of Indians coming from the east. Brown ordered his men forward at a gallop; the hostiles scattered into the dusk,

---

* Rover's real name was Ephraim C. Bissell. Mrs. Carrington said that "a hasty indiscretion impelled him to the army." He was killed three months later in the Fetterman Massacre.

the other Indians remaining where they were. As Brown approached, he recognized the new arrivals as Cheyennes. Some
were holding up the good-conduct passes signed by Carrington
back in July.

There were only nine of them, three chiefs, five warriors and
a squaw. Two Moons was the spokesman. He said Black Horse
was sick, that the old chief and the rest of the band were in the
mountains. Two Moons' party was en route to Fort Phil Kearny
to ask the Little White Chief, Carrington, for permission to
hunt in Tongue River valley.

They were brought back to the fort, and after Carrington
questioned them closely he granted permission to pass on to
Tongue River. He also ordered the quartermaster to issue them
rations of bacon and coffee, and told them they might camp for
the night across Little Piney opposite the sawmills.

By this time wagons from the pineries had come in, and the
story of Private Smith spread rapidly through the fort. Nothing
the Indians had done before had so aroused the anger of the
men as the scalping of one of their comrades and leaving him to
die. Stories of Smith's blood-smeared face, the skin hanging in
strips from his forehead, the broken arrows in his body, were
recounted around all the mess fires that evening. The contract
surgeon, Edwin Reid, marveled that the man was still alive;
Reid had found it almost imposible to remove one arrow deep
in Smith's chest.

From inside the fort the men could see the near campfires of
the Cheyennes down by Little Piney. Those who had ridden
with Brown and Adair that day were skeptical of the Cheyennes'
genuine friendliness. For all they knew, these Cheyennes might
have been the ones who scalped Pat Smith and left him to die.
If the Cheyennes were real friends of the soldiers, why had the
hostile Sioux passed them by without harm?

In the close confines of the 400-foot stockade, the men were
restive, their bitterness deepening with the spreading rumors.
Like General Sherman in his recent letter to Carrington, they
were eager to "strike a blow" against any Indians; as the general had written, it seemed "impossible to tell the true from the
false."

Chaplain David White, closer to the enlisted men than any of the officers, heard enough threats to worry him. Soon after tattoo was sounded, White called on Carrington and warned him that some of the men were talking openly of surrounding and killing the Cheyennes in their camp.

Carrington summoned Captain Ten Eyck immediately, and suggested that the post commander throw a guard around the Cheyenne camp. The colonel as usual went along to see that everything was done properly, and when the two officers and the guard detail marched down toward the Indian campfire, they surprised a mob of some ninety soldiers spread out along the creek. "The troops," Carrington said afterward, "armed themselves and climbed the stockade, or went through the wicket of the quartermaster's gate." Some of them had "cocked their pieces, and were ready to deliver fire, when their muskets were thrown up by two reliefs of the guard sent to quell the disturbance."

The mob broke in the darkness; some started running for the water gate. Ten Eyck cried an order to halt, but this only caused others to turn and run for fear of being recognized and punished. "I ordered them to halt twice," Carrington said, "was disobeyed, but two shots from my revolver halted the men. . . ."[28] In the dim light of the Cheyenne campfires he recognized a few familiar faces. Among them were some of the best men in the garrison. He gave them a brief tongue-lashing, warned against any such demonstrations in the future, and ordered them back to their quarters.

Next morning the colonel interviewed the Cheyennes again, hoping to learn something of the movements of the Sioux and Arapaho. They told him they had heard Red Cloud and Man-Afraid-of-His-Horses were operating from Tongue River valley and that Buffalo Tongue was directing harassment of trains around Reno and Powder River. They also had heard that Bob North, a white man with one thumb, a big medicine man to the Arapaho, had made an alliance with the Sioux in August. Their information tallied with what Jim Bridger had heard from the Crows, and although Carrington could not take the field for punitive action with the small force at his command, he at least was satisfied that he knew where his enemies were.

Entries in post records indicate that the month of September ended routinely. Daniel Bradford, an unlucky Third Class Musician from Pittsburgh, reported his carbine and cartridge box missing, and was listed as owing the "U. S. for one Spencer carbine $30, and one cartridge box, $1.05. Total $31.05."

By the month's end Indian raids had caused serious losses in the beef herd. Six hundred of the seven hundred head brought overland from Fort Kearney were gone, most of them to raiding Indians, and the post's prospects for fresh meat during the winter were poor indeed.

Three enlisted men and five civilians in government employ had been killed; one enlisted man had deserted. Officers and men present for duty totaled 341. One building 50x24 feet for commissary stores, one building 44x52 feet for officers' quarters, and four buildings 84x24 feet for company quarters were approaching completion.

And on the last day of the month, Train No. 33 crossed the ford of Little Piney, ending its long slow journey from Nebraska, loaded with tons of corn and oats for the starving horses and mules of the mounted infantry and wood trains.

Colonel Henry B. Carrington

Margaret Carrington,
wife of Col. Carrington

Frances (Grummond) Carrington

Captain William J. Fetterman

Red Cloud

Captain Frederick Brown   Lieutenant George W. Grummond

Captain Tenodor Ten Eyck

Lieutenant Grummond's hand-to-hand running fight
From a drawing by Charles Schreyvogel, *Pearson's Magazine*, 1904

General Philip St. George Cooke

Jim Bridger

Lieutenant George Templeton

John (Portugee) Phillips *(seated)*
Captain James Powell *(standing)*

EASTERWOOD COLLECTION,
UNIVERSITY OF OREGON

Sitting Bull's drawing of a horse he captured on the Montana Trail in 1866
BUREAU OF AMERICAN ETHNOLOGY, THE SMITHSONIAN INSTITUTION

Fort Phil Kearny, as drawn by Antonio Nicoli, 2nd Cavalry Bugler
U.S. SIGNAL CORPS, NATIONAL ARCHIVES

Two Moons, Cheyenne leader

VII. October:

HARVEST MOON

On the 7th of October I issued an order assuming command of Fort Philip Kearny, to have more immediate personal command of the post, at which were my district headquarters. . . . I took charge of the system of police and discipline of the post, entertaining the idea that the future policy might involve more formidable Indian aggression and require a more exact and careful watchfulness and defense.[1]

AS October came in, frosty mornings and crusted ice on the edges of the Pineys warned of winter's approach. Wagon trains were hurrying north to be clear of the road before the heavy snows fell. Inside the fort's stockade the parade was being closed in by rows of buildings nearing completion.

Two more freighting trains ended their sixty-day runs from Lone Tree, Nebraska, bringing in enough corn and oats to supply the post's livestock into midwinter. As usual there were shortages in bills of lading, and Lieutenants Bisbee and Wands spent three days as a board of survey determining whether Train No. 33's deficiencies of 4,195 pounds of corn from a shipment of 179,882 pounds, and 397 pounds of oats from a shipment of 20,199 pounds, were allowable. After taking testimony from three civilians, the young lieutenants reported that

"Leviticus Carter, James Hill, and James Henning, who have for many years freighted grain over the plains for the Government and private parties, find that the deficiency is only a fair allowance arising from shrinkage and spilling from old and worn sacks and other causes incident to freighting, being only 2¼% of the total delivered."[2]

The survey board consequently exonerated contractor Herman Kountz from all blame and responsibility. After studying the deficiencies of subcontractor W. H. Berger's Train No. 41 and F. M. Square's Train No. 43, Bisbee and Wands reached the same conclusion. Perhaps they felt that any freighters who had the raw courage to risk lives, stock, and wagons hauling grain over the dangerous Montana Road to remote Fort Phil Kearny deserved approbation rather than penalties.

Meanwhile disturbing news had come from Fort Reno. The aging commander, Captain Proctor, had placed Lieutenant Kirtland under arrest, blaming him for losses of the post's mounts to raiding Sioux. On the 4th, Carrington dispatched an urgent communication to Omaha concerning this: "I wish to visit the other posts and inspect them, as soon as I can get a few mounted men. . . . I fear Captain Proctor is too ill and nervous to command, but have no one to succeed him. He has lost nearly all his stock; has arrested his adjutant, Lieutenant Kirtland, without notifying me or furnishing me or the lieutenant with a copy of charges. He may have sent them up direct to you, as he follows no regulations in correspondence with these headquarters. If so, please return them for my action. Gen. Hazen told me that he found the same inefficiency. I hope to go there in a few days and judge for myself."

The colonel also felt that he should make some explanation of the recent uprising of his men against the visiting Cheyennes. "I had trouble to keep my men from killing the Cheyennes, they are so bitter against all Indians; I do not put full confidence in them yet, but those that came seemed faithful to their agreement of July. They are great beggars, and I give them very little, as they can find plenty of game, but they seem to fear the Sioux. . . . I gave the three chiefs one day's ration of flour, but refused any luxuries, and told them they must hunt for their living, and if they kept away from the road and trains I would keep peace with them."³

Next day he was confronted by an angry trio of freighters, the contractors who had delivered the grain from Nebraska. They complained that several of their teamsters had deserted and moved in with the fort's civilian employees. Some had even been given employment by Captain Ten Eyck and Lieutenant Brown.

Sympathizing with the plight of the contractors, whose wagons must be manned on the return journey, Carrington assured them the Army would co-operate. He issued an immediate order establishing the Mountain District's policy, and notified Ten Eyck and Brown to discharge the deserting teamsters without delay.

> The attention of post commander is directed to the constant difficulties arising between owners of trains, or Government contractors, and their teamsters and employés.
>
> Men hire at the Missouri River ostensibly as teamsters, but really to obtain hereby the means of transportation to this new country. Hence it is frequently the case trains are partially deserted and much property exposed to loss by Indians, if the train returns short of men, or the owner is put to great expense by delay in supplying himself with teamsters.
>
> Whenever teamsters desert at any post and a fair examination that they so desert without fault of their employer, and in breach of their contract for the purpose of higher wages, such teamsters will not be hired by any quartermaster or other officer of this command, neither will they be harbored or permitted to remain within the limits of any post.⁴

On the 6th, after more than a week of uneasy peace around the fort, a war party estimated at one hundred Indians ambushed a detachment of twenty enlisted men working at the pinery. In the initial attack one man was wounded and Privates John Wasser and Christian Oberly of A Company were killed. After the survivors fought their way to the nearest blockhouse, some of the Indians boldly rushed the loopholes, firing inside. The Indians finally were driven off, but when the timber cutters attempted to return to work, they were constantly harassed by bullets and arrows fired from woods concealment.

As soon as Carrington learned of the situation, he took a mountain howitzer and a thirty-man detachment out to the pinery and shelled the woods and ravines. After clearing the area, he left the weapon and a gunnery detail on permanent duty, and from that day until late in December the Indians gave the timber cutters very little trouble.

For some time Carrington had realized that his relations with post commander Ten Eyck were becoming awkward and strained. With daily emergencies arising, the colonel often acted without consulting Ten Eyck. It was not always easy to differentiate between matters which concerned the Mountain District alone or the post alone. Under the new security precautions, the District was virtually confined to the stockade and the pinery. The distant posts of Reno and C. F. Smith might as well have been on different continents insofar as Carrington's immediate authority affected them, and as soon as winter halted timber cutting and further isolated the other posts, the Mountain District and Fort Phil Kearny would share the same boundaries.

Aware that such a situation could cause serious command friction, Carrington issued an order on the 7th, assuming command of Fort Phil Kearny, "to have more immediate personal command of the post, at which were my district headquarters." His first action was to reorganize the post's defenses. "Every officer and soldier, every citizen, employé, and teamster, and every clerk in the sutler's store had his loophole, or place at which to report at a general alarm by night or day."[5] He also reshuffled his officers. Ten Eyck was now free to devote all his time to commanding the 2nd Battalion and to reassume command of his old company, H, which had been under temporary command of Lieutenant Wands.

Wands in turn was assigned to duty with the regimental quartermaster, Fred Brown, who had received his captain's commission and was awaiting transfer orders to Laramie. Lieutenant Bisbee became regimental adjutant, replacing John Adair who had announced he would resign his commission as soon as

Lieutenant Bradley returned from escort duty with General Hazen. Carrington also acquired a new orderly, one of the bright young clerks in his office, Private Archibald Sample.

The worst deficiency was serviceable horses. After a personal inspection of all mounts, he pronounced only forty in condition for Indian pursuit. Several were absent, of course, with mail escorts to Laramie and C. F. Smith.

Any hopes he may have had of obtaining replacements from the Department of the Platte were dashed by the next communication he received from General Cooke: "Having one company of cavalry you can probably dispense with your ninety-four horses, after mounting all the cavalry. They could be used for cavalry at Laramie. The same as to any useless horses at C. F. Smith and Reno."[6] If Carrington ever used profanity he must have indulged himself freely at the moment of reading this telegram. In the first place he had no cavalry as yet; secondly, there were no longer ninety-four serviceable horses at Phil Kearny; thirdly, horses were so short at Reno and C. F. Smith that even three-legged ones would not have been considered expendable.

It may seem incredible that Cooke, author of the classic *Cavalry Tactics* and a cavalryman of many years' service, showed so little interest in or understanding of Carrington's need for mounted men. In 1866, however, the general was still suffering bitter disappointment and emotional strain from the Civil War. He felt that his career had been blighted; he was grieving because his son, John Rogers Cooke of the defeated Confederate Army, had broken all relations with him, and because his daughter, Jeb Stuart's widow, was also estranged from him and living in poverty in the ruins of Richmond.

Whatever the reasons for Cooke's appalling indifference to conditions at Phil Kearny, this new evidence of it shook Carrington much more than a second message from the general, a curt order abolishing the Mountain District. In a way this was only a paper adjustment; Carrington still commanded the 18th Infantry Regiment; he would still report directly to Omaha. If he considered the order a reprimand, he never said so. He announced the district's dissolution on October 13, and those of his officers who had been carrying Mountain District assignments as extra duties were happy to be relieved of the paper work.

Reporting compliance of the order to Cooke, Carrington added that "the change to fine weather fills the valleys with Indians who are getting winter provisions, and I expect some trouble with them, but can meet it."[7]

In the midst of these organizational changes, a remarkable cavalcade arrived at the fort—twenty-five cowboys driving more than six hundred head of Texas longhorns. This was Nelson Story's legendary trail drive of 1866, probably the longest continuous overland drive ever made north from Texas.

An enterprising young man in his late twenties, Nelson Story had washed thirty thousand dollars in gold out of a placer claim in Alder Gulch, Montana. By the time the ore was exhausted, Story had had enough of gold mining. But instead of returning to his home in Ohio, he decided to parlay his strike into a larger fortune by venturing into the cattle business. He heard that longhorns could be bought for low prices in Texas, driven north to a railhead, and sold for enormous profits.

With ten thousand dollars sewed in the lining of his clothes, he went to Texas early in 1866. Establishing headquarters at Fort Worth, he collected a herd of about a thousand longhorns, hired a crew of cowboys, and started trailing north. Near Baxter Springs, Kansas, he met opposition from bands of vigilant Jayhawkers who refused to permit any Texas cattle to cross their small farms. Some of the Kansans feared Texas fever, a fatal cattle disease; others were willing to fight to keep the herds from wrecking fences and trampling crops. Instead of battling the Jayhawkers as many of the Texas drovers did, Story detoured. He remembered how hungry he had been for beef when he was digging gold in Montana, and he was certain he could obtain premium prices for every steer he could deliver to the northwestern mining camps. He also must have known what a foolhardy chance he was taking, but he went boldly ahead with his plans.

At Fort Leavenworth he made thorough preparations for the long drive, buying an ox-drawn wagon and loading it with groceries. His little army of cowboys and bullwhackers moved leisurely along the old Oregon Trail across Nebraska to Fort Laramie. Army officers there tried to persuade him to abandon his plans for going on to Montana. They told him that Sioux and Arapahos were swarming all over the north country, attacking everything that moved along the Bozeman Trail, and warned that if he drove north Red Cloud would stampede all his cattle and probably take several scalps to boot.

Story calmly purchased new Remington rapid-fire breech-loaders from the Laramie sutler for each of his twenty-seven men, and started north. Below Fort Reno, they met their first Sioux, a war party that boiled up suddenly over a hill. The Indians' hit-and-run punch left two trail drivers badly hurt with arrows. They also cut away a good slice of the herd, leaving the remainder in a state of stampede.

As soon as Story and his men had quieted the cattle and taken care of their wounded, they organized a war party of their own to pursue the Indians. Dusk was falling, but just before darkness ended the chase, Story and his seasoned trail herders tracked the Sioux into camp. The Indians had the longhorns bedded down in the center of an arc of tepees.

One of the drivers present on this occasion later said: "We surprised them in their camp and they weren't in shape to protest much against our taking back the cattle." Story also told his son some years afterward that he had never killed an Indian before that night attack. "We had to wipe out the entire group to recover our Longhorns," he said.[8]

When the herd was reassembled, the drivers pushed them north to Reno, left their two wounded comrades there, and moved on to Fort Phil Kearny. Carrington, in his new role as post commander, politely informed Story that military regulations forbade movement of trains between Phil Kearny and C. F. Smith unless there were forty armed men in the party. Story had only twenty-five.

The young cattleman replied angrily that he had no intention of halting at Fort Phil Kearny until another Montana-bound train arrived to strengthen his own. As late as the season was, another train might never arrive. He pointed out that his men had Remington breechloaders, giving them firepower equal to a hundred men with old-fashioned Springfields. But Carrington was firm; forty men was the minimum. The colonel advised Story to corral his stock three miles from the fort and await further orders.

When Story demanded to know why he must camp three miles from the safety of the stockade, Carrington informed him coldly that the post's herd needed the grass near the fort.

During these negotiations it is possible that Carrington offered Story the Army's maximum price for his beef cattle; the post was in sore need of the entire herd to replace animals driven off by Indians. If he did make such an offer, Story surely declined it. Story knew he could obtain four or five times the Army's price anywhere in the gold fields. Whether Carrington made the offer or not, Story no doubt suspected the colonel wanted the cattle and was purposely holding the herd at the fort in hopes of obtaining them. A prolonged delay, followed by a series of snowstorms, would jeopardize Story's entire venture, possibly force a sale to Carrington's quartermaster at low prices. Nelson Story knew this, and relations were strained between him and Colonel Carrington. Nevertheless, the young cattleman decided to gamble one week of time before tangling with military authority. He ordered his herd into corral and set up a vigilant guard against Indians.

Shortly after the arrival of Story's cattle herd, a small supply train came up from Laramie with the mail escort. It carried a long-needed shipment of medical and hospital supplies. As usual there were deficiencies in the bill of lading, the largest shortage occurring in a consignment of porter, meant for use as a tonic for invalids: 205 of 258 bottles failed to arrive. The mystery was never cleared up, even thought testimony was taken from a number of men who had access to the mildly alcoholic brew. The official assumption was that the bottles had broken en route, but few believed that. Everyone who had crossed the dry plain below Reno knew how tempting was a bottle of porter in an easily accessible covered wagon.

Among the medicines received by Surgeon Horton for administering to his ailing or wounded patients was ammonial liquor, used as a liniment and for loss of consciousness; asafetida, used as a carminative; ceratum adipsis for dressing wounds, licorice root extract for coughs, ferrous iodide syrup for colds and consumption; castor oil and epsom salts for cathartic use; tincture of peppermint oil for nausea and flatulence; scillae syrupus for use as an expectorant and emetic; chlorinated soda and zinc chloride solution for antiseptics; barley for making malt extract to be used in digestive troubles; beef extract, tapioca, and what was left of the porter, for restoring invalids.

To supply his hospital the surgeon received forty-five yards of adhesive plaster, twenty pounds of lint, eighty pounds of oakum, three hundred dozen roller bandages, seventy-two hair mattresses, one hundred hair pillows, seventy-three dressing gowns, twenty-seven delft bed chambers, and sixty-six meteorological report blanks. One of the extra duties of surgeons at that time on the frontier was recording temperatures, precipitation, and other weather phenomena.

Arrival of these medical and hospital supplies—with the previously received corn and oats, rations and ammunition—brought Phil Kearny's stores to a point where the post could operate well into the winter. The problem of replenishing stores before spring was a formidable one, but Carrington was confident he could solve it.

On the morning of the 22nd, the colonel was notified that Nelson Story's cow camp had vanished during the night. Unknown to anyone in the fort, Story had called his men together the previous evening and asked them to vote on whether they should continue to abide by Carrington's orders or slip away toward Montana. "All in favor of moving out tonight say 'Aye.' Opposed say 'No.' "

One driver named George Dow said "No!"

As soon as the word was out of Dow's mouth, Story had the man covered with his six-gun. "We'll have to tie you up, George, until we're one day gone." In the darkness, Story and his men hitched oxen to wagons, moved the cattle out of corral, and headed for Montana. Next day, Dow was released and informed that he could return to Fort Phil Kearny. He decided to stay with the drive.[9]

Meanwhile Carrington was furious over Story's willful violation of orders. At the same time the colonel remembered his responsibility for civilians' safety, and ordered a fifteen-man detail under a sergeant to move out north, join Story, and bring the party up to regulation strength of forty men. The fifteen soldiers, armed only with muzzle-loading Springfields, were supernumeraries, of course. Story's cowboys pushed the herd through to Montana without a hitch, trailing by night, grazing by day. They beat off two Indian attacks with ease, and lost only one man, a careless cowboy who rode too far ahead and was killed and scalped. On December 9, Story's historic drive reached its goal, the mining country near Virginia City.

During the day following Nelson Story's unauthorized departure from Phil Kearny, Colonel Carrington brooded over this act of insubordination and decided he could not permit its repetition. Such actions would surely weaken his authority over other civilian travelers, possibly over his own men. He decided that personnel of all civilian trains awaiting permits to proceed over the Montana Road would in future be quartered within the stockade. And to ensure that none of them might emulate Nelson Story and depart after nightfall against orders, he issued a new four-point regulation:

I. No citizen will be permitted to enter or leave the gates after retreat, unless connected with the sutler or quartermaster's department, and then to be properly passed by the officer of the day or sergeant of the guard.

II. All gates and wickets will be locked at retreat, except that at the quartermaster's gate, which will be closed at tattoo, and then only will be opened by the officer of the day or sergeant of the guard in their line of duty or for good cause.

III. All soldiers absent from quarters after tattoo will be promptly arrested, and unless sent on messages by officers, or otherwise duly authorized to be absent, will be confined and held to answer to charges before a garrison or general court-martial.

IV. This order is to be read at the first parade after its issue, and posted upon the bulletin board for three days from said issue.[10]

From this time it is evident that Carrington's desire for absolute security became an obsession; he was reaching the point where he could trust no one but himself. A year later, during the inquiry which followed the Fetterman Massacre, he virtually admitted this. "I took charge of the system of police and discipline of the post, entertaining the idea that the future policy might involve more formidable Indian aggression and require a more exact and careful watchfulness and defense."[11] His wife, recalling this period of tension, wrote that he "slept for weeks in succession without removal of garments, and nightly made his rounds to secure personal knowledge of deportment of guards and condition of post."[12]

Meanwhile the weather continued bright, the air cold and crisp, the sky incredibly blue. Most of the post's essential buildings were nearing completion.

On the 27th, after a two-months absence on escort duty with General Hazen, Lieutenant Bradley returned with his detachment of mounted infantry. Four men failed to return. Jim Brannan, scouting ahead, had been killed, between Fort Benton and Fort C. F. Smith in a surprise Indian attack. Surgeon McCleary had his horse shot from under him, but was unharmed. Only one soldier, Private Brooks of Company H, was wounded in the brief engagement. Three others had deserted previously while the detachment was marching through the gold country of Montana.

Carrington was immensely cheered by the return of his best mounted group, and in this temporary mood of elation announced that he was declaring a holiday on the last day of the month to celebrate completion of the fort's construction.

Actually many of the men enjoyed two holidays in succession, the 30th being given over to preparations for ceremonies of the 31st. One small detail spent the morning carrying out a special assignment. They placed dozens of slender poles tipped with strips of white cloth at various distances from the stockade. The poles represented different ranges of the positioned howitzers, including the maximum range, so that gunners could determine instantly whether an enemy was within accurate firing distance and thus not waste time and ammunition finding the range.

Out in the center of the parade, two men were putting finishing touches to a towering 124-foot flagpole. They were Principal Musician John H. Barnes, who had been a ship's carpenter before his army enlistment, and Private William Daley, an expert woodworker and mechanic. They tested and retested the halyards to make certain the new garrison flag would rise smoothly to the masthead.

Most of the men, however, lined up by companies in front of the new quartermaster storehouse, and filed in to receive brand-new uniforms carefully hoarded for the celebration. Returning to their new pine-smelling barracks, they smoothed wrinkles out of trousers and blouses, burnished their boots, polished buttons and belt plates.

Officers also were refurbishing uniforms, those with wives calling upon them to assist in brightening swords and shoulder scales, and seeing that plumes were properly fixed on dress hats. Several had already moved into officers' row, and others were busily transferring from tents into still-unfinished buildings. Frances Grummond was especially proud of her large double bedstead fashioned by the carpenters, "a luxury indeed, with mattress stuffed with dried grass, army blanket and a large gay-colored shawl for counterpane."

The children naturally were caught up in the holiday spirit, and Judge Kinney, the sutler, handed out so many free ginger-snaps and sugar balls to the youngsters that Mrs. Wands and Mrs. Carrington had to interrupt preparations for the big day in order to empty their sons' pockets of this oversupply of un-accustomed sweets.

October 31 was ideal for a celebration day, the sun rising out of a clean azure sky, turning the air soft and balmy and brightening the golden leaves of aspens on the Big Horn slopes.

First order of the day was an inspection and review held in the morning on the level plain between the stockade and Big Piney. Every man, every animal, every weapon, was rigidly inspected by company commanders, and the findings were mixed. In their new uniforms, hard-muscled and ruddy with health from weeks of rough outdoor life, the soldiers met all tests. Horses and mules, however, were suffering from unavoidable overstrain, and serious deficiencies were found among the arms. The few Spencer carbines were in good condition, but many Springfields showed effects of constant wear and tear. Regimental armorers had worked hard to recondition all rifles for this inspection, but more than a hundred were found unserviceable. Lieutenant Grummond, for instance, reported twenty of twenty-seven unfit for use in Company C.

With this bad but not unexpected news out of the way, companies marched back into the fort to prepare for the grand ceremonies. Early in the afternoon the bugler sounded adjutant's call. Companies formed before their respective quarters and moved out to the center of the parade, forming three sides of a square around the octagonal band platform at the base of Barnes and Daley's towering flagstaff. The fourth side of the square was occupied by a temporary platform upon which were seated officers' wives, civilian employees, and children.

On the speakers' platform with Colonel Carrington and his aides were Chaplain White and Judge Kinney. Private William Murphy, recalling afterward the presence of the obsequious sutler, noted: "There was a man who was surely 'on to his job.' He was a good diplomat. He made love to men, women, and children."[13] Mrs. Carrington was less trenchant in her brief comment: "Judge Kinney read an appropriate poem of Miss Carmichael's * chaste and spirited collection." She added: "Chaplain White offered the prayer, and principal musician Barnes presented to be read an original poem of his own, which at least did justice to his patriotic spirit."[14]

Following these preliminaries, the colonel delivered the main address. He began with a salute to those men of the command who had lost their lives since the first stakes were driven at Fort Phil Kearny.

"Fifteen weeks have passed, varied by many skirmishes and both day and night alarms.... In every work done your arms have been at hand. In the pine tracts or hay fields, on picket or

---

* Sarah E. Carmichael, who published her own works "for private circulation."

general guard duty, no one has failed to find a constant exposure to some hostile shaft, and to feel that a cunning adversary
was watching every chance to harass and kill. . . .

"The steam whistle and the rattle of the mower have followed
your steps in this westward march of empire. You have built a
central post that will bear comparison with any for security,
completeness, and adaptation to the ends in view, wherever the
other may be located, or however long in erection.

"Surrounded by temptation to hunt the choicest game, and
allured by tales of golden treasure just beyond you, you have
spared your powder for your foes, and have given the labor of
your hands to your proper work. Passing from guard-watching
to fatigue-work, and, after one night in bed, often disturbed,
returning to your post as sentry; attempting with success all
trades and callings, and handling the broad-axe and hammer,
the saw and the chisel, with the same success as that with which
you have sped the bullet, your work has proven how well deserved was the confidence I reposed in all of you. . . .

"And now this day, laying aside the worn and tattered garments, which have done their part during weeks of toil and
struggle, the veteran battalion of the 18th Infantry . . . puts on
its fresh full-dress attire for muster and review.

"The crowning office, without which you would regard your
work as scarcely begun, is now to be performed, and to its ful-
fillment I assign *soldiers;* neither discharging the duty myself,
nor delegating it to some brother officer; but some veteran soldier of good desert shall share with a sergeant from each of
their companies, and the worthy man whose work rises high
above us, the honor of raising our new and beautiful garrison
flag to the top of the handsomest flag-staff in America.

"It is the first full garrison flag that has floated between the
Platte and Montana. . . .

"With music and the roar of cannon we shall greet its un-
foldings.

"This day shall be a holiday, and a fresh starting point for
future endeavor.

"And yet all is not said that I wish to say! While we exalt the national standard, and rejoice in its glory and its power, let us not forget the true source of that glory and power. . . .

"Let me, then, ask all, with uncovered heads and grateful hearts, to pause in our act of consecration, while the chaplain shall invoke God's own blessing upon that act; so that while this banner rises heavenward, and so shall rise with each recurring sun, all hearts shall rise to the throne of the Infinite, and for this day, its duties and its pleasures, we shall become better men and better soldiers of the great Republic." [15]

At a signal from Adjutant Adair, Private William Daley and a group of sergeants and enlisted men assembled around the flagstaff. While Daley carefully gathered the halyards, Chaplain White offered a brief prayer. Immediately following his loud "Amen!" a succession of commands rang clear in the autumn air: "Attention!" "Present, arms!" "Play!" "Hoist!" "Fire!"

Frances Grummond recorded that emotion-filled scene. "With the simultaneous *snap* of presented arms in salute, the 'long roll' of the combined drum-corps was followed by the full band playing 'The Star Spangled Banner,' the guns opened fire, and the magnificent flag with its 'thirty-six-foot fly' and its 'twenty-foot *hoist*' slowly rose to masthead and was broken out in one glorious flame of red, white, and blue!

"The very shadow of the immense flag, as it floated at full length in the breeze, seemed to answer back our waving handkerchiefs; and while cheers were not permitted to break the dignified exultation of the occasion, we *did* involuntarily clap our hands, and our beating hearts did respond to the vibrations of the guns, whose echoes among the hills seemed to magnify their number as if a battle were raging all about us. Then, every officer on the alert, at the order, 'pass in review' . . . column was formed, the review received, and with the order 'parade dismissed' each company marched to its quarters, the band playing 'Hail Columbia' until the troops disappeared." [16]

It was a great day for Fort Phil Kearny, all officers and men not on guard duty free to loaf away the afternoon under a warm October sun, to view for the first time with casual ease the fruits of their fifteen weeks of labor.

Around the browning turf of the parade a score of buildings

cast their shadows—two 84x24-foot quartermaster warehouses, four company quarters, 60x25 feet; a sutler's store; adjutant's quarters; laundry; a bachelor officers quarters, 44x52 feet; a row of completed and partially completed cabins for married officers. Most of the buildings were faced with half logs, bark sides to the weather. Some were roofed with shingles, others with four-inch poles set close together and covered with corn sacks, grass, and six inches of earth.

Colonel Carrington's headquarters, topped by a lookout tower, faced north along a twelve-foot-wide graveled walk which curved around the flagpole and bandstand and crossed a similar walk running east and west. Under construction in the southeast quadrant of the parade was a 16x16-foot magazine of 14-inch timbers, sunk eight feet below ground, waterproofed and ventilated. Bordering the entire parade was a twenty-foot-wide graded street, and at diagonal corners of the stockade were two massive blockhouses of 18-inch logs. Gates were twelve feet wide of heavy planking, with small wickets in the right halves just large enough for one man to pass in a stooping position.

To the east of the parade cluster, and separated by a solid strip of stockade, lay the quartermaster's yard, six hundred feet long, two hundred feet wide, its ten-foot cottonwood palisade enclosing quarters for civilian employees, a blacksmith and wagon shop, carpenters', saddlers', and armorers' shops, stabling for mules and horses, a woodyard and a hay yard.

According to quartermaster records, more than twelve thousand logs had been cut, hauled and sawed to bring this fort into being, and considering the difficulties under which the work had been accomplished, the men had a right to take pride in the results.

For Henry B. Carrington this fort was the realization of a life's dream, and in summing up the official record of events for his first month as post commander, he noted with gratification that "work at the fort has progressed satisfactorily during the month, the weather being exceedingly favorable. Storehouses, officers quarters and substantial and commodious quarters for the troops, stabling for the public animals are all in a manner completed." [17]

He was also pleased by the number of civilians who had passed safely over the Montana Road since it had come under his responsibility—979 men, 32 women, and 26 children. Yet it was some relief to know that the emigration season was ending and that there would probably be only a few more trains to worry over before another spring and summer rolled around.

On that last day of October the garrison's strength was 360 officers and men, a gain of nineteen during the month. Two enlisted men of the 2nd Cavalry were listed on the muster rolls, casuals from escort duties, but neither of the two full companies promised in August had yet reported.

At three o'clock in the afternoon of the holiday, Indians made their first close appearance in three weeks. They had come up from camps along Tongue River, their curiosity aroused by the massed firing of howitzers during the flag-raising ceremony. They splashed across Big Piney and galloped around the bend of Sullivant Hills so quickly they almost passed the west gate before pickets sounded an alarm. "Others appeared upon the hills, and flashing mirrors were constantly passing signals for nearly an hour," said Margaret Carrington. "They had at least the satisfaction of seeing the stars and stripes, and thus getting new hints as to the proposed length of our visit."[18] As a precautionary measure, extra ammunition was dispatched to each company quarters, howitzer details were called to stations, and a few men were added to the guard. By sundown, however, the inquisitive visitors from Tongue River had vanished back into their hills.

In the evening the Carringtons entertained officers and wives with a levee in their new quarters. It was a full-dress affair, with music, dancing, and party games. In proper military fashion, the merrymaking ended promptly at midnight, the guests strolling to their neighboring quarters under a star-filled autumn sky. Frances Grummond, who had temporarily forgotten her almost constant forebodings, was cheered by the calls of the sentries on the banquette: "Twelve o'clock and all's well." It was the first hour of November, the Deer Rutting Moon.

VIII. November:

DEER RUTTING MOON

Because the country was broken, because most of the officers had not been with me in reconnaissances and had recently arrived at post entirely unused to Indian warfare, because I knew the Indians to be in large numbers, I would not authorize them to make hazardous adventures. . . . I did (as I believed) fail to have the confidence of some officers. Few came from Omaha or Laramie without prejudice, believing I was not doing enough fighting.[1]

LATE on November 1, the last Montana-bound civilian train of the season was camped outside the fort. This party had met with little Indian resistance on the journey up from Laramie, and some of the men had grown careless enough to sit around campfires after dark, playing cards by the light of the flames. About nine o'clock on this evening a band of Indians crept close upon them in the surrounding darkness, and without warning fired upon the card players. Three men were wounded, one fatally, in the first fusillade. A few moments later signal fires appeared on hills around the fort, and Indians could be seen dancing around them.

"Colonel Carrington concluded to try his mountain howitzer on the Indian dancers," teamster John Bratt later recorded.

146

"After a few shots, the gunners got range on some of the Indian fires, and many fires were extinguished and some dancers' lives went out with them." [2] The colonel also dispatched a skirmish party, but no trace of the night attackers was found.

Two days later one of the two cavalry companies assigned to Phil Kearny in August finally arrived from Laramie—sixty-three men of Company C under command of Lieutenant Horatio S. Bingham, a young Minnesotan with Civil War experience. For Bingham and twenty-seven of his men, this would be their last post assignment. The lieutenant had less than a month to live, and Company C would suffer the heaviest loss of any of the five companies represented in the detachment which marched out with Fetterman on December 21. They were armed with obsolete Enfield rifles and Starr carbines.

Accompanying Bingham's cavalrymen from Fort Laramie was the man who would lead so many of them to their deaths— Captain William J. Fetterman. While Carrington as nominal commander of the 18th Regiment had remained in Ohio and Indiana through most of the Civil War, Fetterman had been winning honors in combat. In the spring of 1862, Fetterman commanded Company A of the 2nd Battalion during the siege of Corinth; later that year he was cited for gallantry at Stone's River after thirty-six hours of continuous fighting. As commander of the 2nd Battalion he fought throughout most of Sherman's Georgia campaign of 1864—Resaca, Kennesaw Mountain, Peach Tree Creek, Jonesboro, the siege of Atlanta. Official dispatches were filled with numerous commendatory references: "Captain Fetterman's command marched to my assistance with great promptness . . . conspicuous for gallantry and bravery . . . displayed great gallantry and spirit . . . the conduct of Captain Fetterman in throwing up a salient and maintaining his positions against repeated attempts to dislodge him by the enemy, is worthy of particular notice. . . ." [3] By the end of the campaign he was breveted lieutenant-colonel and assigned to brigade staff.

Brilliant as his record was, Fetterman knew nothing of Indian warfare, and was boastfully contemptuous of the savages' ability to withstand attacks from trained soldiers of the United States Army. Because he had held rank longer than Ten Eyck, Fetterman superseded him as commander of the 2nd Battalion—his old outfit which he had led in the bitterest fighting in Georgia. Ten Eyck thus was dropped another notch in authority; the former post and battalion commander was left with only Company H.

Captain James W. Powell and Major Henry Almstedt, the paymaster, also arrived with this party. Powell was assigned to C Company, which Lieutenant Adair had been commanding in addition to his duties as regimental adjutant.

In the mailbag from Laramie was a scolding telegram from General Cooke, complaining about delays in receiving communications from Fort Phil Kearny, and suggesting that Carrington send mails more frequently. There was also a formal query from The Adjutant General in Washington wanting to know the location of the fort. To this Adjutant Adair replied politely that Phil Kearny was in Dakota Territory, sixty-five miles northwest of Fort Reno.

With restrained impatience, Carrington answered Cooke's complaint by pointing out that he had sent three mails in October, as required by orders. "My mail just received," he added, "was twelve days, on account of snow, bad roads, and weather, and this on return trip alone. It must not be overlooked that our snows, which leave the hills bare, fill the intermediate ravines, valleys, and gulches so that no one can travel. While we had no snow at this post, owing to its position, there were four feet within a mile of it. . . . I believe that the general commanding would prefer to lose a mail occasionally, with the assurance that in an emergency I will advise him at all risk, rather than embarrass me in any skirmish or temporary encounter which calls for use of my present force." [4]

Jim Bridger returned during that first week in November, reporting on his talks with the Crows around Fort C. F. Smith and along Clark's Fork. Old Gabe was confident the Crows would not join the Sioux and Arapaho as allies, but he had heard many disturbing rumors of war plans and of the great strength the hostiles were amassing along Tongue River. The Crow chiefs reported that it took half a day to ride through all villages of war parties there. Sissetons, Bad Faces, Oglalas, Hunkpapas, Arapaho, and some Gros Ventres and Cheyennes were together, and there was big talk of destroying the two new forts in their hunting grounds. Yellow-Face, a Crow warrior, declared that he had passed hostile camps in close array along a forty-mile stretch of the Tongue Valley.

Some of the Crows told Bridger of an interview with Red Cloud. "We want you to aid us in destroying the whites," Red Cloud had said, and then boasted that he would cut off the soldiers' supplies when bad weather came, and would starve them out of the forts during the winter and kill them all.[5]

Bridger also had conferred some weeks earlier with Jim Beck-wourth, who had been living in one of the Crow villages.* Beckwourth told Bridger he had enlisted 250 young Crows who were willing to join the soldiers and go on the warpath against the hostiles. When Bridger mentioned this, Carrington informed the scout that he had authority to enlist only fifty Indian auxiliaries, and had already sent a man (W. B. C. Smith) to Omaha to arrange for enlistment of Winnebagos or Pawnees. After pondering the matter, Bridger allowed that if Pawnees or Winnebagos could be brought from Omaha with rifles, it would be better than enlisting Crows nearer at hand but who possessed only bows and arrows.

When he reported to Omaha on Bridger's findings, Carrington expressed no alarm over Red Cloud's threat to starve the soldiers out of the forts. "He does not comprehend the idea of a year's supplies, nor that we are now prepared to not only pass the winter, but next spring and summer, even if he takes the offensive." This was careless boasting on the colonel's part; supplies on hand were adequate for full rations only into mid-winter.

In this same letter, Carrington repeated his deep disillusionment with the Laramie treaty. "I had not the slightest confidence in the result of the proposed treaty, and so wrote you. And in fact the whole result of the negotiations there [Laramie] was a mere temporary suspension of hostile acts, if it even amounted

---

* Beckwourth never returned from the Crow village, dying there during the autumn under mysterious circumstances; by poison, it was rumored.

to that. . . . I look for this month to determine their purpose, and hope yet to be able to strike a blow which they will feel more than the last, and not risk a single post on the line in the attempt." [6]

His comment, *I hope yet to be able to strike a blow,* may have been a subconscious reply to pressures which had been exerted upon him during the past two days by his ambitious new captain, William J. Fetterman. Since the hour of his arrival at Fort Phil Kearny, Fetterman had given Carrington no peace.

The two men were almost exact opposites in temperament, Fetterman being a man of action, a fighter pure and simple, descended from generations of professional soldiers. Before leaving his eastern assignment to journey to Phil Kearny, he had been informed that in an impending reorganization of the Army he probably would supersede Carrington as commander of the post. (In a move to increase the size of the frontier army, the War Department was planning to use the 18th Infantry's 2nd Battalion as nucleus for a new 27th Infantry Regiment. The 1st Battalion was to be enlarged to regiment strength, retaining the original 18th regimental number.)

Fetterman was eager to further his advancement, and from the first day of his arrival was openly critical of Carrington's cautious policy toward the hostiles. His old comrades of Civil War days, Fred Brown and William Bisbee, quickly sided with Fetterman. Young George Grummond was another supporter of his proposal to attack instead of defend, and a few days after Fetterman's arrival, officers and men were quoting some of the captain's reckless boasts: "A single company of regulars could whip a thousand Indians." "A full regiment could whip the entire array of hostile tribes." "With eighty men I could ride through the Sioux nation." [7]

This was the beginning of a schism between Carrington and his officers which would grow deeper and more dangerous with each passing week until the tragedy of late December.

On the second day after reporting for duty, Fetterman came to Carrington with a plan for tricking the Indians into a night ambush. He had talked it over previously with Brown and Grummond, and both had approved. The plan was to conceal

a heavily armed detachment in a cottonwood thicket along Big
Piney opposite the fort, hobble some mules between the thicket
and the fort as live bait, and thus decoy the Indians into position for a cross-fire attack.

Carrington considered it a risky business, but granted permission after advising Fetterman to exercise the greatest caution
in exposing men needlessly in any such action as a massed charge
out of concealment. The Sioux, he warned, did not fight in the
same manner as Fetterman's recent opponents, the soldiers of
the Confederacy.

Fetterman laid his trap after dark, setting out the hobbled
mules and placing his detachment carefully in the thicket. "The
entire garrison," Frances Grummond wrote, "was keenfully
watchful of this experiment." [8] She was worrying about her husband, George, who was out in the cottonwood thicket waiting
for Indians while she waited for his safe return. Unable to
sleep, she wandered about their three-room pine-log cabin. She
had hung pieces of sheeting over the living room windows for
shades, covered the unglazed kitchen windows with old newspapers, and carpeted her living room with gunny sacks sewn
together. Crude as the cabin was, it seemed like a palace after
six weeks of housekeeping in a tent, a warm dry haven in which
to give birth to her expected child.

Elsewhere in the fort others also stayed up late, waiting for
the Indians to dart into Fetterman's trap. Some played cards
(Authors was a favorite with the women and older children)
and some brought out their musical instruments or sang; others
read books or reread old newspapers from the last Laramie mail.
Most of the women sewed, using patterns swapped back and
forth, fashioning dresses and coats from calico, flannel and
linsey-woolsey procured from the sutler's store.

In the sutler's store, the usual evening crowd stayed late,
talking, drinking, nibbling at cheese and crackers, half listening
for a fusillade from the thicket along Big Piney. Jim Bridger
was in the store, tilted back in a chair with one arm on the
trading counter, his dingy, smoke-stained hat pulled down so
that it half hid his weathered stubbly-bearded face. Squatting
in a corner near Old Gabe was a Crow Indian who had come

down with him from Fort C. F. Smith to serve as an interpreter. Almost every evening for hours at a time the Crow took this same position, speaking to no one, no one speaking to him. Bridger had neither offered nor been invited to participate in Fetterman's ambush scheme. His rheumatism was bothering him, and since his return from the north he had been in a somber mood. "Bridger would walk about, constantly scanning the opposite hills that commanded a good view of the fort," Frances Grummond wrote of him at this time, "as if he suspected Indians of having scouts behind every sage clump or fallen cottonwood." [9]

After midnight the unofficial post watch diminished in numbers as most of them gave up and went to bed. Bright moonlight exposed the hobbled mules grazing quietly between the fort and the shadowed ambush. A few meteors streaked across the sky, wolves howled back in the hills, but not one Indian appeared on the Big Piney side of the fort.

They struck instead on the opposite side, stampeding a small herd of cattle belonging to James Wheatley, by daylight soon after Fetterman quit in disgust and led his sleepy-eyed men back into the fort. That should have been Lesson Number One for Fetterman (the Indians would give him the benefit of only two more lessons). But at this time in the short life of William J. Fetterman his cocksureness would not admit that anything could be learned from a savage Indian.

For several days after the unsuccessful decoy attempt, life in the fort fell into an even pattern of military routine. Fifty of the sixty-three recently arrived cavalrymen departed on escort duties, ten accompanying a mail carrier to Fort Casper, and forty forming a heavy guard for Paymaster Almstedt en route to Fort C. F. Smith.

On the 11th an incident involving two men of Company A further deepened the rift between Carrington and Fetterman. For reasons not clear, Sergeant Garrett attacked Private Thomas Burke, verbally and physically, in full view of several officers and their wives. When a guard was summoned to put the combatants under arrest, the commanding officer of Company A interceded, resorting to violent profanity himself as he endorsed the actions of his sergeant. The commanding officer of Company A was Captain Fetterman.

Carrington, who witnessed part of the incident, was horrified, especially because the fighting and profanity occurred on a Sunday morning and in sight and hearing of women who were on their way to church services. The colonel walked on with his wife to the building which was then being used for Sunday services, listened to Chaplain David White's sermon and the music of a string band, and joined in the spirited singing of such familiar hymns as "Old Hundred," "Gloria in Excelsis," and "There Is a Light in the Window."

After services he returned to his headquarters, summoned Adjutant Bisbee, and issued a sternly worded general order (No. 38) condemning "profane swearing, verbal abuse, kicks, and blows," and declaring that such "perversion of authority . . . will be dealt with in the most decided manner." While most of his order was directed toward noncommissioned officers, one paragraph was surely aimed at Fetterman:

> Officers at this post will communicate and carefully enforce this order, seeking to inspire among non-commissioned officers, by precept and example, that calm and steady habit of command which will surely secure implicit obedience, and no less augment respect for authority requiring obedience.[10]

Although Lieutenant Bisbee's name was signed to the order as post adjutant, Bisbee recognized the implied reprimand to his old friend, Fetterman, and lost no time in informing the latter that he thoroughly disapproved of it. In a few hours, the pro-Fetterman group was referring to General Order No. 38 as "Bully 38," and not a few profane jokes about it were being privately passed around officers' row. Those who now sided openly with Fetterman against Carrington included Captains Brown and Powell, Lieutenants Bisbee and Grummond, and one of the contract surgeons, C. M. Hines.

Ironically, the officer who had twice been demoted in authority, Captain Ten Eyck, was perhaps most loyal to Carrington. Ten Eyck's nature was introspective as was Carrington's. Although he had served in the field with the 18th Regiment during the war, Ten Eyck had been wounded and captured at Chicka-mauga, and was not bound to Fetterman by shared hardships in the long Georgia campaigns as were Brown, Powell and Bis-bee.

For various reasons there was a great deal of discontent at this time among officers of the frontier army. Most of them had held brevet ranks in the Civil War much higher than their permanent ranks. It was not easy for a brevet lieutenant-colonel to resume the duties and pay of a mere lieutenant without ex-pectations of immediate promotion, and by late 1866 it was evident that promotions would be very hard to come by in this vastly shrunken army. A letter from one of Carrington's junior officers who signed himself "Dacotah" appeared in the *Army and Navy Journal* in November, decrying inadequate army pay. "There is not an officer in the Army but will testify that it is next to an impossibility to live like an officer and a gentleman on his pay. Pay of a second lieutenant amounts to $110.80 for a 31-day month, tax off. On this one must live, clothe ourselves and appear like gentlemen. When uniform suits cost $100, over-coats from $125 to $150, boots $17 . . . what is left to pay board bills and mess bills and where and how are we to obtain a cigar if we desire to smoke after our scanty meals?" [11]

At Fort Phil Kearny there was also a sharp differential in civil-ian pay and officers' pay, which led to added dissatifaction among the latter. Civilian guides received three times as much money as lieutenants, civilian clerks more than captains. Blacksmiths, carpenters and wagon masters were almost as well paid as second lieutenants and they had no problems of dress uniforms or bur-dens of extra military duties. As for teamsters and laborers, they were far better off economically than noncommissioned officers.

The blame for slow promotions, for inequitable pay, had to be placed somewhere, and naturally it fell upon the symbol of army authority nearest at hand, the colonel of the regiment, Henry B. Carrington.

As if to compound the dissociated position in which Carring-ton now found himself, a telegram arrived on November 12 from General Cooke, casually threatening him with a general court-martial. The message and one other were brought by a special express from Laramie, the lone courier risking his life to cross 236 miles of snowdrifts, with hostile war parties all along the route. The first telegram demanded copies of the post's monthly and trimonthly returns since July. "If not immediately sent, with explanation, this matter must be brought before a general court-martial." [12] The second telegram was less ominous. It acknowledged previous receipt of the missing returns, and according to the courier, had been received at Fort Laramie after his departure, then had been rushed up to Bridger's Ferry by another messenger who there overtook the first rider. Such was the state of communications between Fort Phil Kearny and Omaha headquarters in November.

During the week of the 12th, Carrington lost two of his best junior officers, Lieutenant John Adair resigning his commission to return to civilian life, and Lieutenant James Bradley transferring to the 3rd Battalion in Utah. Five enlisted men deserted that week to seek their fortunes in the Montana gold fields. The civilian master of transportation also left without notice. "In his pockets went the money for our supply of wood and hay," Private Murphy noted. "It was reported that he went to Canada." [13] Another indication of a slackening of discipline within the garrison was a report on the 18th of pilfered stores and forage. An extra guard had to be placed over the quartermaster buildings and corn piles.

To add to these mounting internal troubles, the Indians began showing themselves in strength again, and on the 21st attacked a beef contractor's train coming up from Reno. Company C under Captain Powell beat off the attack and no cattle were lost, but the men were unable to overtake and punish the raiders.

Next afternoon Captain Fetterman made his first visit to the pinery, accompanying the regular escort which was to return with the wagons. With Fetterman was his close friend, Lieutenant Bisbee, and as the two officers approached the timber of Piney Island ahead of the escort, they halted to water their horses. "Suddenly from behind a huge log fifty yards away," Bisbee wrote later, "came yells and shots from ambushed redskins. Taking immediate shelter under the bank of the creek for better observation and to await reinforcements from the train guard in rear, we plainly discovered larger parties of Indians in the timber waiting our further approach. One lone 'buck' only came into the open, plainly a decoy tempting us to a trap. It was not accepted, but in temptation to see what the young brave was really made of I charged him. Zip, zip, came several shots from concealed Indians in the woods to which he escaped in great haste." [14]

From this account it is clear that Bisbee had learned something of Indian fighting; he recognized a decoy trap when he saw one. Perhaps he passed a warning to Fetterman on that day, and restrained the overconfident captain from dashing on into the woods. But whether he did so or not, Fetterman must have received the lesson with skepticism, or soon forgot it.

Soon after the sounds of firing rang through the woods, a false alarm was somehow carried to the fort, spreading by word of mouth until the post bugler dashed up to Carrington's headquarters with the startling news that Indians had attacked the wood train and "all were killed." Frances Grummond and Mrs. Bisbee were both nearby and heard the announcement. "I recall as if yesterday, the blanched face of Mrs. Bisbee, knowing as she did that her husband was with the wood party." [15]

Within a few minutes Carrington himself formed a relief party and dashed out the gate at a gallop. A mile or so from the fort he met Fetterman and Bisbee, both completely unaware of the false report of their deaths. They passed it off as a joke, and as they approached the fort and saw the flag at half-mast, began swapping banter as to which of their brother officers would receive promotions now that they were no longer among the living. To Carrington such talk was in extremely bad taste, and he called the officers up sharply. Carrington was not a humorless man, but he had seen too much of death since July to joke about it in November.

A mail arrived from Laramie on Sunday the 25th with another of those oddly unrealistic messages which were coming with increased frequency from General Cooke:

COLONEL: You are hereby instructed that so soon as the troops and stores are covered from the weather, to turn your earnest attention to the possibility of striking the hostile band of Indians by surprise in their winter camps, as intimated in telegram of September 27 ultimo from these headquarters.

An extraordinary effort in winter, when the Indian horses are unserviceable, it is believed, should be followed by more success than can be accomplished by very large expeditions in the summer, when the Indians can so easily scatter into deserts and mountain hiding places almost beyond pursuit.

Four companies of infantry will be available, besides some cavalry. You have a large arrear of murderous and insulting attacks by the savages upon emigrant trains and troops to settle, and you are ordered, if there prove to be any promise of success, to conduct or to send under another officer, such an expedition.[16]

By this late date Carrington had almost despaired of ever making General Cooke understand the realities of the situation at Fort Phil Kearny. But once again he wrote of arms shortages, of the demands upon his single cavalry company for almost constant escort service. He pointed out that the cavalry's promised new carbines had not arrived; they were armed only with obsolete rifles and antiquated Starr carbines. The infantry companies required at least one hundred Springfields to replace broken and worn-out pieces. "I shall look for another company of cavalry soon," he added, "as mentioned in previous telegram." And then because there was nothing else he could do in the face of a direct order, he concluded: "I will, in person, command expeditions, when severe weather confines them [the Indians] to their villages, and make the winter one of active operations in different directions, as best affords chance of punishment." [17]

Before that Sunday ended, the Indians gave Carrington a chance to strike a blow. They made a daring raid upon the beef herd, cutting out sixteen head of cattle. In a mood of extreme anger, the colonel took charge of the pursuit, ordering out every available mounted man. Lieutenant Bingham led off with his cavalry company, and Fetterman, Brown and Grummond commanded separate mounted detachments. None of them overtook a single Indian, but they recovered eight steers, and found five others slaughtered and partially butchered.

On the 27th, Lieutenant Bingham and a detachment of twenty-four cavalrymen departed for Fort C. F. Smith with dispatches and mail, and on the 29th a sergeant and ten men left for Fort Reno on a similar assignment. With these men and others absent, post returns for the last day of the month showed 427 officers and men, a gain of sixty-seven over October.

Another routine item which Carrington entered in his post records for November concerned the transfer of Lieutenant-Colonel Henry Walton Wessells, Brevet Brigadier-General of Volunteers, from Omaha to Fort Reno to replace the ailing Captain Proctor. In a time when brigadier-generals of Volunteers were as numerous as regular army lieutenants, Carrington probably gave little thought to the rank of his new Reno commander. He could not anticipate that dark twenty-first day of December, in the Moon When the Deer Shed Their Horns, nor could he have believed that in another month Wessells would replace him as commander of Fort Phil Kearny.

IX. December:

MOON WHEN THE DEER SHED THEIR HORNS

Fort Phil Kearny was established amid hostilities. Fifty-one skirmishes have occurred. No disaster other than the usual incidents to border warfare occurred, until gross disobedience of orders sacrificed nearly eighty of the choice men of my command....Life was the forfeit. In the grave I bury disobedience.[1]

1.

ON December 3, Lieutenant Horatio Bingham set a new record for a round-trip escort to Fort C. F. Smith by returning to Phil Kearny seven days after departure. Later that same day, Lieutenant Wilbur F. Arnold arrived from Laramie with forty-three infantry recruits; most of these men were formed into a new unit designated as Company K. Although these infantrymen were "perfectly new recruits from the general depot," they were given a warm welcome as well as immediate assistance in completing a new barracks for their use.[2]

On the same day in Washington, President Andrew Johnson was delivering a message to Congress. "The Army has been promptly paid," he declared, "carefully provided with medical treatment, well sheltered and subsisted, and is to be furnished with breech-loading small arms ... Treaties have been concluded with the Indians who ... have unconditionally submitted to our authority and manifested an earnest desire for a renewal of friendly relations." [3]

The President was many hundreds of miles from Fort Phil Kearny, of course, but had he been there on December 6, he might have been surprised at the "friendly relations" manifested by a large band of Sioux which attacked a wood train that day.

Around one o'clock in the afternoon, pickets on Pilot Hill began waving signal flags around their heads, repeating the warning five times in succession to indicate large parties were engaged in the attack. As soon as he was apprised of the action, Carrington climbed to his lookout tower and swept the horizon with his field glass. The wood train was four miles west of the fort, just south of Sullivant Hills. Off to the north along Lodge Trail Ridge, other Indians were flashing mirror signals. Several mounted warriors were within two miles of Big Piney, moving down the ridge toward the fort.

In keeping with his new policy of striking a blow at every opportunity, Carrington immediately ordered all serviceable horses saddled. To Captain Fetterman he assigned Bingham's cavalry company and one squad of mounted infantry, and ordered the captain to gallop straight west, relieve the wood train, and drive the Indians back across the Piney. At the same time Carrington with Lieutenant Grummond's mounted squad would sweep around to the north between Sullivant Hills and Lodge Trail Ridge and endeavor to cut off the Indians' retreat.

After five months of directing pursuit of the hostiles, Carrington could assume that "there was no outlet for the attacking force, except across Lodge Trail Ridge or between that ridge and Peno Head, about nine miles distant from the fort." [4] With Lieutenant Grummond at his side, the colonel led his twenty-four mounted men rapidly up the valley of the Piney, keeping to the south bank. The temperature was below freezing, with a cold wind off the Big Horns. As soon as the column came opposite the slope of Lodge Trail Ridge, he signaled for a crossing of the Piney. The mounted Indians previously sighted along the creek had disappeared, and only three were visible on the upper ridge.

Big Piney was sheeted with ice, but Carrington turned his horse into the creek, hoping its hoofs would break the crust.

Instead the animal floundered, and Carrington slid from his saddle. He kicked disgustedly at the ice with his boots, breaking a passage for the others as he waded the nervous mount across in three feet of freezing water.

When all were across, he ordered march resumed up the eastern slope of Lodge Trail Ridge. They were now four miles from the post, and in a few minutes the Bozeman Road came into view off to the right. Four Indians, widely spaced, held their horses on the road while a war party attempted hurried concealment in a nearby ravine. Carrington saw all of them clearly, quickly counting thirty-two. "At the same time I saw on the hills across the creek over one hundred Indians descending to the creek, followed by . . . Fetterman's command, which had properly carried out the original order on the left. Delivering a sharp fire at a small party in my way, who instantly fled, I pushed on at a gallop westward along the ridge." [5]

Reaching the end of Lodge Trail Ridge, the colonel saw that he must bring his men down at full speed if he hoped to intercept the Indians being driven by Fetterman. At the same time he warned his men not to scatter as they guided their horses down the rough terrain. During the descent, Lieutenant Grummond's eagerness overcame his caution. He galloped so far ahead that Carrington sent an orderly after him, with an order to "keep with me and obey orders or return to the post." The orderly, Private D. Harman, failed to overtake the lieutenant.

"Upon descending the ridge," Carrington later reported, "I found to my surprise fifteen cavalry, dismounted and without an officer. I passed through them, ordering them to mount and follow upon the gallop." Before the colonel could slow his horse to a walk, the trail jogged sharply, and he found himself suddenly blocked by a band of yelling Indians spread along a low hill. He swung in his saddle. Only six men were still with him, one of them being Bugler Adolf Metzger of Bingham's cavalry.

"Where's Lieutenant Bingham?" Carrington demanded.

Metzger replied that Bingham had gone down the road around a hill to the left, and Carrington realized then that the cavalry leader must have dashed ahead, the Indians deliberately allowing him to pass through into a trap. He ordered Metzger to sound recall, the bugle notes echoing back from the hills in the cold air.

Meanwhile several mounted infantrymen strung out behind Carrington had come up, and he was ordering them to spread out in skirmish formation just as the first wave of Indians swarmed from the base of the hill and began attacking. Private James McGuire, one of Bingham's troopers, was thrown from his wounded mount. A warrior dashed forward, intent upon counting coup with a raised war club. Carrington swung over toward McGuire, dismounted, and drove the Indian away. At least one hundred warriors were circling and yelling, but the soldiers had dismounted and formed a defensive front. Firing was steady, the carbines crackling, the rifle fire slower spaced, ramrods glistening in the pale sunlight. Along the ridges to right and left, Indian lookouts were flashing mirror signals and waving white flags. There was still no sign of Bingham or Grummond.

For twenty minutes Carrington was engaged in what would be the only real military action of his entire career. "One saddle," he reported afterward, "was emptied by a single shot fired by myself." [6] At the end of the twenty minutes, Captain Fetterman's slow-moving squad arrived, and the attackers immediately vanished over the hill.

Conferring briefly with Fetterman, Carrington informed him that Bingham and Grummond and probably several men were missing somewhere off to the right, and he ordered an immediate movement in that direction. A few minutes later a drumming of hoofs sounded on their front, and Lieutenant Grummond and three men dashed suddenly into view, closely pursued by seven Indians, who veered away, shaking their lances, as they sighted the oncoming relief force.

Exactly what words Carrington and Grummond exchanged as they brought their sweated horses together are unrecorded, but if one may believe hearsay accounts, the young lieutenant was more angry than frightened, and "very hotly asked the colonel if he was a fool or a coward to allow his men to be cut to pieces without offering help." [7] If Grummond did say this, Carrington never made public record of it, possibly out of deference to the lieutenant's widow, who in after years became the colonel's second wife. At that moment on the field of action, Carrington was more interested in finding Lieutenant Bingham who undoubtedly was in trouble. Grummond told Carrington that as he was descending Lodge Trail Ridge he had sighted Bingham and hurried forward to join him, assuming that Bingham's cavalry company was close behind.

Bingham's cavalrymen, however, had fallen back "in the most unaccountable manner," as Fetterman put it in his report. "I, assisted by Captain Brown and Lieutenant Wands," the captain added, "used every exertion to check [the retreat]. The Indians, corralling and closing around us, it was plain the retreat, if continued, would be a rout and massacre." Instead of staying with his men, Bingham chose to dash forward. "I cannot account for this movement on the part of an officer of such unquestionable gallantry," Fetterman declared, somewhat with the same puzzlement that his surviving fellow officers would ponder his own fatal actions two weeks later.[8]

Of this same incident, Lieutenant Wands said that he and Captain Brown, "leveling their guns" at the cavalrymen, warned them they would shoot if the retreat was not halted. At the same time, according to Wands, Bingham called back, "Come on," beckoned, and went ahead with some of his men in the direction of Carrington's squad which could be seen a half mile away descending Lodge Trail Ridge.[9]

While it was never possible to determine why Bingham acted as he did, the reason could be blamed upon his lack of experience in Indian warfare. The same excuse could be given for the actions of his men, most of whom were green recruits, some untrained even in horsemanship. They had made several escort journeys with the mail, but this was their first close encounter with armed hostiles. Like most newcomers to the frontier, they attributed almost superhuman powers to the Indians and dreaded close fighting with them.

When Grummond overtook Bingham on that narrow twisting trail beyond Lodge Trail Ridge, the cavalry officer and the few men still with him were pursuing a single dismounted Indian. This Indian was performing the oldest trick of frontier warfare, the decoy trap, and as the soldiers galloped down Peno Valley, dozens of warriors began springing from concealment in their rear. One of the men in the trap who lived to tell the tale was Private John Guthrie of Bingham's C Company. Bingham, said Guthrie, was the first to be hit. "He fell off his horse, shot in the head. This was a bad place to be, as we could not use our arms very well on the Indians. The red skins tried to save our horses for their own use. This move is what saved our lives, they tried to lasso us from the horses." [10]

In the confusion of hand-to-hand fighting, Grummond and three men broke out of the surround, the lieutenant using his saber, the men swinging their rifles as clubs. They were in pell-mell flight from seven Indians armed with lances when they met Carrington's search party.

The search for Bingham now continued, and within an hour they found his body "in the brush . . . shot with over fifty arrows, lying over an old stump." [11] Nearby was Sergeant G. R. Bowers, E Company, an experienced Civil War veteran. He had slain three Indians with his revolver, but his skull was split with a hatchet, and he died before an ambulance could arrive from the fort.

It was midafternoon, only two hours having passed since the two mounted forces left the fort, but the cold was intensifying, the low December sun hidden by hills, a gray cloud scud covering the sky. Not an Indian was in view anywhere. Carrington called off the pursuit, asking for a casualty count. Bingham and Bowers were dead, one sergeant and four privates wounded. Eight horses were out of action, three so badly wounded they had to be destroyed.

As for the hostiles, no one could be sure of their losses, as all casualties had been carried from the field. Carrington estimated ten enemy killed, several wounded. But not an officer or man in the field that day could take any pride in his accomplishments. Blunders, disobedience of orders, misunderstandings, recklessness, cowardice, had almost brought disaster to the fort's defenders. Bingham had left his confused company of green recruits to ride to his death; Grummond had disobeyed Carrington and almost met the same fate as Bingham. Lieutenant

Wands, who had been ordered to ride with Carrington's party, had instead joined Fetterman. (He claimed afterward he misunderstood Carrington's order.) When Carrington dispatched a written order to Fort Phil Kearny for reinforcements and an ambulance, he specifically asked for Captain Powell to head the relief. But Powell remained in his quarters, ordering Lieutenant Wilbur Arnold to go in his place. Carrington himself was not blameless. When he came off Lodge Trail Ridge, he outrode his own men, galloped through Bingham's disorganized cavalry, and almost ran headlong without support into an Indian ambush. Not every one of this succession of military discords could be laid to the wide cleavage between Carrington and his officers, but most of them could be. The pattern for disaster on December 21 was laid on that afternoon of December 6.

After returning with their casualties to the warmth and security of post quarters, the participants in the day's blunders spent the remaining hours before taps in recounting and reassessing their experiences. One of the cavalrymen, offering a reason why Bingham left his disorganized command, said that the lieutenant's horse "ran away with him and he could not restrain him." Another declared that "Bingham lost one pistol, and after firing the other, so excited did he become that he threw it away." Private John Donovan, who had been riding in the front of the action, said that Lieutenant Bingham was armed only with a saber, and that both the lieutenant and Sergeant Bowers had been pulled from their horses by Indians. Frank Fessenden's later account corroborates Donovan's: "The savages attempted to catch several of our boys by trying to put their strong bows over their necks and drag them off their horses." Fessenden also reported that Lieutenant Grummond told him "that he shut his eyes and literally slashed his way out, as did many of the others. Grummond said he could hear his saber 'click' every time he cleaved an Indian's skull." [12]

In recording the reunion with her husband after the fight, Frances Grummond wrote: "We both sat for a long time in silence, then mingled our tears in gratitude for the wonderful deliverance . . . he said that he abandoned the use of spurs and jammed his sword into the weary beast to urge him to greater effort, followed by the chief, in full war-dress, with spear at his back so near that but for his good horse he would then and there have met a terrible fate. . . . A sense of apprehension that I seemed to have been conscious of ever since my arrival at the post, deepened from that hour. No sleep came to my weary eyes, except fitfully, for many nights, and even then in my dreams I could see him riding madly from me with the Indians in pursuit." [13]

Even the cocky Captain Fetterman seemed to be sobered by the day's events. When he handed his official report to Carrington he professed to have learned a lesson. "This Indian war," he said, "has become a hand-to-hand fight, requiring the utmost caution." [14]

Unfortunately, Fetterman forgot this lesson, the last he would learn from the Indians. Jim Bridger, growing more melancholy every day, must have sensed that he would. "Your men who fought down south are crazy," he told Carrington. "They don't know anything about fighting Indians." [15]

But if Fetterman forgot what he learned, the Indians remembered everything which happened that day. From the high ridges, Red Cloud and other leading chiefs had observed the foolish actions of the soldiers, and later that week in the Sioux lodges along Tongue River, they heard many details of the fighting from a subchief, Yellow Eagle, who had led the main attacks. Years afterward, white men would learn from the Indians that the fight of December 6 convinced the hostiles that they could overpower and destroy any force sent out from the fort to fight them. They decided that on the first auspicious day after the coming of the next full moon they would lay a great trap of more than a thousand warriors, make another feint at the wood train, work the decoy trick, lure as many men out as possible, kill them all, and then burn the fort.

As the gloomy hours of December 6 dragged toward midnight, voices of sentries on the stockade echoed "All's well!" But the fate of eighty-one men in Fort Phil Kearny was already cast. Doom waited for them only a fortnight away, along the frozen flats of Peno Creek.

2.

They buried Lieutenant Bingham and Sergeant Bowers on Sunday the 9th. As Bingham had been a Mason, he was accorded the honors of that society, Lieutenant Grummond conducting the rites with the assistance of six other members. Chaplain White led the religious services, and when the chaplain came to speak of Sergeant Bowers, Captain Fred Brown stepped forward and placed his long-treasured Army of the Cumberland badge upon the breast of the dead sergeant. Brown, Bisbee, Powell and other veterans of the regiment had soldiered with Sergeant Bowers from Stone's River to Atlanta and held him in high regard.

In wooden boxes lined with tin, the dead were buried in the little cemetery at the foot of Pilot Hill; their graves were mounded with frozen earth and then covered with stones against the wolves.

Letters had to be written to relatives, and the duty of informing Miss Stella Bingham, St. Charles, Minnesota, of the death of her brother, Horatio, was assigned to Captain Fetterman.

> I send you herewith an Inventory of his Effects taken by me by virtue of my position as his Military Administrator. The money has been forwarded to the Adjutant General, U. S. Army, Washington, D. C., by applying to him it can easily be obtained by his heirs . . . the sword, sash and epaulettes, with private correspondence etc. have been sent to you. His other effects were sold at auction & the proceeds as before stated sent to the Adjt. Gen. . . . This is the customary manner of disposing of the effects of deceased officers, which it is supposed his heirs will not want, and which cannot be easily sent to them. Your brother was much esteemed by all who knew him, and his death is severely felt by all. He was buried with military and Masonic honors and the whole garrison attended his remains to the grave, all being desirous to pay their last tribute of respect to one whom all esteemed so highly.
>
> I am madam,
> Very Respectfully
> Your Obt. Svt.
>
> WILLIAM J. FETTERMAN [16]

Ironically, only a few days later another appointed military administrator would be writing a similar letter concerning the composer of this one.

As soon as funeral services were ended, a mail escort of one corporal and eight troopers from the cavalry gathered in front of headquarters. Joining this escort were Lieutenant Bisbee and his wife and son, who boarded a canvas-topped army wagon which had been especially prepared for winter travel to Laramie. Floor and sides were double-boarded, and a stove had been placed inside. "My outfit," wrote Bisbee, "consisted of buffalo skin cap, two woolen shirts under a heavy blanket suit, buffalo-lined hip boots over two pairs of woolen socks, two pairs of gloves. . . ." [17] All of Bisbee's fellow officers were on hand to wish him luck in his new assignment at department headquarters in Omaha, and Bisbee in turn gave his blessing to the lieutenant succeeding him as post adjutant, Lieutenant Wilbur F. Arnold.

In the mailbag for Omaha were Carrington's full reports of the "skirmish with a body of Indians, numbering in the aggregate not less than three hundred warriors," with accounts of the deaths of Bingham and Bowers. "I need mittens for the men," he added, "and especially do I need every officer I can get. The cavalry has none. There are but six for six companies, including staff. . . . This is all wrong. There is much at stake; I will take my full share, but two officers to a company is small allowance enough, with mercury at zero and active operations on hand." [18]

Beginning the second week of December, Carrington tightened the duties of his "six officers for six companies." Captain Powell was assigned to drill C Company, 2nd Cavalry, in such basic elements as mounting and dismounting, forming columns of twos and fours, and firing carbines and pistols by command. Daily at retreat, Captain Fetterman drilled the infantry in loading and firing by file and by numbers. Lieutenant Grummond was given full command of the mounted infantry, with orders to keep all serviceable horses—about fifty—saddled and ready for pursuit from dawn to dusk.

During the fortnight following the fight of the 6th, the Indians did not approach the fort or the pinery, yet scarcely a day passed without their scouting parties appearing on distant hills, signaling with mirrors or flags. Carrington doubled the guards assigned to wood trains, and maintained a state of watchful waiting. The weather continued bitter cold, and Surgeon Horton's hospital records showed a sharp increase in rheumatic complaints and frostbitten ears.

The Indians made their long-planned decoy attack on the 19th, and as soon as the vigilant Carrington saw the picket on Pilot Hill signaling "wood train under attack," he ordered his most cautious officer, Captain Powell, to command the relief party. Orders were explicit: "Heed the lessons of the 6th. Do not pursue Indians across Lodge Trail Ridge." [19] Powell performed his task to the letter, keeping his well-drilled cavalry company and Grummond's mounted infantry in check and permitting no individual dashes or pursuits. Neither he nor Carrington knew, of course, that the Indians wanted no fight near the pinery; their objective was the same as that of the 6th—to draw the soldiers off, scatter them with decoys, and attack the small parties in force. But Powell did not pursue, and the hostiles withdrew without inflicting or suffering any casualties.

A fight had been avoided, yet as if anticipating criticism from those of his officers who believed in taking the offensive at every opportunity, Carrington explained to his staff that he intended to continue his policy of caution until more reinforcements arrived. The immediate objective, he added, was to continue movement of timber supplies from the pinery to the fort so as to complete winter quarters for such troops as the Department of the Platte might later send him. He also covered his policy of restraint by dispatching a special courier to Laramie with a telegram for transmittal to Omaha: "Indians appeared today and fired on wood train, but were repulsed. They are accomplishing nothing, while I am perfecting all details of the post and preparing for active movements." (At the time of his appearance before a court of inquiry in the spring of 1867, Carrington told of sending Captain Powell to relieve the train. "He did his work —pressed the Indians toward Lodge Trail Ridge, but having peremptory orders not to cross it, he returned with the train, reporting the Indians in large force, and that if he had crossed the ridge he never would have come back with his command.") [20]

Snow fell that night, light and powdery, the sun rising in a clear sky at dawn upon a glittering-white world. The air was bracing, and Carrington decided to ride out to the pinery with the wood train. "On the morning of the 20th, very early," he later told the court of inquiry, "I had both saw-mills at work upon 3-inch plank, and at 9 o'clock, with sixty infantry and twenty cavalry, and the ordinary train guard, I went myself to the woods to test the animus and force of the Indians, and to build a bridge across Piney Creek, to facilitate the passage of the wagons off Pine Island.... Trees were felled for stringers; the bridge, forty-five feet long and sixteen feet wide, was built; the wagons were loaded, and the train reached the fort at 6 P.M. without casualty. I saw no Indians, and no fresh trail upon the snow which had fallen the night before." [21]

That evening Captains Fetterman and Brown called unexpectedly upon the colonel in his headquarters. Brown was in a genial mood. He had slung his spurs carelessly in the buttonholes of his greatcoat, and wore a pair of revolvers at his waist. Acting as spokesman, he told Carrington that he and Fetterman had secured the promises of fifty civilian employees to join an equal number of mounted soldiers in an expedition to Tongue River to clear out the Indians. Both men were convinced that if the hostile villages were destroyed, the fort could settle down to a peaceful winter.

Carrington listened politely, then picked up his morning report for that day and handed it to Brown. If he let fifty seasoned men go to the Tongue, the colonel pointed out, he could not keep the mails moving, or maintain adequate picket and guard assignments. Fifty veterans were the core of his strength; most of those left behind to defend the fort would be untried recruits. Also, he added soberly, only forty-two horses had been reported serviceable that morning, and if he let them go, he would have none left at the fort.

Fred Brown was disappointed. He had almost completed his quartermaster records, and expected to be leaving for Laramie after Christmas to report for his new assignment. He wanted one more good fight, a smashing victory such as the one he had led against the Arapaho back in September.

Fetterman had little to say during this interview, and when it was clear that Carrington had no intention of authorizing a Tongue River expedition, he rose to go. As he and Brown left, the latter admitted that "he knew it was impossible, but that he just felt he could kill a dozen himself."[22] Scarcely twelve hours later, Captain Brown would know—too late—just how impossible it was.

On the eve of the massacre which would bear Fetterman's name, the weather was remarkably fine, almost temperate, the sky faintly hazed but casting enough light to outline the sturdy stockade and buildings. All warehouses were completed; the last barracks was habitable; one more load of logs from the pinery should finish up the hospital. Military strength was slightly above four hundred, but many men carried faulty arms, and ammunition was in short supply.

In the rarefied atmosphere of that high country, sounds carried for long distances, and when there was no sound the stillness was almost overpowering. The Pineys were frozen across, their waters moving quietly below the ice. Except for the occasional howl of a wolf, the night was broken only by monotonous calls from the sentry posts: "All's well!"

3.

From early autumn into December, Red Cloud and other hostile chiefs had been assembling recruits along the headwaters of the Tongue, not more than fifty miles north of Fort Phil Kearny. Visiting Crows, who had been welcomed in the lodges and invited to join the hostiles, reported tepees spread out over a stretch of forty miles, and the number of warriors gathered there in mid-December probably totaled almost four thousand.

Although his military opponents considered Red Cloud the commanding general of all hostile operations in the Powder River country, certainly by December such was not the case. Opposition inspired during the summer by this relentless Oglala leader had grown to such proportions by late autumn that it was beyond control of one tribal chief. Roman Nose and Medicine Man of the Cheyennes, and Little Chief and Sorrel

Horse of the Arapaho had joined Red Cloud's camp along the Tongue as allies, not as subordinates. Nor did the six hereditary chiefs of the Miniconjous, including Black Shield, yield any authority to Red Cloud.

In the days following the fight of December 6, however, the chiefs came to a general agreement; they would combine to lay a great ambush of many warriors, then send out a few young men on fast ponies to lure the soldiers from the hated fort on the Pineys into their trap.

When the moon was at the full in the third week of December, detachments of Oglalas, Miniconjous and Cheyennes began moving south out of the lodges along the Tongue. How many warriors made this journey is not certain, estimates ranging from fifteen hundred to two thousand, the latter figure being more often mentioned by the few white men who saw them and survived.

Black Shield led the Miniconjous, Crazy Horse the first war party of young Oglalas. The weather was very cold and the warriors wore buffalo robes with the hair turned in, leggings of dark woolen cloth, high-topped buffalo-fur moccasins, and carried red Hudson's Bay blankets strapped to their saddles. Most of them rode pack horses, leading their fast-footed war ponies by lariats. Some had rifles, but most were armed with bows and arrows, knives and lances. They carried enough pemmican to last several days, and when an opportunity offered, small groups would turn off the trail, kill buffalo or deer, and take as much meat as could be carried on their saddles.

When they were about ten miles northwest of Fort Phil Kearny, the first detachments made camp and waited for the others to come down and join them. As more warriors arrived, the camp spread out in three circles of Sioux, Cheyennes and Arapaho. While the chiefs held council, scouts moved out along the high ridges to watch the soldiers in the fort. It was decided that the best place to lay an ambush was in the forks of Peno Creek, about halfway between camp and the fort.*

---

* Peno Creek, named for a French trapper, was later changed to Prairie Dog Creek.

On the morning of the 19th, they made their first decoy attack, but that was the day Captain Powell obeyed Carrington's strict orders and refused to follow the warriors. Snow fell during the night, and the Indians stayed in their camp on the 20th, warming themselves by fires inside saddle-blanket windbreaks. Much of the powdery snow melted except along shadowed slopes, and by the morning of the 21st, the chiefs again decided to send decoys out against the soldiers' wood train.

This time the most daring of the young braves were chosen to tantalize the soldiers into pursuit. The medicine men were certain that this time the soldiers would come running into the trap, and while the decoys rode off toward the fort a great ambush was laid on each side of the Bozeman Road where it ran along a narrow ridge and descended to Peno Creek. The Cheyennes and Arapaho took the west side. Some of the Sioux hid in a grassy flat on the opposite side; others remained mounted and concealed themselves behind two rocky ridges. By midmorning almost two thousand warriors were waiting there for Captain Fetterman and his eighty men.

4.

When Colonel Carrington stepped out of his quarters early on the morning of the 21st, he found the day bright and clear, the air cold and dry. Most of the snow was gone from the ground around the fort, but it lay on the ridges, ice-sheeted in places where the previous day's sun had partially melted it. Big Piney was still frozen from bank to bank. The snow, he knew, would still be deep in the pine woods, and he notified Lieutenant Wands to delay departure of the wood train until there was some indication the good weather would hold through the day.

About ten o'clock Carrington ordered the train to move out. As though he had some premonition of danger, he attached an extra guard from E Company under Corporal Legrow so that soldiers and civilian teamsters together formed an armed force of almost ninety men. Less than an hour later, as the post guard was changing, pickets on Pilot Hill began wigwagging the signal for many Indians attacking the train. Companies were bugled out immediately, and as the men hurried to assigned positions, two Indians appeared on the slope across Big Piney. They dismounted beyond rifle range, wrapped themselves in red blankets, and sat down near a tree to watch the action inside the fort. The time was now almost eleven o'clock.

At the first alarm, Carrington ordered Captain Powell to take command of the relief party. The colonel had been satisfied with the efficient yet cautious manner in which Powell had handled the Indians on the 19th, and saw no reason to use another officer now. When Captain Fetterman reported in front of headquarters with Company A, however, he reminded Carrington that he outranked Powell and demanded firmly that he be given the relief command.

With some misgivings Carrington acquiesced, and told Fetterman to move out with his own company, A, and a detachment of C Company. Lieutenant Grummond would follow with the cavalry in time to overtake the infantry before they reached the besieged wood train. "Support the wood train," Carrington ordered. "Relieve it and report to me. Do not engage or pursue Indians at its expense. Under no circumstances pursue over the ridge, that is, Lodge Trail Ridge."[23]

Fetterman saluted and turned back to the assembled infantrymen. Sergeants began barking orders, and Companies A and C moved out on the double for the south gate. Carrington turned to his acting adjutant, Lieutenant Wands, and asked him to hurry after Fetterman's troops, halt them at the gate, and repeat the orders. The time was now 11:15.

Meanwhile Lieutenant Grummond had formed his horsemen for a hurried inspection. Carrington himself walked down the line of dismounted men, inspecting rifles and carbines. A number of the mounted infantry were dismissed from formation because of ammunition shortages or faulty weapons, but all of the twenty-seven cavalrymen reporting for duty passed inspection. Only a few days earlier Carrington had transferred the regimental band's Spencer carbines to the troopers.

During the inspection Private Thomas Maddeon, the regimental armorer, stepped forward and asked permission to join the relief party. Maddeon, a favorite of the colonel, had often expressed a desire for action. Carrington glanced at his rifle and told him to join a small detail from H Company. Captain Brown also appeared, eager for "one more chance," as he expressed it, "to bring in the scalp of Red Cloud myself."[24] He added with a smile that he had arranged to borrow a mount from Jimmy Carrington—the mottled pony, Calico. Two other eager volunteers were James Wheatley and Isaac Fisher, civilian employees, both of whom had been officers during the Civil War. They were armed with new 16-shot Henry rifles, and were the envy of the infantrymen with their obsolete single-shot muzzle-loading Springfields.

"I was standing in front of my door next to the commanding officer's headquarters," Frances Grummond recorded, "and both saw and heard all that transpired. I was filled with dread and horror at the thought that after my husband's hairbreadth escape scarcely three weeks before he could be so eager to fight the Indians again. . . .

"To my husband was given the order, 'Report to Captain Fetterman, implicitly obey orders, and never leave him.' Solicitude on my behalf prompted Lieutenant Wands to urge my husband 'for his family's sake to be prudent and avoid rash movements, or any pursuit,' and with these orders ringing in their ears they left the gate. Before they were out of hearing Colonel Carrington sprang upon the *banquet* inside the stockade (the sentry walk), halted the column, and in clear tones heard by everybody, repeated his orders more minutely, 'Under no circumstances must you cross Lodge Trail Ridge;' and the column moved quickly from sight."[25] As Grummond's mounted men left the gate, the time was nearing 11:30.

Carrington, watching from the sentry platform, saw that Fetterman was not following the wagon road which led south of Sullivant Hills but had turned into the north trail which ran between the hills and Lodge Trail Ridge. This was the same route which Carrington himself had followed on the 6th when the objective had been to take the Indians in reverse, and the colonel assumed now that Fetterman had a similar plan in mind. Within a minute or so, Grummond was swinging his mounted column into the trail; he overtook Fetterman's foot soldiers at the crossing of Big Piney just south of Lodge Trail Ridge.

"I remarked the fact," Carrington reported later, "that he [Fetterman] had deployed his men as skirmishers, and was evidently moving wisely up the creek and along the southern slope of Lodge Trail Ridge, with good promise of cutting off the Indians as they should withdraw, repulsed at the train, and his position giving him perfect vantage ground to save the train if the Indians pressed the attack. It is true that the usual course was to follow the road directly to the train, but the course adopted was not an error, unless there was then a purpose to disobey orders."[26]

At about this same time Carrington suddenly remembered that no surgeon had been assigned to Fetterman's command, and he immediately ordered Assistant Surgeon C. M. Hines and two orderlies to mount up and ride directly for the wood train. If a surgeon was not needed there, Hines was to swing around Sullivant Hills and join Fetterman. The surgeon and his escort had scarcely galloped out of the gate when the pickets on Pilot Hill signaled that the wood train was no longer under attack, that the wagons had broken corral, and were proceeding unmolested toward the pinery.

During the next few minutes, Carrington's attention was distracted by a party of about twenty Indians which appeared across Big Piney near the Bozeman Road ford. Noting that they were within howitzer range, he ordered the gunners to drop a few case shot among them. At the first explosion, thirty more Indians were flushed out of the brush, one falling from his pony. The party scattered, fleeing toward the valley north of Lodge Trail Ridge.

For the first time since the alarm, Carrington relaxed. He stepped down from his position on the banquette and walked across the graveled street before officers' row and entered the rear of his headquarters. He did not know, of course, that the Indians at that moment were engaged in decoying Fetterman's men over Lodge Trail Ridge.

5.

A few minutes before twelve o'clock, Fetterman's command was moving up Lodge Trail Ridge, with Grummond's cavalry out on the flanks and advancing ahead of the infantry. Along the slope, little bands of decoys raced ponies back and forth, the young warriors yipping their wolflike barks, taunting the soldiers, waving blankets to frighten the soldiers' horses. When Fetterman gave orders to the infantry to fire, the decoys danced their ponies away, but as soon as the firing stopped, the Indians darted back into range, daring the soldiers to follow and shoot again.

Fetterman had seen no fighting such as this when he soldiered with Sherman in Georgia. He was accustomed to orthodox lines of battle. He knew how to form salients for defense, to storm rifle pits, to handle men under heavy artillery fire. But these Indian warriors, unlike his former Confederate adversaries, refused to follow the rules laid down in military manuals.

As he urged his infantrymen forward to overtake the cavalrymen on the crest of the ridge, the small party of Indians which had been fired upon by Carrington's howitzers came galloping along the Bozeman Road just below. These Indians slowed and joined the decoys. For a short while Fetterman held his position, the fort yet in view, his infantrymen still firing by command at an occasional daring Indian who rode within easy rifle range. When the decoys saw that the soldiers were reluctant to pursue, they became more reckless than ever, zigzagging their ponies and screaming insults.

By this time the warriors who had made the original attack upon the wagon train appeared to the south, some following Peno Creek valley, while many were beginning to ascend the slope of Lodge Trail Ridge in Fetterman's rear. It is possible that at this moment Fetterman made a hasty decision to drop north off Lodge Trail Ridge, kill as many of the outnumbered decoys as possible, and then swing back east along the Bozeman Road to the fort.

But if he intended to turn east when he struck the Bozeman Road, he changed his mind and turned west. Perhaps the tantalizing decoys offered too many easy targets to disregard. At high noon Fetterman gave the command to move, the cavalry at a walk so the infantry could keep closed up. They entered the Bozeman Trail where it ran along a narrow ridge sloping to the northwest, and followed this descent past a few large boulders toward the flats of Peno Creek. There were eighty-one men, about half of them mounted, the cavalrymen so eager to overtake the decoys that the gap began widening between horsemen and infantry. The firing was fairly regular now and several decoys were wounded, some fatally. Every hoofbeat, every footfall, however, brought these eighty-one men closer to the great ambush—two thousand Sioux, Cheyennes and Arapaho, waiting in concealment in the high grass of the flats and behind the rocky ridges on either side of the trail.

Among the individual Sioux and Cheyenne warriors who risked their lives to lure the soldiers into the trap were several who during the next decade would become famous chiefs— Crazy Horse, Dull Knife, Black Shield, Big Nose, White Bull. Crazy Horse won a great name for himself that day with his acts of defiance, sometimes dismounting within rifle range and pretending to ignore the presence of the soldiers and the screams of their bullets.

Years later in his old age Red Cloud claimed to have directed the fighting, but the testimony of several Indian participants indicates that the Oglala leader was not present. On that day, they said, he was either on his way down from Tongue River, or on a recruiting mission to the north. But whether he was there or not, the ambush was the fruition of Red Cloud's long summer campaign of harassment, put into execution by such leaders as High Back Bone, Red Leaf and Little Wolf.

A few minutes past noon, the decoys were beginning to ford the broken ice of Peno Creek, with Grummond's cavalry pressing pursuit. The infantrymen, now well within the silent ambush, were marching rapidly. As soon as all the decoys were across the creek they separated into two parties, riding away from each other, and then turning, came back and crossed files. This crossing of files was the prearranged signal for attack.

A moment later it seemed that every clump of yellow grass

on the Peno flats had been transformed into a hostile Indian, the mass swarming up on foot like a gale-blown prairie fire toward the road. Beyond them other warriors on horseback also sprang from concealment, their hoofbeats like sudden thunder. And from the left came the Cheyennes, most of them mounted. The Indians' concentrated yelling drowned out commands from Fetterman and the other officers.

At the first assault Grummond managed to halt the cavalry, Fetterman quickly closing the gap with his foot soldiers. The civilians, Wheatley and Fisher, and four or five mounted infantrymen, all seasoned Civil War veterans who were riding the point, dismounted quickly. These men formed a defensive ring and delivered such concentrated fire that the first wave of attack was blunted. In that first minute of confusion a lone mounted Miniconjou, impelled by some mystical dream of glory, charged down the Bozeman Road from the rear, racing right into the infantrymen until he was slain. A moment later another Sioux on foot performed a similar act of reckless courage, and also died.

The air was now filled with arrows, warriors on foot closing in, pony riders circling, their war whoops reverberating in the cold damp wind. Yet Fetterman somehow managed to start his infantrymen back upslope to the nearest cover, a collection of flat boulders.

Whether Lieutenant Grummond ordered the cavalry to cover the infantry is not certain; the horsemen may have broken formations in terror. They swung up the hill to the left, all except Wheatley, Fisher, and the handful of men who had dismounted and formed a circle of defense. Nor can anyone be certain when or how Grummond died, but it is probable that he was killed early in the fighting, either in a vain effort to keep the cavalry with the infantry, or in a gallant rear-guard covering action. Long afterward some of the Indians who were there said a pony-soldier chief was killed on the road and that his men then gave way and fled up the ridge. Others told of a soldier chief on a white horse who fought a brave delaying action, cutting off an Indian's head with a single stroke of his saber. All that is known for certain is that Grummond's body was found on the road

beside that of Sergeant Augustus Lang of Company A, somewhere between the infantry's position and the defensive ring
of Wheatley and Fisher.

In any case, cavalry and infantry were separated in the first
fury of attack, the men on foot facing a thousand warriors so
close it was possible to see the color of their war paint and the
metal ornaments and brass studs of their shields. Feathered
arrows streamed like flights of bright speeding birds, and the
trapped soldiers felt the pains of sharp heads wrapped in sinew,
driving deep into flesh, drawing warm blood to trickle along
the grooves of shafts until it froze in the bitter air. Neither
Sioux nor Cheyennes carried many rifles that day, but their
quivers were filled with arrows which they had learned from
boyhood to drive with accuracy into the thickest buffalo hides.

How the eighty-one trapped men died, the order of their
dying, can only be reconstructed from the positions of the dead,
the record of cartridge shells, the bloodstains of the enemy, and
later accounts of Indian survivors. As soon as the retreating infantry reached the rock formation, they flung themselves down
and began firing. Fetterman then formed a thin skirmish line
facing the Oglalas and Cheyennes to north and east, the Miniconjous to south and west, and ordered his men to fire at will.
For several minutes fighting was intense, the infantry firing volleys from their muzzle-loaders while the cavalry floundered
about without an officer, a hundred yards above on the hillside,
their Spencer carbines scarcely used.

Farther down the road, Wheatley and Fisher, supported by
the Springfields of five or six soldiers who had joined them, kept
up a rattling fire with their Henrys. They knocked down several
Indian ponies whose riders tried to rush them, and then used
the animals' bodies as cover. Dead and wounded Indians were
ringed around them.

For fifteen or twenty minutes, the rock-sheltered infantrymen
were able to hold the attackers off. Then their ammunition
began to run short. Men bunched together, and the Indians
sensing their growing panic moved in closer, Miniconjous on
one side, Oglalas on the other—so close that Miniconjous were
killing Oglalas, and Oglalas were killing Miniconjous, with

their own arrows. The Sioux leaped over the rocks, using lances and war clubs, and some of the infantrymen broke away and started running up the hill toward the cavalry position. Indians pursued them. One warrior running with a raised bow to count coup came within two steps of a soldier before one of the man's comrades shot the Indian down.

Some time during the fighting, Captain Fred Brown released his borrowed pony, Calico, and joined Fetterman among the boulders. The two officers were together at the last, their ammunition exhausted, capture and torture almost inevitable. As they had sworn to do, each man saved one unexpended cartridge. At the end they faced each other—the ambitious, good-natured, balding quartermaster, and the determined and over-confident infantry veteran who had boasted that eighty men could ride through the Sioux nation. With revolvers held against each other's temple, they counted quickly in unison to three, and squeezed triggers.

About this time, the position held by Wheatley and Fisher and the six infantrymen was overrun. The defenders fought with gunstocks, bayonets and knives until the last man was slain.

The cavalry, knowing that they would be next, had already dismounted and started climbing farther up the ridge, leading their horses. A handful of infantrymen joined them, and two or three surviving noncommissioned officers tried to keep some sort of military order. On the high slope, snow had formed ice sheets which made walking difficult, and when they reached the rocky summit they abandoned any hopes they may have had of descending the south side and racing for the fort. The south slope was alive with Indians coming up from the other fork of the Peno.

There was nothing the survivors could do now but seek cover among the rocks and try to keep alive until help could come from the fort. They turned their horses loose (there was no place for horse holders to go) and moved along the ridge toward a cluster of large boulders. For a few minutes the showers of arrows lessened as the Indians devoted their attention to capturing abandoned cavalry horses. Then the fight was resumed with renewed fury along the ridgetop, a narrow forty-foot shelf swept by icy winds that froze blood in wounds.

As they took cover among the massive boulders, these inexperienced cavalrymen must have felt a momentary revival of hope. They formed into compact units, firing carbine volleys downslope into their besiegers, the rear guard kneeling for accuracy, sometimes half hidden in powder smoke. One of the men fighting this delaying action was running backward, yelling, swinging his carbine in an arc as he fired, reloaded, and fired again. It was told later among the Miniconjous of how White Bull rushed this brave pony-soldier, shooting him through the heart with an arrow, and when he fell on his back White Bull struck him across the head with his lance, knocking his cap off, counting coup.

By this time, Indian scouts watching from hills near Phil Kearny had signaled that reinforcements were coming from the fort, and chiefs passed the word that the pony-soldiers must all be killed as quickly as possible. The leaders knew it would not be easy; the cavalrymen were in a much better position than the infantrymen had been. But enough warriors crawled and darted forward among the rocks until they were in sufficient numbers to charge. Heedless of screaming bullets, they rushed in among the dismounted pony-soldiers, fighting and scuffling hand to hand in the carbine smoke, swinging bludgeons and hatchets, scalping men alive. Years afterward the Sioux showed a knotted war club of bur oak, driven full of nails and spikes, still clotted with dried blood and hair of cavalrymen who died that day on Massacre Hill. But the Indians paid dearly for this quick victory, many more dying among the boulders on the ridge than had lost lives against the infantrymen on the road below.

One of the last soldiers to die was Adolph Metzger, the little German-born bugler, an army veteran since 1855. Metzger beat off his assailants with his bugle until the instrument was a battered, shapeless mass of metal, until his body was bleeding from a dozen wounds. He fell on the ridge near where a monument now stands to mark the Fetterman Massacre, his dead comrades all about him, their ammunition boxes still half-filled. The fighting was all over. Forty minutes had passed since the Sioux first sprang their trap and surged up out of the grass flats at the forks of Peno Creek.

As the last carbines were fired, a relief party from the fort was reaching high ground east of the scene of fighting. Along the road and down in the valley, hundreds of Indians circled their war ponies and jeered at the cautious bluecoats. Others of the victors stripped uniforms off the dead and began mutilating the bodies according to tribal rituals. Trouser legs were cut off to use for leggings; paper money and coins were shaken from pockets. The coins were kept, the paper money discarded. Soldier overcoats were fastened to saddles or donned as replacements for buffalo robes.

When a dog belonging to one of the dead soldiers came running and barking out of the rocks, one of the warriors cried: "All are dead but the dog. Let him carry the news to the fort." But another warrior shot the animal through with an arrow. "No," he said. "Do not let even a dog get away." [27]

The last task of all was recovering arrows from the field of battle. Almost forty thousand had been fired, a thousand for each minute of the fighting, and those which had not found a human target or were not blunted or broken were quickly collected and replaced in quivers.

Among the Indians were many wounded and dead, although exactly how many will be never be known. Estimates of the participants varied from ten to a hundred dead, and from sixty to three hundred wounded. The more reliable informants believed at least sixty were killed on the field, and of about three hundred wounded probably a hundred more died. Many years later, Red Cloud would recall the names of eleven Oglalas killed in the fighting and several others of the tribe who died later of wounds. White Elk, a Cheyenne, often said that more Indians were killed in the Fetterman fight than in the Custer fight ten years later. But whatever the casualties, the victory was not a cheap one for the combined tribes of Tongue River.

6.

After Assistant Surgeon Hines left the fort some minutes before noon, he proceeded rapidly with his escort along the road toward the pinery. Hines' orders were to join the wood train, and if not needed there to find Fetterman and return with him. The surgeon, of course, discovered that the attack on the train had already ceased; the wagons were moving unmolested toward Piney Island. Requesting two additional escorts from the train guard, Hines hurried on west, expecting to meet Fetterman coming around the end of Sullivant Hills. Instead, as soon as Lodge Trail Ridge came into his view, Hines saw hundreds of Indians swarming in the valley and up the slopes of the ridge. He saw no trace of Fetterman's detachment, and as there were too many Indians between him and the ridge to move in that direction, he turned back at a fast gallop toward the fort.

A few minutes later Hines was back in the fort reporting to Carrington. Neither the surgeon nor the colonel was especially concerned as yet over the whereabouts of Fetterman, each probably assuming the soldiers were returning along the Bozeman Road or by one of the trails north of Big Piney.

Hines had scarcely left post headquarters, however, when sounds of heavy rifle fire came from the northwest. "Just about dinner call," Carrington recorded later, "or near twelve noon . . . my office orderly told me that the sentry at the door reported firing. I went to the top of the house, on which was a lookout, and heard a few shots, apparently in the direction of Peno Creek. With my glass I could see neither Indian nor soldier. I think I counted six scattering shots at first, succeeded by more rapid firing.* I directed the orderly, then in front of the house, to notify the officer of the day; had sentry call the corporal of the guard, and the guard formed immediately. Sent one man who was bringing boards into the unfinished part of the house, to the quartermaster's office, to have wagons and ambulances hitched, and to immediately go and notify every unarmed man in the quartermaster's employ to report at once to the magazine for arms.

"Lieutenant Wands, Captain Ten Eyck, and another officer

---

* Others in the fort reported hearing four volleys in succession, each time the sound seeming farther away—then a continuous and rapid fire with a fierceness indicating a pitched battle. "At the noon hour we could hear volleys plainly," said Private William Murphy, "and they continued for a long period of time."

whose name I do not recollect, were in sight from the top of the house.

"I directed Captain Ten Eyck to be prepared to move at once. I called Lieutenant Wands to the top of the house to watch the firing and went in person to hasten and organize the detail that was to move. It moved in a very few minutes. I rejected some men from the detail after it was formed, taking those only who had most ammunition and had reported promptly, not wanting to have any boxes re-supplied."[28]

Less than a quarter hour after the first alarm, Ten Eyck marched with seventy-five officers and men, including Lieutenant Winfield Scott Matson and Surgeons Hines and Ould, "being all the men for duty in the fort."[29] Most of these men were on foot, but among those mounted was Carrington's orderly, Private Archibald Sample, who was to act as messenger. They were under orders to join Fetterman's troops and return with them to the fort. According to Private Murphy, "they went at a double-quick or as fast as they could, until they came to the crossing of the Piney." Big Piney was never easy to cross on foot, and with the added hindrance of broken ice, "the men had to remove their shoes and stockings to get across."[30]

After fording the creek, Ten Eyck followed the Bozeman Road for a short distance, then turned right, seeking high ground on the north. For taking this less direct route to the scene of the fighting, Ten Eyck would suffer bitter condemnation in years to come. Accused of cowardice, shunned by fellow officers, he turned to alcohol and quit the Army. Yet it is very probable that any responsible officer operating under the same conditions would have made a similar move to higher ground, and it is most likely that had Ten Eyck not done so, his detachment would have met the same fate as Fetterman's.

By the time Ten Eyck was across the Piney, sounds of firing were lessening, and he must have assumed that Fetterman either had beaten off the foe or was beyond retrieval. When he reached the summit of the ridge, about 12:45 P.M., all firing had ceased. According to Surgeon Hines, they were "just in time to see the last man killed."[31] Peno Valley was swarming with more Indians than any man in the detachment had ever seen gathered in one place.

As soon as the victorious hostiles sighted this relief force, scores of mounted warriors galloped up the Bozeman Trail to the base of the ridge, daring the soldiers to come down, slapping their buttocks, calling obscenities. Ten Eyck held his position, dispatched a messenger to the fort, and waited.

In the meantime Carrington had already started more reinforcements and ammunition. "I sent immediately after Ten Eyck moved, the remainder of Company C, 2nd U. S. Cavalry, dismounted (nearly thirty men in all), having the new carbine, requiring them to fill their pockets with all the surplus ammunition they could carry." Convinced that Fetterman's men had suffered casualties and were in need of ammunition, he also ordered an ambulance and two wagons to join this detachment. "In the first wagon that reported I placed three thousand rounds Springfield and two cases of Spencer, to give this command, and also Fetterman's, additional ammunition. I sent Williams, master of transportation, in charge of the wagons and ammunition, with forty-two men, they quickly following the details that had already left."[32] Most of the men in this latter group were civilian teamsters from the quartermaster department, some mounted on their own horses, others on broken-down cavalry horses.

By now an hour had passed since the first alarm, and there were no longer any sounds of firing. In the words of Frances Grummond who was anxiously awaiting news of the fate of her husband, "the silence was dreadful."[33] She and other wives in the fort had gathered near the headquarters building, watching the hills to the northwest.

A few minutes past one o'clock, they sighted a lone horseman galloping furiously down the slope beyond Big Piney. As the rider crossed the stream, they recognized him as the colonel's orderly, Private Sample. Without checking the speed of his horse, Sample swept through the gate and crossed the parade. Carrington was waiting for him in front of headquarters as he dismounted.

"Captain Ten Eyck says he can see or hear nothing of Captain Fetterman," Sample reported. "The Indians are on the road challenging him to come down."

Carrington asked how many Indians there were. Sample replied that the valleys for miles around were filled with them, and added quickly that Captain Ten Eyck requested reinforcements and one of the mountain howitzers. Carrington began scrawling a message on a sheet of paper, and as he wrote, Sample said quietly: "The Captain is afraid Fetterman's party is all gone up, sir." The colonel continued writing:

> CAPTAIN: Forty well-armed men, with 3,000 rounds, ambulance, etc., left before your courier came in.
>
> You must unite with Fetterman, fire slowly, and keep men in hand; you could have saved two miles toward the scene of action if you had taken Lodge Trail Ridge.
>
> I order the wood train in, which will give 50 more men to spare.
>
> H. B. CARRINGTON
> Colonel Commanding [34]

Afterward Carrington explained that he made no mention of the howitzer because the gun could not be sent. No fit horses were left in the fort, he said, nor did Ten Eyck have any men with him who knew how to cut a fuse or handle the piece. "If he were compelled to fall back I was prepared to support him to better advantage, and I deemed the gun useless to him." [35]

Sample started back immediately on a fresh horse—riding Carrington's favorite mount, Grey Eagle—and reached Ten Eyck's position about the time the Indians began leaving Peno Valley. While the victors were still streaming westward, an enlisted man called out suddenly, pointing to the Bozeman Road: "There're the men down there, all dead!"

Private Murphy afterward described the scene: "There was at that time a large stone that had the appearance of having dropped from a great height and thereby split open, leaving a space between the pieces men could pass through, which made a good protection for a small body of men, I should say for about twenty-five or thirty. Around this rock was where the main body of the men lay. There were just a few down on the side of the ridge north of the rock, not more than fifty feet from the main body."[36]

As soon as the last of the Indians had forded Peno crossing and vanished beyond the ridges, Ten Eyck ordered his men to march, foot soldiers advancing cautiously toward the road, mounted soldiers and civilians riding flanks. The boulders where the infantrymen had died were surrounded by dead Indian ponies and army horses, the latter with their heads pointing toward the fort. Many broken arrows, some with points deep in the earth, littered the ground. All Indian casualties had been removed, numerous bloodstains marking the grass where they had lain. The dead soldiers lay in a space no more than forty feet in diameter, most of the bodies stripped naked and mutilated, and beginning to freeze in the bitter air. "The greater number," Surgeon Hines noted, "were in one heap."[37] Most of them had been killed by arrows. Several unexpended cartridge shells were scattered near the rocks.

Private Murphy told of finding a man of his company "scalped, stripped and mutilated. . . . It looked as though they had first stripped him and then filled his body with arrows, as they were sticking out of him all over like porcupine quills . . . all of the bodies were stripped, scalped and mutilated with the exception of two who were not scalped, but the Indians had drawn a buffalo bag over their heads."[38]

In Colonel Carrington's official report, suppressed and unpublished until twenty years after the event, no details were spared in describing the mutilations: "Eyes torn out and laid on rocks; noses cut off; ears cut off; chins hewn off; teeth chopped out; joints of fingers, brains taken out and placed on rocks with other members of the body; entrails taken out and exposed; hands cut off; feet cut off; arms taken out from sockets; private parts severed and indecently placed on the person; eyes, ears, mouth, and arms penetrated with spear-heads, sticks, and arrows; ribs slashed to separation with knives; skulls severed in every form, from chin to crown, muscles of calves, thighs, stomach, breast, back, arms, and cheek taken out. Punctures upon every sensitive part of the body, even to the soles of the feet and palms of the hand."[39]

Captains Fetterman and Brown had suffered similar treatment, the latter's body, according to Private John Guthrie, "hacked up and a lot of arrows in him (he had a little tuft of hair back of the ears and was nicknamed by the Indians 'Bald Head Eagle') and scalped."[40] The two officers were found together, each shot through the left temple, with powder burned into the skin and flesh about the wounds. They had carried out their often expressed declaration that they would never be taken alive by Indians.

Only one living being was found on that field of death—a gray mount named Dapple Dave, belonging to the 2nd Cavalry. The horse lay near the boulders, blood oozing from a dozen arrow wounds. Ten Eyck ordered a soldier to put the animal out of its misery, and then signaled the ambulance and wagons down from the ridge. The December afternoon was waning and the sun would be gone before other vehicles could be brought from the fort. The dead would have to be packed aboard like butchered animals. "We brought in about fifty in wagons," wrote Surgeon Hines, "like you see hogs brought to market."[41]

7.

In the fort, after Ten Eyck's relief forces departed, the anxieties of those left inside soon deepened to an awful apprehension of what must have happened beyond Lodge Trail Ridge. Carrington was acutely aware of how small his remaining force was; almost three-fourths of his combatant strength was in the field, divided between the pinery, Fetterman's detachment, and Ten Eyck's relief column.

He placed the entire garrison under arms, including all civilians and several prisoners released from the guardhouse. He suspended all activities of a nonmilitary nature, and ordered arms stacked before quarters.

"This occupied not a very few minutes," he later reported, "and I joined Lieutenant Wands upon the house to watch indications of the position of the parties out. There had been a short lull in the firing (namely, only scattered shots here and there), succeeded by a very brisk firing, apparently by file at first, and quite regular, and an occasional volley, followed by indiscriminate firing, gradually dying out in a few scattered shots. Being satisfied that the affair was occurring beyond the range of Brevet Lieutenant-Colonel Fetterman's instructions, I became apprehensive of disaster, and directed Brevet Captain Arnold, post adjutant, to determine and report to me at once the number of men remaining at the post—soldiers and civilians —who were armed, to determine whether I had any force to spare for further operations outside. He reported the number at 119, including guard. . . ."[42]

An observer of these grave developments was Frances Grummond, whose earlier concern for her husband had turned to bitter anguish. "I shall never forget the face of Colonel Carrington as he descended from the lookout when the firing ceased. The howitzers were put in position and loaded with grape, or case-shot, and all things were in readiness for whatever might betide. He seemed to try to impress us with the assurance that no apprehension could be entertained for the safety of the fort itself, but encouraged all to wait patiently and be ready for the return of the troops. How different was the reality, soon to be realized!"[43]

To increase his defensive force, Carrington next sent couriers to the pinery, ordering all men there to return immediately to the fort. The woods detail had been completely unaware of the Fetterman fight, being too far away to hear the rifle fire. They came in well before twilight, with most of their wagons empty, and took up positions around the banquette.

As darkness was falling guards sighted the first horsemen of Ten Eyck's forward scouts on the Bozeman Trail, and in a few minutes they could hear the rumble of wheels on axles. Ten Eyck had recovered forty-nine bodies, filling his wagons, and had started back for the fort in the biting cold of the early December dusk. A few Indians appeared on the ridges, but no fight was offered, and the relief force returned without firing a shot.

Musician Frank Fessenden was among those at the gate when the wagons came in with their gruesome cargo of naked mutilated bodies, "arms and legs in all shapes, divulging the horrible manner in which our brave comrades had died. It was a hor-rible and a sickening sight, and brought tears to every eye, to see those men, many of whom had served four years in the War of the Rebellion, meeting such an awful death on the western plains. Some of these men had but ten days more to serve, when their enlistment would have expired, and they could have re-turned to their homes."[44]

Young Jimmy Carrington also witnessed the arrival of the wagons. "How many times later," he wrote as an adult, "I awoke in the dark in terror, to see again the tortured bodies and bloody arrows of that night."[45]

For all in the fort the night of that Black Friday was long and terrible—filled with bitter gloom, anxieties and alarms. Indian signal fires ringed the hills, and every enlisted man was assigned to guard watches. Few slept even when off duty, shocked by the loss of their comrades, aware that there was not a single full cartridge box left in the garrison. Carrington and his officers were so certain of an impending direct attack upon the stockade that none of them slept at all.

"We had orders to bar up our windows and doors," said Frank Fessenden, "but to leave port-holes in the windows to fire through. There was a magazine in one corner of the parade ground, which was a large hole in the ground, well supported with heavy timbers and covered with earth and sodded over. This magazine was well supplied with ammunition of all kinds. Wagons were hauled in; the beds taken off their gears and placed on their sides and surrounded this magazine. Then more wagons were placed in a circle, until we had three circles sur-rounding the magazine. The soldiers were then placed three in number at every port-hole around the inside of the stockade.

"We had ten women and several children with us. The colonel gave orders that as soon as the Indians made the expected attack, the women and children should enter the magazine, and the men should hold the fort as long as possible. When they could hold it no longer, they were to get behind the wagons that surrounded the magazine, and when the colonel saw that all was lost, he would himself blow up the magazine and take the lives of all, rather than allow the Indians to capture any of the inmates alive."[46]

For Frances Grummond the events of the day were only a confirmation of the forebodings which had filled her thoughts since the September day when she and her husband had arrived at Phil Kearny. All through the late afternoon, the officers' wives had waited in the Wands' quarters, and soon after the arrival of the wagons, Margaret Carrington came to inform Frances that Lieutenant Grummond had not been found alive. Nor was he among the recovered dead. Certain there was little hope that Frances would ever see her husband alive again, Margaret insisted that she move into the Carringtons' quarters so that she would not be alone.

Early in the evening Frances received an unexpected caller, a swarthy man in his middle thirties, tough and wiry of frame, with a pointed black beard and bright piercing eyes. He was John (Portugee) Phillips, a mining partner of James Wheatley and Isaac Fisher, all of whom had come to Phil Kearny in August and accepted jobs with the quartermaster. Had he not been engaged in hauling water to fill the post's water barrels at the time of the Indian alarm, Phillips no doubt would have volunteered and met the same fate as his partners.

Although he was an admirer of Lieutenant Grummond, Phillips had never before so much as spoken to Frances. Perhaps he felt it his duty now to reassure her that she and her unborn child would be protected. He began speaking in his strange soft accent (Phillips was born in the Azores of Portuguese parents), explaining that he had offered his services as a messenger to Laramie for reinforcements. "I will go if it costs me my life. I am going for your sake."

Writing of this moment in later life, Frances Grummond recalled that Portugee Phillips had tears in his eyes as he handed her a wolf robe in a sort of symbolic gesture. "Here is my wolf robe. I brought it for you to keep and remember me by it if you never see me again."[47]

While this interview was in progress, Colonel Carrington was in his adjoining lamplit office, penning dispatches to General Cooke in Omaha and to General Grant in Washington.

These messages were almost incoherent, hastily written attempts to report the disaster, combined with desperate pleas for help. "Do send me reinforcements forthwith," he begged General Cooke. "Expedition now with my force is impossible. I risk everything but the post and its stores. I venture as much as any one can, but I have had today a fight unexampled in Indian warfare." As yet, he knew only that forty-nine bodies had been recovered, but company roll calls had not yet been taken, and he estimated thirty-five dead still to be brought in, three more than the actual number. He listed Fetterman, Brown, and Grummond among the dead, although the latter's body had not yet been found. "No such mutilation as that today is on record. Depend upon it that the post will be held so long as a round or a man is left. Promptness is the vital thing. Give me officers and men. Only the new Spencer arms should be sent; the Indians are desperate; I spare none, and they spare none."

To a copy of this plea, he attached a covering message direct to General Grant:

> I send copy of dispatch to General Cooke simply as a case when in uncertain communication, I think you should know the facts at once. I want all my officers. I want men. Depend upon it, as I wrote in July, not treaty but hard fighting is to assure this line. I have had no reason to think otherwise. I will operate all winter, whatever the season, if supported; but to redeem my pledge to open and guarantee this line, I must have re-enforcements and the best of arms up to my full estimate.[48]

In the folklore of the western frontier, the ride of Portugee Phillips from Phil Kearny to Laramie has achieved a status equal to that of Paul Revere's ride. And as in the case of the New Englander's exploit, there also seems to have been more than one rider. A sergeant writing from Phil Kearny on December 28 said that "Colonel Carrington sent citizen couriers to Laramie with dispatches to department headquarters for re-enforcements."[49] John Hunton, a Fort Laramie sutler's store clerk who knew Phillips well, listed four riders, including a sergeant "and a man named Gregory."[50] John Friend, the telegraph operator at Horseshoe Station, said that when Phillips arrived there on Christmas Day he was accompanied by William Bailey and George Dillon. Colonel Carrington in his testimony before a commission of inquiry in the spring of 1867 stated that he "hired two citizens to take dispatches to Laramie."[51]

It appears likely that Carrington selected both Phillips and Bailey for the ride, and it is logical that he would have ordered them to leave the fort separately on the theory that if one did not make it through to Laramie, the other might. Also it is probable that other riders joined one or both of them en route —at Fort Reno or Bridger's Ferry—which explains the presence of the veteran wagon train captain, George Dillon, when Phillips and Bailey rode into Horseshoe Station.

That Phillips left Phil Kearny alone, that he traveled most of the 236-mile journey alone through raging blizzards, that he rode alone the last forty miles from Horseshoe Station to Laramie—all appear to be facts. It was an almost incredible feat of horsemanship, a heroic four-day ride.

On that cold dark evening of December 21, Phillips stuffed his saddlebag with hardtack, took a quarter of a sack of oats for his mount, and went with Colonel Carrington to the stables. There by lantern light he saddled one of Carrington's horses, variously described as a "thoroughbred charger," "a Kentucky saddle horse," "a white horse."[52] The two men then walked together, Phillips leading the horse, to the water gate at the southeast end of the quartermaster yard.

Since sundown Private John C. Brough had been posted at the water gate, and as the two men approached, Brough challenged them. A moment later the sergeant of the guard called out: "Attention! It's the commanding officer." Carrington spoke up then: "Never mind, sergeant, open the gate." The sergeant unlocked the padlocks and Carrington and Phillips stepped forward, pulling out the bars and pushing the gate open.

"I recovered arms," Private Brough recalled afterward, "stepped back and stood at present arms while the two men walked to the gate opening. . . . They conversed for a minute or two, and finally one of them mounted the horse, which was restive and prancing around. The other man . . . he was Colonel Carrington . . . reached up, took the man's hand, and spoke a few words. I could not hear all he said, but did hear him say, 'May God help you!'

"The horseman wheeled and started off on a trot. For about thirty seconds we could hear the hoof-beats, and then they ceased. The colonel stood with his head bent on one side, as if listening intently, and then straightening up and speaking to no one in particular, said, 'Good, he has taken softer ground at the side of the trail!' "

Wind gusts swirled bits of sleet and snow around Carrington's lantern as he and the sergeant closed the gate and replaced the bars. The colonel turned back toward his headquarters, the sergeant accompanying him. Private Brough slapped at his tingling ears, and continued walking his post in the below-zero temperature.[53]

8.

Carrington waited impatiently for daylight on the morning of the 22nd. He had not slept, indeed had scarcely rested at all during the night, and having learned the ways of the Indians he expected a dawn attack, perhaps a massive assault against the stockade at the earliest show of light.

In occasional interludes of self-examination during that long night, he had attempted to adopt the viewpoint of the hostiles, tried to reason what he would do if he were an Indian. "I could not but feel that if I had been a red man," he admitted later, "I would have fought as bitterly, if not as cruelly, for my rights and my home as the red man fought."[54]

But when daylight came, pale gray and bitter cold, not an Indian was visible anywhere, in the valley or on the ridges. The sky was heavy with snow, warning white man and red man to seek shelter from a threatening blizzard. The morning gun echoed back from the hills; bugles and drums sounded reveille.

Soon after breakfast, Carrington summoned his four surviving officers for a council. Company roll calls had shown thirty-one enlisted men and Lieutenant Grummond still missing, and as none had come in during the night, they were all assumed to be dead. The first order of business, as Carrington saw it, was to recover the bodies of these dead comrades. Ten Eyck,

Powell, Wands, and Matson listened respectfully, then each in turn offered his opinion. It would be hazardous for any small party to return to the battlefield while the Indians were still celebrating their victory. If a large party left the stockade, the lives of all left behind would be in peril.

In the room adjoining this meeting, Frances Grummond and Margaret Carrington could hear every word spoken. "I will not let the Indians entertain the conviction that the dead cannot and will not be rescued," the colonel declared. "If we cannot rescue our dead, as the Indians always do at whatever risk, how can you send details out for any purpose, and that single fact would give them an idea of weakness here, and would only stimulate them to risk an assault."[55] Carrington concluded by announcing that he would lead the expedition himself. He wanted eighty picked men, soldiers and civilians. Ten Eyck, Matson, and Surgeon Ould would accompany him. He dismissed the group and turned immediately to the door of the adjoining room, knocking on the panel.

"Mrs. Carrington was sitting near the window," Frances Grummond recorded, "deep in thought . . . I was lying down, equally absorbed by the momentous question at stake. . . . When the door opened, we sprang trembling to our feet. The Colonel advanced to his wife and quietly announced his decision. . . .

"Turning to me, he said, 'Mrs. Grummond, I shall go in person, and will bring back to you the remains of your husband.' "[56]

While his eighty men were assembling and awaiting inspection, Carrington penciled two separate orders, delivering them in person to Captain Powell, who was officer of the day. The first order concerned communications arrangements between the fort and the expedition while it was in the field. "Fire the usual sunset gun, running a white lamp to mast head on the flag-staff. If the Indians appear, fire three guns from the twelve pounder at minute intervals and later substitute a red lantern for the white."

The second order was to be a secret between Carrington and the officer of the day. "If in my absence, Indians in overwhelming numbers attack, put the women and children in the magazine with supplies of water, bread, crackers and other supplies that seem best, and, in the event of a last desperate struggle, destroy all together, rather than have any captured alive."[57]

To make certain that Powell could carry out this last order, Carrington opened the magazine (which was surrounded by a circular defense of upturned wagon beds), cut the Boorman fuses of spherical case shot, and laid a train of powder which would blow up everything at the touch of a match.

Under a darkening winter sky, the eighty men marched out to the Bozeman Road and turned west. The cavalrymen moved briskly to the flanks. A few of the infantrymen rode in the mule-drawn wagons. As soon as the last man was through the gate, Carrington signaled for it to be closed and bolted, and then galloped forward to the head of the column.

Jim Bridger, although suffering from arthritis, had volunteered as a scout, and he assisted in placing pickets along the ridges so that a surprise attack might be avoided. On every high point two men were posted, each pair in sight of two other guard positions so as to form a continuous signal link to the fort. The temperature held around zero; there was still no sign of hostiles.

Among the boulders on high ground to the left of the road they found most of the remaining dead. "It was terrible work to load the frozen corpses into the wagons," said Finn Burnett, one of the volunteer civilians in the party. "The ground was fairly sodden with blood, the smell of which frightened the mules until they were well-nigh unmanageable. A man was obliged to hold the head of every animal while other teamsters loaded the naked, mutilated remains like cordwood into the wagon-boxes.

"When the first wagon had been half loaded, the mules began to lurch and kick, until they succeeded in throwing the men aside. Turning the wagon around they overturned it in their frenzy, and the bodies were dumped out before the animals could be recaptured and subdued. It was a terrible sight and a horrible job."[58]

John Guthrie, hard-bitten little cavalryman of the 2nd, described the same scene in his crude but vivid vernacular: "Some had crosses cut on their breasts, faces to the sky, some crosses on the back, faces to the ground, a mark cut that we could not find out. We walked on top of their internals and did not know it in the high grass. Picked them up, that is their internals, did not know the soldier they belonged to, so you see the cavalry man got an infantry man's gutts and an infantry man got a cavalry man's gutts."[59]

Carrington was shocked by what he saw, yet in his introspective way sought a reason for such evidences of savagery as the methodical removal of dorsal, thigh and calf muscles, of arms and limbs torn from sockets. Not until many years afterward, when he talked with a survivor of Red Cloud's Oglalas, did he learn the answer—a variation of the white man's myth of Tantalus. "The key to the mutilations were startling and impressive. Their idea of the spirit land is that it is a physical paradise; but we enter upon its mysteries just as in the condition we hold when we die. In the Indian paradise every physical taste or longing is promptly met. If he wants food, it is at hand; water springs up for ready use; ponies and game abound, blossoms, leaves, and fruit never fail; all is perennial and perpetual. But what is the Indian hell? It is the same in place and profusion of mercies, but the bad cannot partake. . . . With the muscles of the arms cut out, the victim could not pull a bowstring or trigger, with other muscles gone, he could not put foot in a stirrup or stoop to drink; so that, while every sense was in agony for relief from hunger or thirst, there could be no relief at all."[60]

According to Finn Burnett, only the body of the bugler, Adolph Metzger, was left untouched. "His heroism had aroused the admiration of the savages, they covered his corpse with a buffalo robe as a symbol of extreme respect."[61] John Guthrie, however, said that Metzger's body was never found, and a few weeks after the fight the Helena (Montana) *Herald* reported an interview between fur trappers and a band of Crows who had heard from the Sioux a story of the last survivor, who may have been Metzger. "He stood up and fought hand to hand till overwhelmed by their closing upon him, and carrying him off a prisoner to their camp where he was finally tortured to death."[62]

After loading all bodies found on the high ground, Carrington ordered the wagons moved cautiously along the road toward Peno Creek. Over a distance of three-quarters of a mile they recovered six more dead, including Lieutenant Grummond and Sergeant Augustus Lang. The lieutenant's head was almost severed from his body; his fingers had been chopped off, his naked body filled with arrows. Along this same stretch of road, they also found Jimmy Carrington's calico pony, which had been hastily borrowed by Captain Brown. The pony was dead, its head badly cut up, and someone remarked that the Indians must have scalped it out of hatred for Captain Brown.

A few hundred yards farther on, they found Wheatley, Fisher and "four or five of the old long-tried and experienced soldiers. A great number of empty cartridge shells were on the ground at this point." In front of the bodies, the last to be recovered, was a ring of dead Indian ponies, and "sixty-five pools of dark and clotted blood" on the ground and grass.[63] Wheatley had 105 arrows in his body and had been scalped.

The cautious march out, and the tedious and painful search for the dead, which was made even more difficult by bitter cold, occupied most of the day. As they were turning back from Peno Creek they heard the fort's sunset gun, and a black wintry darkness settled over the land before they sighted the gleam of a lantern on the flagstaff. It was a white light, signaling the reassuring news that Indians had not attacked the fort in their absence.

"We hauled them all into the fort," said John Guthrie, "and made the guard house at the fort a dead house." [64]

The first act of the colonel when he returned was a sentimental gesture. He visited Frances Grummond, handed her a sealed envelope, then left her to a moment of private grief. "I opened the envelope," she wrote afterward, "with eager but trembling hands. It contained a lock of my husband's hair." [65] She suddenly remembered, then, another memento, an encased miniature portrait of herself which George Grummond had worn since their wedding, and she wondered sadly if some Indian warrior carried it in his possession as a trophy of the battle.

Another who had to be consoled was the nineteen-year-old widow of James Wheatley.* Wagoner Finn Burnett described her as "a beautiful girl, a fine woman . . . a brave splendid little soldier." [66]

On the night of the 22nd, the blizzard which had been threatening for two days began in earnest, its fierce winds sweeping a blinding snow across the land and dropping temperatures to twenty below zero. Arm-length mittens, thigh-length leggings, buffalo boots, and a variety of fur hats were issued to the guards, and shifts were cut to one-half hour. At daylight of the 23rd the storm still raged, and snowdrifts crested the west flank of the stockade, packed so tightly that guards could walk from the parade directly over the upright posts. As a security measure, Carrington ordered a ten-foot trench cleared outside, but the biting winds refilled it almost as fast as men could dig.

That day and Christmas Eve were devoted to the melancholy task of preparing the dead for burial. Bodies were cleaned, mutilated fragments put together, arrows drawn out or cut off. Because most of the dead were left naked by the Indians, their comrades volunteered uniforms to clothe them. While this work went on in the hospital, carpenters constructed coffins. And in spite of the weather, a grave-digging detail cleared snow from the burial ground and started digging a trench for interment.

"One-half of the headquarters building, which was my temporary home," wrote Frances Grummond, "was utilized by carpenters for making pine cases for the dead. I knew that my husband's coffin was being made, and the sound of hammers and the grating of saws was torture to my sensitive nerves. . . . During the nights I would dream of Indians, of being captured and carried away by Red Cloud himself while frantically screaming for help, and then awaken in terror only to spring from my bed involuntarily to listen if the nearby sentry would still voice

---

* Burnett said that Mrs. Wheatley remained at the fort until the following spring when her brother came for her and took her back to the family home in Ohio. William Murphy, however, stated that she later married a man by the name of Breckinridge and lived on a ranch about five miles from Fort Laramie.

the welcome cry, 'All's well.' Sleeping draughts and the kind ministrations of Dr. Horton seemed rather to aggravate than reduce the nervous tension. . . . " [67]

On Christmas Day, the burial detail placed lines of pine cases by companies along officers' row. Two enlisted men were sealed in each box; the three officers rated separate coffins. Cases were carefully numbered to identify the occupants.

Carrington had hoped to bury the dead in solemn Christmas Day services, but the gravediggers, even though working in continuous half-hour shifts, were unable to complete excavation of the trench. Not until Wednesday, the 26th, five days after the battle, was burial completed, in a pit fifty feet long, seven feet deep, seven feet wide. "The severity of the weather," [68] a sergeant wrote two days later, "and probability of immediate attack upon the fort compelled us to bury our dead in trenches, without ceremony or military honors." *

On that same day—December 26—the War Department in Washington received the first telegraphic dispatches of the Fort Phil Kearny disaster. From General Cooke in Omaha: "On the 21st instant three officers and ninety men, cavalry and infantry, were massacred by Indians very near Fort Phil Kearny." [69] At 3:15 that afternoon direct from Fort Laramie, General Grant received Carrington's dispatch pleading for reinforcements.

To give this news to the outside world, John (Portugee) Phillips had forced his way through almost continuous blizzards, riding only at nights, rationing oats carefully to his horse, sometimes digging tufts of grass for it from under the snow. Late on Christmas morning he rode into Horseshoe Station, accompanied by William Bailey and George Dillon, and handed his dispatches to the telegraph operator, John Friend. Phillips had crossed 190 miles of snow that was in some places four or five feet deep.

After Friend had tapped out a condensation of the messages, Phillips rebound his legs with sacks, wrapped himself in a buf-

---

* These bodies with those of thirty-seven other soldiers buried at Fort Phil Kearny were exhumed in October 1888 and reburied in the National Cemetery at Custer Battlefield.

falo coat, saddled up, and prepared to ride the forty remaining miles to Fort Laramie. He had promised Colonel Carrington he would deliver the dispatches to the commander at Laramie, and neither his companions nor the telegraph operator could dissuade him from completing his mission.

After riding all afternoon across a dazzling-white land that blinded him, he welcomed the relief of nightfall even though more snow began falling and the temperature dropped far below zero. Between eleven o'clock and midnight he arrived at Fort Laramie. Icicles were hanging from his clothing; snow and ice matted his beard. From lighted windows of the main officers' quarters, he could hear gay dance music.

Phillips slid out of his saddle, staggering from exhaustion, and a minute later the officer of the guard, Lieutenant Herman Haas, was at his side, asking his name and what he wanted. Phillips was so weak he could barely reply that he wanted to see the commanding officer.

Lieutenant David Gordon (who later became a brigadier-general) was stationed at Laramie with a company of the 2nd Cavalry. "It was on Christmas night, 11 P.M.," Gordon later recorded, "when a full-dress garrison ball was progressing and everybody appeared superlatively happy, enjoying the dance, notwithstanding the snow was from ten to fifteen inches deep on the level and the thermometer indicated twenty-five degrees below zero, when a huge form dressed in buffalo overcoat, pants, gauntlets and cap, accompanied by an orderly, desired to see the commanding officer. The dress of the man, and at this hour looking for the commanding officer, made a deep impression upon the officers and others that happened to get a glimpse of him, and consequently, and naturally, too, excited their curiosity as to his mission in this strange garb, dropping into our full-dress garrison ball at this unseasonable hour.

"As we were about to select partners for another dance word was passed into our ball-room that General Palmer desired to see me...." [70] A few moments later, Lieutenant Gordon met Portugee Phillips face to face.

During the preceding forty-eight hours, Laramie officers had been hearing rumors from Indians around the fort of a great battle which had supposedly taken place near Phil Kearny. At two o'clock that afternoon, General Innis N. Palmer, the new commanding officer, had received a garbled telegram from Horseshoe Station, reporting a massacre. Palmer had immediately forwarded the message to Omaha, but evidently he still considered the massacre a rumor until Phillips arrived with Carrington's dispatches. Not until early in the morning of the 26th did Carrington's full report go to Omaha, and Lieutenant Gordon afterward stated that Fort Laramie received "nothing authentic until the dispatch was handed the commanding officer by one Portuguese Phillips, who was employed by Colonel Carrington at Fort Phil Kearny." *

Thus the world outside Dakota Territory learned of the incident which would be known thereafter as the Fetterman Massacre.

----

* The horse used by John Phillips on his four-day, 236-mile ride died soon after arriving at Fort Laramie. Phillips himself collapsed from exhaustion and exposure, suffering for weeks from severe frostbite. Lieutenant Gordon said that Phillips was paid one thousand dollars for the ride, but official records indicate that the amount he received for quartermaster services at Fort Phil Kearny and for the ride totaled only about three hundred dollars. Thirty-three years later, in 1899, his widow received five thousand dollars in partial recognition of Phillips' ride from Phil Kearny to Laramie.

X. *January:*

MOON OF STRONG COLD

Upon being relieved I moved to Fort Casper with regi-
mental headquarters, staff, and officers' families, with
mercury at 38° below zero (the second day), and having
more than half my escort of sixty men frosted the first
sixty-five miles, requiring two amputations at Reno.[1]

ON December 27, the day following the mass burials at
Fort Phil Kearny, a small party of soldiers appeared unexpectedly on the snow-drifted road east of Little Piney. They were
three officers and twenty-two enlisted men who upon reaching
Fort Reno had learned of the Fetterman disaster, and instead
of waiting at Reno for the weather to improve had pushed on
through blizzards to Phil Kearny. Senior officer of the group was
Captain George B. Dandy, who some weeks earlier had been
assigned to replace Captain Brown. Accompanying him were
Lieutenant Thomas J. Gregg, 2nd Cavalry, replacement for the
late Lieutenant Bingham, and Lieutenant Alphonse Borsman.

Borsman's orders were for service with the 27th Infantry Regiment, which after weeks of rumors was now a fact—created from
the 18th's 2nd Battalion. The mail from Omaha informed Carrington that new headquarters for the 18th Infantry would be
Fort Casper, where companies of the 1st Battalion would become
cadres for new battalions of the 18th.

This news was not unexpected. Following the arrival of Captain Fetterman in November, Carrington had assumed there would be a change eventually. But after Fetterman's death, Carrington probably clung to a hope that he might be permitted to remain in command of the fort he had so painstakingly designed and constructed, and which had become so vital a part of his existence.

He welcomed the arrival of Captain Dandy and the reinforcements, but he knew he needed ten times their number as well as replenishment of his arms and ammunition if he hoped to equal the power demonstrated by the Indians on December 21. His enlisted men also knew this, and some indication of their morale at this time is revealed in a letter written by a sergeant on the night of December 28:

> It is now past tattoo; the night is cold; the men are sleeping in their clothes, and accoutrements on. Indian signals have been seen, and we don't know what hour the post may be attacked. Self and two soldiers are keeping watch so as to awake the men in case of alarm. At midnight I shall have Sgt. Clark and three others to relieve us. So you can imagine the state of affairs here.
>
> We are fighting a foe that is the devil. In your last you spoke about some newspapers which you had sent me. I did not get them. Please write soon, and pray God to hasten the day when I shall get out of this horrible place. Goodbye; this may be my last letter; should it reach you, don't forget your friend. ...[2]

By New Year's Day, however, fears of an Indian attack had diminished. Valleys and trails were deep with snow, and Jim Bridger assured Carrington that even the most hostile of Indian bands would hesitate to go on the warpath under such conditions. It was Bridger's opinion that most of the warriors were holed up in their villages on Tongue River.

(Bridger's surmise was good, as far as it went. Actually there had been no danger of attack upon the fort since the day of the Fetterman fight. As soon as the fight ended, the main body of warriors departed for Tongue River, leaving a few scouts behind to watch movements around the fort. Red Cloud and other chiefs expected retaliatory measures from the soldiers before winter ended, and in spite of bitter weather, the leaders decided to abandon their Tongue River stronghold. The Arapaho went to the Yellowstone, the Cheyennes into the Big Horns, the Sioux scattering down the valleys of the Powder and Tongue.)

On New Year's Day Carrington issued his first general order of 1867, offering a solemn memorial to the men who fell in the Fetterman fight. "As a feeble tribute to their memory, their names are published in this order, so that the records of the post shall bear them in remembrance so long as the post shall remain ... a copy of this order shall be read before each company and at the first garrison parade...." [3]

In addition to the three officers and seventy-six enlisted men killed in Peno Valley, Carrington included the names of Lieutenant Bingham and Sergeant Bowers, killed on December 6. Had he summed up losses from the day of Fort Phil Kearny's establishment, he would have listed five officers, ninety-one enlisted men, and fifty-eight civilians killed, with many additional wounded. Indians had attacked almost every wagon train and traveler attempting to pass over the Montana Road.

By January 4 the weather had moderated sufficiently for a mail party to start for Laramie, and Carrington composed a long report for General Cooke in which he claimed the Fetterman disaster confirmed his previous judgment as to the hostility of the Indians. "It vindicates every report from my pen," he wrote. "It vindicates my administration of the Mountain District.... It vindicates my application so often made for reinforcements ... it proves correct my report of 1,500 lodges of hostile Indians on Tongue River."

Having thus attempted to justify his position in the disaster of December 21, Carrington added significantly: "My duty will be done when I leave, as ordered to my new regimental headquarters, Fort Casper." [4]

This transfer order, which he must have dreaded, came with the arrival of his replacement, Lieutenant-Colonel Henry W. Wessells, on January 16. First to sight this long-awaited relief column from Laramie and Reno was the picket on Pilot Hill, who immediately signaled the lookout on Carrington's headquarters tower. "The bugle call and the long roll were never more gladly echoed in hearts," wrote Frances Grummond. "Our spontaneous cry was 'Open wide the gates, and admit our deliverers!' We hardly had patience to don protective outer-garments because of the flow of our quickened blood, and our common outbreak of joy was simply, 'At last! At last! We are saved! We are saved! Phillips was saved, saved for us!' ... The band was on hand with its preparations for a share in that welcome and an escort was hastened from the gates to facilitate their arrival. As for myself, I felt that I could have hugged every half-frozen man as he entered, and I still feel that their story as it unfolded would have justified the impulse, if not the action." [5]

The relief column's story had begun unfolding on December 26 a few minutes after General Cooke in Omaha received the first authentic telegraph report of the Fetterman disaster. Without waiting for Carrington's full report, Cooke dispatched a curt order to Laramie:

> Brevet Brigadier General I. N. Palmer, commanding Fort Laramie will send from the garrison of that post two companies of the second cavalry and four companies of the eighteenth infantry, to report to Brevet Brigadier General Wessells at Fort Reno.
>
> Brevet Brigadier General Wessells will proceed with the reenforcements and assume command of Fort Philip Kearny, and will also have authority to order such movements of the troops at Forts Reno and C. F. Smith as he may find necessary. The commanding officers at Forts Reno and C. F. Smith will obey all orders they may receive from Brevet Brigadier General Wessells.
>
> Colonel H. B. Carrington, 18th United States Infantry, will be relieved from the command of Fort Philip Kearny by Brevet Brigadier General Wessells, and will proceed immediately to Fort Casper, to which post the headquarters of the new 18th Regiment have been heretofore ordered, and assume command of the post and that regiment.[6]

When General Palmer received this message, Laramie was experiencing its worst weather of the winter. He waited hope-fully for the blizzard to pass, then replied on the 27th: "The most violent blinding storm now raging; there would be nothing gained by moving in such a snow storm; meantime all preparations which can be made in-doors are going on." [7]

Cooke meanwhile continued to counter any possible criticism of his own responsibility in the Fetterman affair by directing blame toward Carrington. "Colonel Carrington is very plausible," he wrote General Grant on the 27th, "an energetic, industrious man in garrison; but it is too evident that he has not maintained discipline, and that his officers have no confidence in him." [8]

Not until New Year's Day were the first relief units able to leave Fort Laramie—four companies of the 18th Infantry's 1st Battalion under Major James Van Voast. Forty-eight hours later, two companies of the 2nd Cavalry under Lieutenant Gordon moved out, and overtook the infantry January 5.

"On account of the severity of the weather and deep snow," said Gordon, "there was no grazing for the animals, a scarcity of wood, and the water in the streams that we crossed was partly frozen to the bottom, except in the deep holes, where we were compelled to chop holes in the ice and water the animals out of buckets. . . . Our long forage gave out after being on the road ten days and the mules were cold and hungry for hay . . . they broke their halters, eat at wagon tongues, manes and tails of each other. Had to replace some tongues and ridge poles on wagons." [9]

At Fort Reno, Wessells was informed of Cooke's order naming him as Carrington's replacement. He took command of the expedition, which reached Fort Phil Kearny on the 16th, "with but one casualty, a man being frozen to death." [10]

Carrington reacted mildly to the news that one of his subordinates, Lieutenant-Colonel and Brevet Brigadier-General Wessells, was replacing him. He had suffered so many frustrations from department headquarters that one more scarcely mattered, although he was bitter over the way Cooke had deliberately worded the replacement orders to make it appear "that the purpose of changing my post occurred simultaneously with report of the massacre, before receipt of my telegram." [11] He may have taken some satisfaction from the War Department's abrupt removal of General Cooke himself from command of the Department of the Platte shortly afterward, but thirty years would pass before Carrington could forgive Cooke for the manner in which he handled his transfer from Fort Phil Kearny.

On the day that General Christopher C. Augur reported as Cooke's replacement in Omaha, January 23, Carrington was making an emotional departure from the fort he had dreamed all his life of building and commanding. The dream had come to fruition, flourished, and died all within six short months. He later summed up the midwinter change of stations in a single trenchant paragraph: "Upon being relieved I moved to Fort Casper with regimental headquarters, staff and officers' families, with mercury at 38° below zero (the second day), and having more than half my escort of sixty men frosted the first sixty-five miles, requiring two amputations at Reno." [12]

Margaret Carrington and Frances Grummond both recorded much more detailed accounts of this harrowing march. Frances was in an advanced state of pregnancy by this time, sensitive to every movement of the jolting wagon in which she rode. She had insisted on taking her husband's body with her to Tennessee, and Carrington had arranged for George Grummond's pine box to be disinterred and placed in one of the wagons.

In preparation for the journey, wagon covers were doubled, and carpenters boarded up sides and ends of wagon beds, leaving only a tiny window at each end. They placed a hinged door at the back of each vehicle for entry, and near the door a small sheet-iron stove made from a stovepipe, with a smoke vent through the wagon cover. Pine knots and short blocks of wood for fuel were packed in one corner. Women and children huddled themselves into cloaks, shawls, beaver hoods, buffalo boots, and all the furs they owned or could borrow.

Snow was falling at 1:30 P.M. on the 23rd when Carrington gave the order to march. The first afternoon and on into the dark night, the column struggled against the storm and the snow-packed road. A pioneer corps was formed and sent in advance to shovel out the deepest drifts. By ten o'clock that night, they had made only six miles. Carrington ordered a corral on a summit for defensive reasons, leaving the party open to fierce gusts of wind which almost swept the sentries off their feet.

At one o'clock in the morning the moon rose, casting a cold blue light across the frozen land. Carrington ordered the bugle sounded, and by three o'clock they were moving again. The sky was clear, the stars brilliant, the aurora borealis dancing weirdly behind them in the north sky. The thermometer in Margaret Carrington's wagon dropped to thirteen below zero.

On through the moonlit night the column crawled, wheels creaking, the cold intense. When Frances Grummond looked out her peephole window at dawn, she saw hundreds of buffalo wallowing in the snow. All that day the column was surrounded by buffalo, twenty-five miles of buffalo—a cheering sight, for it indicated lack of Indians in the vicinity.

At duskfall they halted on Crazy Woman's Fork and formed a corral in a grove beside the stream. Pickets were stationed on an adjoining bluff. The men dug wood out of the snow for night fires; as the wood burned the snow melted, then turned to ice, forming a crystal ring around each fire. They had to use axes to break their bread; coffee taken from the fires turned to frozen slush before it could be swallowed. From each wagon vent, smoke poured in plumes, but Margaret Carrington's children were crying from the cold. The turkey she had cooked before leaving the fort was frozen so hard she had to chop pieces from it with a hatchet, then soften them over her little stove before they could be eaten.

Reveille again was at one o'clock in the morning. As the moon rose, the half-frozen men began shoveling snow off the stream, broke through the ice for water to refill the kegs. A cavalyman had to be lifted from the saddle, his legs frozen from toes to knees. To keep other mounted men from suffering a similar fate, Carrington ordered their legs lashed with whips to start the circulation going.

Inside the wagons, the women wrapped themselves in buffalo skins and beaver hoods and sat with their feet to the tiny red-hot stoves. Margaret Carrington's thermometer dropped to forty below; then the mercury congealed in the bulb.

As soon as teams were hitched, the column crossed the creek, moved forward to a sixty-foot bluff and began a slow ascent. Only one wagon could go up at a time, details of men tugging at the wheels, others pulling with ropes.

"When my turn came," Frances Grummond said, "I rolled over on my bed, clung for dear life to the sides of the wagon, with eyes shut and jaws clamped, to assist or ignore the situation, both being equally ineffective, for it all depended upon those mules. . . . Of all rides I ever had taken in army life or out of it, this one in an army wagon without springs, with mules on a gallop over such a road, or no road, exceeded all in utter misery. One learns something from such an experience and I had learned to seize the sideboards of the wagon firmly, half reclining on the mattress with pillows compactly adjusted, and holding my breath abide the result." [13]

Dawn was breaking when the last wagon reached the crest of the bluff. Fort Reno and temporary security still lay twenty miles to the south. By midmorning the sun's glare was blinding and those who had goggles put them on. All day buffalo herds moved alongside, occasionally coming close as if seeking company, the bulls tearing at the snow to uncover grass. Carrington passed along an order forbidding drivers to crack their whips lest the buffalo become frightened and stampede the train. There was one false alarm of Indians attacking the rear wagons, and an hour was lost in preparing defenses.

At dusk the first wagon rolled into Fort Reno, ending a sixty-five-mile journey that had required almost three days' time. They were all thankful to be alive, even the men who must lose fingers, toes and legs by amputation in the post's hospital.

After three days' rest in the warm quarters of Reno, they took the trail again, this time to Fort Casper, a march that was without perilous incident until the final day. As they neared the fort, Frances Grummond noted that her wagon was moving with increasing speed, and looking out her window she discovered the whole train at a trot, in column of six wagons front, moving all in mass. Indians had approached the train, stealing some of the led horses, but they dashed away without a fight.

At Casper, Carrington learned that the unpredictable higher command back in the States had changed its bureaucratic mind

and transferred the 18th Regiment's headquarters to Fort Mc-
Pherson. With the weather still formidable, he had to lead his
little column back over a long stretch of rough trail already
traveled. Near Sage Creek, while he was galloping his horse,
his revolver was accidentally discharged, wounding him seriously in the thigh. Luck seemed to have run out for the Little
White Chief. The surgeons prepared a sling for him in his wife's
wagon, and thus he was carried on to Fort Laramie. After a two-
weeks convalescence, he traveled by ambulance to Fort McPherson, where he reassumed command of the 18th Infantry. And
there at McPherson during the early weeks of spring, he faced
the ordeal of a special commission formed to fix responsibility
for the Fetterman disaster.

XI:

AFTERMATH

1.

WHILE Colonel Carrington was marching his headquarters complement through the blizzards of Wyoming, recovering from his wound at Fort Laramie, and proceeding to his new headquarters at Fort McPherson, he was also becoming a national figure. In newspapers and illustrated weeklies he was in most cases the target of uninformed journalists who held him solely responsible for the "Fetterman Massacre." In the War Department he was rapidly assuming the role of scapegoat. The Department of Interior's Office of Indian Affairs issued statements absolving the "friendly Indians" and placing all blame on Carrington. He was the victim of a public trial of which he was unaware for some weeks, and in which he was given no opportunity to present his side of the affair.

One correspondent for a New York newspaper described the fight as taking place at the gates of the fort. "When the last band of survivors were driven to the gates of the fort, knocking and screaming in vain for admission; when the last cartridge for revolver, carbine, and rifle was expended; when the sabers and butts of muskets were broken; and when, leaning against the gates, weary and bleeding and all resistance fruitless, all fell in one heap of mangled humanity, unsupported and uncared for." While all this was occurring, the writer continued, Carrington and two full companies were looking on, afraid to fire or open the gates lest the garrison within be massacred by the attacking

Indians. An illustrated weekly carried a report from "the only eye witness of the massacre" who supposedly was cut off by Indians, and watched the fight from a nearby thicket. This survivor vividly described repeated cavalry charges and saw "the last shot discharged by the last survivor through his own brain." [1] Newspapers in New York and Washington also accused Carrington of giving gunpowder to his enemies, and said he permitted officers' wives to toss packages of sugar and coffee over the stockade to passing squaws.

Not to be outdone by these lurid stories in the press, the Commissioner of Indian Affairs, Lewis V. Bogy, issued a statement claiming that the Indians around Fort Phil Kearny had been provoked into attacking Carrington's forces. "These Indians being in absolute want of guns and ammunition to make their winter hunt," he said, "were on a friendly visit to the fort, desiring to communicate with the commanding officer . . . so that they might be enabled to procure their winter supply of buffalo." [2] In a later statement Bogy declared "the whole affair seems incredible . . . and I find it difficult to account for the tragedy upon any other theory than that heretofore advanced by this office, to wit: that the Indians, almost in a state of starvation, having made repeated attempts at a conference, that they might make peace and obtain supplies for their families . . . were rendered desperate, and resorted to the stratagem which proved too successful. It seems as if the officer commanding could have avoided the catastrophe; and it seems also that men thus armed could have repelled an attack by all the Indians in Western Dakota." [3]

Commissioner Bogy ridiculed Carrington's estimate that three thousand Indians could have assembled in one place to attack Fetterman's detachment. "An enormous exaggeration," he charged, and then also expressed disbelief that three hundred Indians would have attacked the wood train and withdrawn without inflicting casualties. Clearly the Commissioner knew nothing of Indian decoy fighting or very little else about affairs in Dakota Territory.

His statements, however, precipitated Carrington into the midst of the perennial political struggle between the War Department and the Office of Indian Affairs. This struggle had been raging off and on since 1849 when control of Indian affairs was transferred from the War Department to the Interior Department. It was the viewpoint of the military that the bureau had been corrupted by politicians who were dishonest, inefficient, and working at cross purposes with national policy. It was the viewpoint of the Interior Department that Indian affairs could be better administered by civilians with humanitarian objectives. Each frequently accused the other of endangering lives, and neither overlooked an opportunity to make the other appear blameworthy.

General Sherman, who had recently completed several months' inspection of western frontier posts, advised General Grant that "if our troops are to keep open a highway of travel they must be allowed to take their own precautions and make their regulations for the guardianship of the Indians. The Indian Bureau should be transferred to the War Department." [4] On February 1, Grant himself expressed this same view in a letter to Secretary of War Stanton, claiming that events at Fort Phil Kearny "show urgent necessity for an immediate transfer of the Indian Bureau to the War Department." [5] The *Army and Navy Journal* leaped into the fight with bitter editorials denouncing the Indian Bureau's practice of issuing arms to Indians, "thus supplying the Indians with the means of repeating indefinitely the scenes of Fort Phil Kearny." [6]

Reacting to pressures from the civilian population which had been aroused by shocking accounts of the Fetterman disaster, the United States Senate on January 30 passed a resolution requesting the Secretaries of War and Interior "to furnish the Senate all official reports, papers, and other facts in possession of their respective departments which may tend to explain the origin, causes and extent of the late massacre of United States troops by Indians at or near Fort Phil Kearny, in Dakota Territory." [7]

While Colonel Carrington still lay recuperating from his thigh wound at Fort Laramie, Washington bureaucracy became more deeply involved over what he had or had not done at Fort Phil Kearny. A few days after the Senate's demand for an explanation of the causes of the Fetterman disaster, the President appointed a special commission "to visit the Indian country in the neighborhood of Fort Phil Kearny, for the purpose of ascertaining all the facts." [8] The commission, ordered to meet at Omaha on February 23, was composed of four army officers, Generals Alfred Sully, J. B. Sanborn, N. B. Buford and Colonel E. S. Parker; and two civilians, G. P. Beauvais and J. T. Kinney. Beauvais was a St. Louis trader who had lived among the Sioux for many years; Kinney had held the sutlership at Phil Kearny (and was no friend of Carrington).

By late March the commission was at Fort McPherson taking testimony from Colonel Carrington. For the first time he had an opportunity to present his side of the controversial incident, offering in evidence official messages and letters which he had sent and received, and patiently explaining all his actions from the time he received orders at Fort Kearney to the last day of his command at Fort Phil Kearny. "I close by stating," he said, "that if further testimony should be deemed necessary there are at this post the following witnesses." And he listed the names of his orderly, Archibald Sample, three other enlisted men who had been present at moments of crucial decision, and William Bailey, the civilian guide who had come with him to Fort McPherson.[9] The commission, however, called none of these witnesses, and as soon as hearings were declared closed, departed for Laramie and Fort Phil Kearny to continue its investigations.

While Carrington waited anxiously through the spring for the commission's verdict of responsibility—a verdict which might exonerate him or be "fatal to his reputation," [10] he received support from an unexpected source—Jim Bridger. Bridger had disagreed with Carrington on some actions at Phil Kearny, but when the scout learned of the colonel's difficulties, he prepared a statement for the *Army and Navy Journal*:

> Now as to the Philip Kearny massacre, it has been said that the Indians did not approach with hostile intent, but that the commanding officer, mistaking their intentions, fired on them, and thus brought on a fight. This is preposterous. Up to that time the Indians had been hanging around the fort every day, stealing stock on every opportunity, attacking the trains going

to the woods, and even stealing up at night and shooting men connected with passing trains, while they were sitting around their camp fires, within one hundred yards of the fort. But a few days before the massacre a train going to the wood was attacked, and in defending it, Lieutenant Bingham, a promising young officer of the 2nd Cavalry, and one Sergeant, lost their lives. This may be a sign of friendship, but I don't think so. Every person that knows anything of affairs in this country knows very well that the massacre at Fort Philip Kearny was planned weeks before, and that the Sioux, Cheyennes and Arapahos had been collecting together, in preparation for it, on Tongue River, until they numbered 2,200 lodges. The intention was to attack Fort Philip Kearny first, and if they were successful to then attack Fort C. F. Smith. At the present time the entire tribe of the Northern Sioux are collecting on Powder River below the mouth of Little Powder River, and their vowed intention is to make a vigorous and determined attack on each of the three posts, and on all trains that may come along the road. Friendly Indians report that they are being supplied with ammunition by half-breed traders connected with the Hudson's Bay Company. There is no use sending out commissioners to treat with them, as it will be only acting over again last Summer's scenes. They would be willing to enter into any temporary treaty to enable themselves to get fully supplied with powder with which to carry on the war. The only way to settle the question is to send out a sufficient number of troops to completely whip the hostile Sioux, Cheyennes and Arapahos and make them sue for peace. Unless this is done the road had better be abandoned and the country given up to the Indians.

I have been in this country among these Indians nearly forty-four years, and I am familiar with their past history, and my experience and knowledge of them is greater than can be gained by commissioners during the sittings of any council that may be held. I know that these Indians will not respect any treaty until they have been whipped into it.

May 4, 1867   JAMES BRIDGER [11]

At last on July 8, General Sanborn as spokesman for the investigating commission issued a report on the causes and circumstances which led "to the horrible massacre of Brevet Lieutenant-Colonel Fetterman's party, December 21, 1866." Sanborn reported the facts as he saw them, and instead of censuring Carrington, gently absolved him from blame. "The difficulty 'in a nutshell,' " said Sanborn, "was that the commanding officer of the district was furnished no more troops or supplies for this state of war than had been provided and furnished him in a state of profound peace. In regions where all was peace, as at Laramie in November, twelve companies were stationed, while in regions where all was war, as at Phil Kearny, there were only five companies allowed." [12]

Unfortunately for Carrington, Sanborn's favorable report was buried among derogatory statements from the Commissioner of Indian Affairs, comments of biased Indian agents, letters from personal enemies such as Surgeon C. M. Hines and an unidentified sergeant, excerpts from unfriendly newspapers, and the damning comments of General Cooke. All these were published a few months later by the Senate's Committee on Indian Affairs.

As for Carrington's own testimony with its supporting documents, these papers were conveniently stored away by someone in authority in the Department of the Interior. For twenty years they would remain hidden in the files, and for twenty years Henry B. Carrington would fight a continuing battle to clear his tarnished reputation as a soldier.

2.

At Fort Phil Kearny, after Carrington departed in January 1867, bitter winter weather sealed the Montana Road to north and south, and for weeks at a time until spring Lieutenant-Colonel Wessells was without communication with the outside world. Old-timers afterward remembered that winter as being unusually severe in the Wyoming country—"cold, and a great deal of snow." [13] One of the men at the fort noted that "the thermometer most of the time was from 25 to 40 degrees below zero." [14]

Wessells had come up from Reno determined to conduct a punitive winter campaign against the hostiles, but the terrible weather combined with shortages of supplies forced him to abandon his plans. From the day of his arrival the supply shortage grew rapidly more acute. Private William Murphy said the additional reinforcements from Laramie "made our condition, if anything, worse, for they had no provisions, and no feed for stock." [15] Reluctantly Wessells ordered Captain James Peale to take the two companies of the 2nd Cavalry back to Laramie in an attempt to save the horses from starvation. Peale and his men reached Laramie, but "without the animals, 150 in number; as evidence of that march, their carcasses could be seen many years afterward strewn along the road." [16]

In February, ration allowances of hardtack, coffee, salt pork and flour were cut drastically. Supplies in the commissary were dwindling, and no one could foresee how many weeks would pass before supply trains could move again from the south. Corn supplies for the mules were still relatively abundant in February, and Finn Burnett told of burning ashes for lye, and then soaking corn in it to loosen the hulls. After removing the lye, he fried the softened corn in bacon grease. "Others learned the trick," he said. "Many in garrison that winter lived on mules' corn." [17]

Another narrator who endured the winter at Phil Kearny complained of the lack of fresh meat and vegetables. "One small loaf of bread was issued to us daily—just enough for one meal. After we had eaten that, we had to fall back on the musty hardtack and frowsy bacon or salt pork with black coffee. Sometimes we had bean soup." [18]

By late winter all corn and forage for the livestock was exhausted, and Private Murphy said the mules began eating holes through the logs in their stables. "It was pitiful to witness the suffering of these poor patient animals," wrote Frank Fessenden, who had remained at Phil Kearny with the regimental band. "At night, especially, we could hear them fairly moan and groan like a human being in their agony of hunger." [19] As soon as weather permitted, Quartermaster Dandy sent teams up Big Piney to cut green cottonwood limbs which the animals consumed avidly, and he risked one small expedition to Fort Reno for corn. "The snow was very deep," said Private Murphy, "and it took several days to make the trip." [20]

Other discomforts came from lack of warm clothing and firewood. "Our shoes were made of cheap split leather," Murphy recorded, "and the shoddy clothes that were furnished at that time were not any protection. One thing in our favor was that after the first few days' storm we had very little wind. Burlap sacks were at a premium and saved our lives. We wrapped them about our shoes to keep from freezing, for there were no over-shoes or rubbers to be had at the fort." [21] Because of the continuous below-zero temperatures the huge pile of billets and slabs in the woodyard vanished long before winter's end, and the wagons going up Big Piney for cottonwood branches for the mules began bringing back logs for fuel. "We often had to saw wood," one enlisted man recalled, "for our heating stoves in the barracks until after tattoo at 9 P.M." [22]

After weeks of poor diet, lack of proper exercise, and exposure to cold, the physical condition of officers and men began declining. "There was no place in the barracks to wash, and after the creeks were frozen over we could not take a bath until they thawed out the following spring." [23] Scurvy cases began showing up at the hospital, and according to Frank Fessenden few men escaped the disease. "For lack of vegetables," Lieutenant Gordon noted, "the hospital was crowded to its limits by men down on their backs with scurvy and no special remedy other than drugs to prevent the entire garrison being afflicted. It was indeed a pitiable sight to see some of these poor soldiers so emaciated and weak and afflicted to that extent that their teeth were ready to drop out of their mouth." [24]

Lieutenant-Colonel Wessells reported in his official record of events at the end of February: "Health of garrison not good, scurvy prevailing complaint." On March 17 he recorded: "Train with antiscorbutants arrived from Laramie, weather extremely cold, snow storms frequent, forage exhausted, wood, fuel, exhausted. Outdoor drill impossible." [25] In April, cases of sickness were the highest for any month since establishment of the fort.

Morale collapsed of course, and with the coming of spring several men deserted. Some disappeared at night, over the stockade; others were more ingenious, Wessells recording in his May report that two men deserted with a party of Crow Indians, "painted and dressed in Indian costumes." [26]

As bad as conditions were at Phil Kearny during that agonizing winter, the garrison was convinced that Fort C. F. Smith was worse off. From November 1866 until late March 1867, the fort on the Big Horn River was completely isolated, and a soldier writing from Laramie in midwinter reported pessimistically: "We have heard nothing from Fort C. F. Smith since the massacre, and we fear it has 'gone up.' "²⁷

However, when Wessells dispatched a small mail party to C. F. Smith in March "to see what had become of the men there," his messengers returned with the news that C. F. Smith had survived the winter far better than Phil Kearny. The soldiers there had lived for weeks on a basic diet of corn, but their provident quartermaster had stocked a supply of potatoes and cabbages—secured from Bozeman in the autumn—and these vegetables were sufficient to keep down scurvy. More than anything else, the men had missed their mail and tobacco.²⁸

Perhaps the single individual who suffered most acutely during the winter at Phil Kearny was not a victim of disease, malnutrition, exposure, or physical wounds. His was an ordeal of the spirit, a mental desolation. In January when Carrington was preparing to leave, Lieutenant-Colonel Wessells had requested that Captain Ten Eyck be temporarily detached from the 18th Infantry so that he might remain at the fort as commander of Company H, recently transferred to the newly formed 27th Infantry.

Exactly what happened to Ten Eyck after Carrington departed probably will never be known. Undoubtedly some of the new officers up from Laramie believed certain whispered allegations that Ten Eyck had acted in a cowardly manner when he was sent in relief of Fetterman. Some may have avoided his society from the time of their arrival; others may have shunned him because he had begun to drink heavily. Ten Eyck seemed to lose the confidence of the men under him; Wessells shifted him from H Company to F, then to A in February, and to C in March.

Late in the summer Ten Eyck transferred to Fort McPherson, rejoining the 18th Infantry, but the change brought no halt to his drinking. He reported for duty one day in a state of drunkenness so advanced that his commanding officer, Colonel William Dye, preferred charges against him. After Ten Eyck became sober, he promised to abstain thereafter from similar conduct, and the charges were withdrawn. A few days later he became drunk again, was charged with "conduct unbecoming an officer and a gentleman" and ordered to a general court-martial, which found him guilty.

When General Grant reviewed the court-martial proceedings he directed that the finding be set aside. "Captain Ten Eyck," Grant wrote, "will resume his sword and report for duty." [29]

For Tenodor Ten Eyck this was but a temporary reprieve. He was plagued by chronic diarrhea, hemorrhoids, and rheumatism. And the whispers—real or imagined—followed him whereever he went. Five years after the Fetterman fight he quit the Army. Like Carrington he was a victim of rumors to which he had no opportunity of replying, but unlike Carrington he engaged in no campaign to clear his record, preferring a straitened civilian life to continuous abuse in the military.

3.

As Jim Bridger predicted in his May letter to the *Army and Navy Journal,* Fort Phil Kearny was destined for more Indian troubles. In June, Red Cloud's hostiles began a steady harassment of the fort, with occasional darting raids against wood trains. In July they became so dangerous in the pinery that Wessells assigned full companies to guard the woodcutters.

For defense, fourteen wagon boxes were formed into an oval-shaped corral on an open plain near the pinery. Tents were pitched just outside the ring of boxes so that the soldiers and civilian wood choppers could remain overnight outside the protection of the fort.

Early on the morning of August 2, several hundred Indians appeared suddenly on the foothills north of this wagon-box corral. As the Indians approached, wood choppers and soldiers rushed to the corral to take up positions. In command was Captain James Powell, who had remained at Phil Kearny as an officer of the 27th Infantry Regiment, and as he watched the waves of hostiles riding swiftly up from the creek he must have recalled the recent fate of Fetterman's command.

Unlike Fetterman, however, Powell had the advantage of cover, and he also had a second advantage—each man of his command was armed with a new breech-loading Springfield rifle. Inside the corral were several carefully arranged boxes filled with several thousand rounds of ammunition. "Instead of drawing ramrods and thus losing precious time," said Sergeant Samuel Gibson, "we simply threw open the breech-blocks of our new rifles to eject the empty shell and slapped in fresh ones." [30]

In their first assault the Indians were mounted, circling the soldiers' position, then charging in, expecting to overrun the wagon boxes when the defenders paused to reload. To the vast surprise of the attackers, the soldiers' fire was continuous. Many ponies went down, screaming in agony, and many braves died within a few yards of the wagon boxes.

Driven back, the hostiles dismounted, sent their surviving horses to the rear, stripped themselves, and returned to resume the fighting. "It chilled my blood," Sam Gibson said, on recalling his first sight of the naked Indians attacking on foot. "Hundreds and hundreds of Indians swarming up a ravine about ninety yards to the west of the corral . . . formed in the shape of a letter V . . . immediately we opened a terrific fire upon them. . . . Our fire was accurate, coolly delivered and given with most telling effect, but nevertheless it looked for a minute as though our last moment on earth had come. Just when it seemed as if all hope was gone, the Indians suddenly broke and fled." [31]

According to Sergeant Gibson, Red Cloud was in the field that day directing the fighting from a ridge just out of rifle range. Years afterward Red Cloud said he lost the flower of his fighting warriors in the Wagon Box Fight.

That hostile forces of the Powder River country were operating in concert is indicated by the fact that on the day preceding the Wagon Box Fight, a similar attack was made against soldiers and civilians working in a hayfield near Fort C. F. Smith. As at Phil Kearny the men were prepared, having constructed a barricade of willow matting, and they were armed with the new repeating rifles. Three soldiers were killed, four wounded, in the Hayfield Fight; Indian losses were much heavier.

These two crushing defeats of the Indians came too late, however, to save the Montana Road. Fetterman's disaster had shaken the nation; its military and political effects ran so deep that once the machinery of appeasement was set in motion, the midsummer victories could not reverse the course of events. Fort Phil Kearny's days were numbered, and so were C. F. Smith's and Reno's.

In October, Captain Dandy, quartermaster at Fort Phil Kearny, met with a group of Sioux, Cheyenne and Arapaho leaders on Big Piney, five hundred yards from the fort. Here were held the first preliminary talks toward an agreement for eventual abandonment of the three forts and closing of the Montana Road. The Indians agreed to cease all hostilities if the soldiers would leave the country north of the Platte and west of the Black Hills.

Red Cloud, however, was not a participant in this first council, and when the recalcitrant Sioux leader was sent a second invitation to come to Laramie in the spring for further talks, he replied disdainfully that he would sign no treaty until the garrisons at all three forts were withdrawn.

In April 1868, a full-fledged peace commission gathered at Laramie, and after lengthy parleys, representatives from the Brûlés, Oglalas, Miniconjous, Yanktonais, and Arapaho signed the new treaty. Again Red Cloud stayed away, and again he sent down word that he would not sign a peace treaty until the forts were abandoned and the road closed through the Powder River country.

On May 19, Major-General Augur issued an order to abandon "the military posts of C. F. Smith, Phil Kearny and Reno, on what is known as the Powder River route. . . . The public property at Fort C. F. Smith will be sold at public auction, and that at Fort Phil Kearny and Reno—commencing and finishing first with the former—will be transferred to such of the lower posts as the chief quartermaster of the department shall direct." [32] At last after two years of unyielding resistance, the enduring Sioux leader, Red Cloud, had won his war.

Dismantlement of the three forts began in early summer, and in August the last wagon train rolled out of Fort Phil Kearny. Records vary as to the exact date of abandonment—probably August 18 or 20—and there is also disagreement as to whether the soldiers or the Indians burned the fort. Some accounts say the soldiers put torches to the buildings; others say that Little Wolf led a party of warriors down from the hills and burned the fort before the departing wagons were out of sight on the Reno road. It must have been a cruel shock to Colonel Carrington when he learned that his beloved fort was gone. Under his exacting and proprietary eye, every post, board and shingle had been fashioned with mathematical exactness and placed in assigned positions to form his dream of an architecturally perfect fort. Now it was ashes.

By the end of August, the last soldiers had left Fort Reno, and the Montana Road was closed. On November 6, Red Cloud arrived at Fort Laramie, surrounded by a coterie of warriors. He had won everything he had fought for. Now, a conquering hero, he would sign the treaty.

For the first time in its history the United States Government had negotiated a peace which conceded everything demanded by the enemy and which exacted nothing in return. Through another stormy decade the Powder River country would belong to the Indians.

4.

In 1868, the year of the peace, Margaret Carrington published her story of Fort Phil Kearny, *Absaraka; Home of the Crows,* basing it largely upon the daily journal of experiences which she had kept at the suggestion of General Sherman. Two years later, Colonel Carrington retired from active military service and became a professor of military science at Wabash College, Crawfordsville, Indiana. That same year, 1870, Margaret Carrington died.

One of the interested readers of *Absaraka* was Frances Grummond, who after bidding the Carringtons farewell at Fort Laramie had continued her sad journey home to Franklin, Tennessee, to bury her husband and rejoin her family. In 1868, Frances traveled to Cincinnati to visit her sister, and there obtained a copy of the book, learning for the first time that the Carringtons were living in Indiana. When she later heard of the death of Margaret Carrington, she wrote a letter of condolence to the colonel. Ensuing correspondence between the two led to their marriage in 1871.

During the decade that Carrington spent at Wabash College, he continued his campaign to clear his reputation of all blame for the Fetterman Massacre. Even after Custer's disaster, which replaced the Fetterman affair in the public's memory, he persisted in bringing out new editions of his first wife's book (there were seven in all), revising and adding to the text so as to present his side of the story in minute detail.

In 1887, twenty years after the event, he at last persuaded the United States Senate to make public his official report and the transcript of his remarks before the commission of inquiry at Fort McPherson. After three strong demands from the Senate, these papers were finally dredged out of the cellar files of the Department of the Interior. With their publication, Carrington felt that he had secured at least a belated vindication.

By this late date many of the actors in the tragedy were dead or forgotten. Old military feuds, however, die hard. William Bisbee, for one, never forgave Carrington. Bisbee and Fetterman had been close friends during the Civil War, and Bisbee preferred to believe that Fetterman was blameless, and that Carrington had tried to shift the blame on Fetterman who was dead and could not reply. After leaving Phil Kearny in December 1866, Bisbee moved up in rank rapidly, becoming a brigadier-general in 1901. In later life he devoted considerable effort to defending Fetterman's reputation, even going so far as to gather statements from witnesses who contradicted Carrington's charge of disobedience, and placing these papers in the files of the Indian fighters' organization in Washington, the Order of Indian Wars.

The man who had done most to impugn Carrington's command abilities, General Philip St. George Cooke, waited until 1890 before admitting that he might have been wrong. "The country was greatly excited, and the government very urgent, so I endorsed the papers for transmission by one of my staff," Cooke explained to Carrington when the latter visited the general in Detroit. "I can do nothing more now than to express my deep pain at what transpired. My memory recalls nothing of the details, except that it was hurried off to General Sherman, and you must take my regrets as sincere, and my congratulations, that in the end you were fully vindicated."[33]

5.

In 1908 all survivors of the Fort Phil Kearny garrison of 1866 were invited to attend a special Independence Day celebration in the town of Sheridan, Wyoming. The Carringtons, well along in years by then, responded with enthusiasm, and at Sheridan they were joined by a small group of former enlisted men, scarcely enough to form a corporal's guard. Among those present were S. S. Peters, Sam Gibson, William Murphy, and William Daley.

On July 3 these honored guests were taken to the scene of the Fetterman disaster, to a monument which was to be dedicated on the slope where the last troopers of the 2nd Cavalry had died on December 21, 1866. A large crowd assembled there, most of them young men and women from the new towns which had been founded in the area during the four decades since Fort Phil Kearny had blazed into oblivion. They came in the rackety open touring cars of the period, on horseback, and in buggies gaily bedecked with holiday bunting.

The former enlisted men wore plain civilian suits, but Carrington was dressed in his old blue uniform, every brass button of his frock coat freshly burnished. His wide-brimmed campaign hat was set squarely on his head; his white beard was trimmed to a neat military cut. Standing straight as a parade-ground soldier, he launched into a dedicatory address, an hour-long speech which was essentially a spirited defense of his actions at Fort Phil Kearny, embroidered with a few mild attacks upon his ancient critics.

Those few in the audience who had been with him in 1866 listened patiently, but the thoughts of most of them must have gone rushing back to that other time. Surely it all seemed like a strange dream to Frances Grummond Carrington. She sat in the seat of a buggy drawn up near the small stone monument, a sturdy little old lady in a starched white shirtwaist and a dark ruffled skirt. Her hat—a sort of toque with a magnificent plume—was set at a jaunty angle. She listened to the words of the man who was her husband, but he spoke of a time when the love of her life had been George Grummond, long dead, George Grummond who had died bravely on the rocky slope where the crowd—so lighthearted, so free of danger—listened now in the glaring summer sunlight.

Former Private William Murphy remembered the hard days of toil, the hot summer, the cold bitter winter, scanty rations, the constant dread of Indian attack. For Sam Gibson, the scene deepest seared into his memory was the day of the Wagon Box Fight, when he had watched the Indians charge and charge again, and each time they came on with their war cries he had said what he thought was his last prayer on earth. S. S. Peters remembered Crazy Woman's Fork, every detail of every minute of that long day-and-night surround which began with the ambush of Lieutenants Daniels and Templeton and ended with Chaplain White's dash for help. The high moment in William Daley's memory was the bright October day when he had raised the first flag above Fort Phil Kearny.

They waited respectfully until Carrington closed his speech, his voice showing weariness at the end, his shoulders stooping a little. When a bugler sounded taps and Carrington uncovered, someone stepped forward with a parasol to shield the old man's head from the sun.

As soon as the dedication formalities ended, the crowd moved to the site of the fort where a staff had been erected on the former parade ground for a flag-raising ceremony. The tall pole stood in the midst of a field of alfalfa growing lush and green from the waters of irrigation ditches. Few traces remained of the stockade, quartermaster yard, officers' quarters and barracks. It was as if the fort had never existed, had been only a dream common to those who remembered it.

Standing knee-deep in alfalfa, the survivors gathered at the base of the flagstaff, and William Daley—who had raised the first flag—was given the honor of raising this one. Afterward the colonel politely pointed out landmarks for the young spectators; the former enlisted men recalled a few incidents long forgotten. The guests of honor seemed to enjoy their day of glory.

But they knew it was all gone, the old harsh leathery life, the sweet zest of danger, the toil and uncertainty. It was all gone and soon they would be gone, too, with the vanished fort. Only a myth remained, a few dreamlike memories of the saga they had helped to create.

Bibliography

Army and Navy Journal, Volumes 4–5, 1866–68.

Birge, Julius C., *The Awakening of the Desert.* Boston, Richard G. Badger, 1912.

Bisbee, William H., "Items of Indian Service." Order of Indian Wars of the United States, *Proceedings,* 1928.

Bisbee, William H., *Through Four American Wars.* Boston, 1931.

Boehmer, George A., Unpublished notebook. Bureau of American Ethnology, Smithsonian Institution.

"Bradley Manuscript." *Contributions to the Historical Society of Montana,* Vol. 8, 1917, 223–24.

Brady, Cyrus T., "Indian Fights and Fighters; the Tragedy of Fort Phil Kearny," *Pearson's Magazine,* Vol. 11, 1904, 211–24.

Bratt, John, *Trails of Yesterday.* Lincoln, Nebraska, University Publishing Co., 1921.

Brown, Dee, and Martin F. Schmitt, *Trail Driving Days.* New York, Scribner's, 1952.

Brown, Jesse, "The Freighter in Early Days." *Annals of Wyoming,* Vol. 17, 1947, 112.

Bryant, Thomas J., "Harry S. Yount." *Annals of Wyoming,* Vol. 3, 1925, 164–75.

Burt, Struthers, *Powder River.* New York, Farrar and Rinehart, 1938.

Carrington, Frances C., *My Army Life.* Philadelphia, Lippincott, 1911.

Carrington, Henry B., *The Indian Question.* Boston, De Wolfe and Fiske, 1909.

Carrington, James B., "Across the Plains with Bridger as Guide." *Scribner's Magazine,* Vol. 85, 1929, 66–71.

Carrington, Margaret Irvin, *Absaraka, Home of the Crows.* Philadelphia, Lippincott, 1878.

Cook, James H., *Fifty Years on the Old Frontier.* New Haven, Yale, 1923.

David, Robert B., *Finn Burnett, Frontiersman*. Glendale, Calif., A. H. Clark, 1937.

De Land, Charles E., "The Sioux Wars." *South Dakota Historical Collections*, Vol. 15, 1930.

Dunn, J. P., *Massacres of the Mountains; a History of the Indian Wars of the Far West*. New York, Harper, 1886.

Ellison, R. S., "John 'Portugee' Phillips and His Famous Ride." *Old Travois Trails*, Vol. 2, No. 1, 1941.

Evans, Major W. H., Letter to Major Roger Jones, May 21, 1866. *Annals of Wyoming*, Vol. 9, 1932, 752–54.

Fox, George W., "Diary." *Annals of Wyoming*, Vol. 8, 1932, 580–601.

Frackelton, William, "Prelude to Fred Newcomer." *Old Travois Trails*, Vol. 2, No. 2, 1941.

Gatchell, T. J., "Events of the Year 1865." *Annals of Wyoming*, Vol. 27, 1955, 142–58.

Gatchell, T. J., "Life of John Ryan." *Annals of Wyoming*, Vol. 31, 1959, 48–52.

Glover, Ridgway, Letters to Editor of *Philadelphia Photographer*, Vol. 3, 1866.

Gordon, David S., "The Relief of Fort Phil Kearny." *Journal of the Military Service Institutions of the U. S.*, Vol. 49, 1911, 281–84.

Grinnell, George B., *The Fighting Cheyennes*. Norman, University of Oklahoma Press, 1956.

Guthrie, John, "The Fetterman Massacre." *Annals of Wyoming*, Vol. 9, 1932, 714–18.

Hafen, LeRoy R., and F. M. Young, *Fort Laramie and the Pageant of the West*. Glendale, Calif., A. H. Clark, 1938.

Hebard, Grace R., "James Bridger." *The Frontier*, Vol. 9, 1929, 145–48.

Hebard, Grace R., and E. A. Brininstool, *The Bozeman Trail*. Cleveland, A. H. Clark, 1922. 2 vols.

Hunton, John, "History of the Old Sutler Store Coins." *Fort Laramie Scout*, Dec. 12, 1928.

Hunton, John, Letter to Grace Raymond Hebard, Fort Laramie, Wyoming, February 20, 1919. *The Frontier*, Vol. 11, 1931, 176.

Jones, Hoyle, "Seth E. Ward." *Annals of Wyoming*, Vol. 5, 1927, 5–12.

Murphy, William, "The Forgotten Battalion." *Annals of Wyoming*, Vol. 7, 1930, 383–401.

Ostrander, Alson B., *An Army Boy of the Sixties*. Yonkers, N. Y., World Book Co., 1924.

Palmer, H. E., "History of the Powder River Indian Expedition of 1865." *Nebraska State Historical Society, Transactions*, Vol. 2, 1887, 197–229.

Parry, Henry C., "Letters from the Frontier." *Annals of Wyoming,* Vol. 30, 1958, 127–48.

"Peno Creek." *Annals of Wyoming,* Vol. 4, 1926, 317.

Richardson, Warren, "Tribute to John Phillips." *Annals of Wyoming,* Vol. 27, 1955, 183–86.

Robinson, Doane, "A History of the Dakota or Sioux Indians." South Dakota Department of History, *Collections,* Vol. 2, 1904.

Schreibeis, Charles D., "The Old Saw Mill." *Old Travois Trails,* Vol. 1, No. 3, 1940.

Schreibeis, Charles D., "The Tragedy of Fort Philip Kearny." *Old Travois Trails,* Vol. 1, No. 6, 1941.

Schreibeis, Charles D., "The Tragedy of Fort Philip Kearny." *Westerners' Brand Book,* Denver Posse, Vol. 7, 1951, 337–62.

Shockley, Lieutenant P. M., "A Forgotten Hero; a Tale of Old Phil Kearny." *Quartermaster Review,* Vol. 12, July–August, 1932, 17–20.

Shockley, Lieutenant P. M., "Fort Phil Kearny, the Fetterman Massacre." *Quartermaster Review,* Vol. 11, May–June 1932, 27–32.

Story, Byron, "The First Cattle up from Texas." *American Cattle Producer,* Vol. 20, No. 6, November 1938, 6–7.

U. S. Congress. 39th. 1st sess. House. *Wagon Road from Niobrara to Virginia City.* (Executive Document 58) Washington, D. C., 1866.

U. S. Congress. 39th. 2nd sess. House. *Message of the President.* (Executive Document 1) Washington, D. C., 1867.

U. S. Congress. 40th. 1st sess. Senate. *Indian Hostilities.* (Executive Document 13) Washington, D. C., 1868.

U. S. Congress. 50th. 1st sess. Senate. *Indian Operations on the Plains.* (Executive Document 33) Washington, D. C., 1888.

U. S. Interior Department. *Annual Report on Indian Affairs, 1867.* Washington, D. C., 1868.

U. S. War Department, Department of the Platte. Letter Book No. 1, 1866. National Archives.

U. S. War Department, 18th Infantry Regiment. Muster Rolls and Record of Events, April 1866–July 1867. National Archives.

U. S. War Department, Fort Philip Kearny, Dakota Territory. Board of Survey Orders, September 1866–July 1867. National Archives.

U. S. War Department, Fort Philip Kearny, Dakota Territory. Post Returns, July 1866–July 1867. National Archives.

U. S. War Department. *The War of the Rebellion: A Compilation of the Official Records,* Series I, Vol. 38, Pt. 1; Vol. 48, Pt. 2.

Vestal, Stanley, *Jim Bridger.* New York, Morrow, 1946.

Vestal, Stanley, *Warpath, the True Story of the Fighting Sioux*. Boston, Houghton Mifflin, 1934.

Watson, Elmo Scott, "The Bravery of Our Bugler Is Much Spoken Of." *Old Travois Trails*, Vol. I, No. 6, 1941.

Wellman, Paul, *The Trampling Herd*. New York, Carrick and Evans, 1939.

Young, Otis E., *The West of Philip St. George Cooke, 1809–1895*. Glendale, Calif., A. H. Clark, 1955.

Notes

CHAPTER I: APRIL

1. U. S. Congress. 50th. 1st sess. Senate executive document 33, 1.
2. Murphy, 390.
3. U. S. Congress. 39th. 1st sess. House executive document 58.
4. U. S. War Dept. *The War of the Rebellion ... Official Records*, Ser. I, Vol. 48, Pt. 2, 356.
5. *Army and Navy Journal*, October 13, 1866, Vol. 4, 125.
6. U. S. Congress. 50th. 1st sess. Senate executive document 33, 51.
7. *Ibid.*, 53.
8. Young, 323–25.
9. U. S. Congress. 50th. 1st sess. Senate executive document 33, 2.
10. *Ibid.*, 2–3.

Other sources used for background material: Birge, 188; Bisbee, "Items," 23; Brady, 213; M. Carrington, 263; Dunn, 479, 483; Grinnell, 208, 230; Hafen and Young, 351; Hebard and Brininstool, Vol. I, 342; Ostrander, 266–67; Palmer, 219, 221.

CHAPTER II: MAY

1. U. S. Congress. 50th. 1st sess. Senate executive document 33, 3.
2. Bisbee, *Through Four American Wars*, 161.
3. M. Carrington, 42.
4. *Ibid.*, 41.
5. Murphy, 383.
6. M. Carrington, 38.
7. J. Carrington, 70.
8. M. Carrington, 43.
9. Bisbee, 162–63.
10. J. Carrington, 71.
11. *Kearney Herald,* January 6, 1866.
12. Bisbee, 162.
13. Palmer, 213.

14. Murphy, 383.
15. Bisbee, "Items of Indian Service," 26.
16. Hebard and Brininstool, II, 89–90.
17. Murphy, 383.

Other sources used for background material: Brady, 224; Parry, 131; U. S. War Dept., 18th Infantry Regiment, Muster Rolls and Record of Events, April–May 1866; Vestal, *Jim Bridger*, 224, 246.

CHAPTER III: JUNE

1. U. S. Congress. 50th. 1st sess. Senate executive document 33, 5.
2. M. Carrington, 59.
3. Bisbee, *Through Four American Wars*, 163.
4. Murphy, 383.
5. M. Carrington, 46.
6. U. S. Congress. 50th. 1st sess. Senate executive document 33, 3.
7. M. Carrington, 70.
8. U. S. Congress. 50th. 1st sess. Senate executive document 33, 3–4.
9. *Ibid.*, 4.
10. *Ibid.*, 5.
11. *Ibid.*, 6.
12. *Ibid.*, 8.
13. M. Carrington, 76.
14. Hunton, John, "History of the Old Sutler Store Coins," *Fort Laramie Scout*, Dec. 12, 1918.
15. U. S. Congress. 50th. 1st sess. Senate executive document 33, 18; M. Carrington, 79.
16. H. B. Carrington, 3; M. Carrington, 79–80.
17. F. Carrington, 124–25.
18. *Ibid.*, 125.
19. Birge, 181.
20. Murphy, 384.
21. Bisbee, "Items of Indian Service," 26.
22. Glover, 239–40.
23. U. S. Congress. 50th. 1st sess. Senate executive document 33, 6.
24. M. Carrington, 80.
25. Dunn, 485.
26. M. Carrington, 94.
27. *Ibid.*, 83.
28. *Ibid.*, 84.
29. U. S. Congress. 50th. 1st sess. Senate executive document 33, 4–5.
30. Murphy, 384.
31. M. Carrington, 90.

32. *Ibid.*, 91–92.

33. Gatchell, "Events of the Year 1865," *Annals of Wyoming*, Vol. 27, 1955, 156.

34. Gatchell, "Life of John Ryan," *Annals of Wyoming*, Vol. 31, 1959, 48–52.

35. Murphy, 384.

36. U. S. Congress. 50th. 1st sess. Senate executive document 33, 7; M. Carrington, 95.

37. Murphy.

38. U. S. Congress. 50th. 1st sess. Senate executive document 33.

Other sources used for background material: Brady, 211–213; David, 120; Evans, 752; Fox, 589; Hafen and Young, 341–50; Jones, 6; Ostrander, 101–114, 134–141; Schreibeis, "The Old Saw Mill," 21; U. S. Congress, 40th, 1st sess., Senate executive document 13, 61–63, 106–108, 134; U. S. War Dept., 18th Infantry Regt., Muster Rolls and Record of Events, June 1866; Vestal, *Jim Bridger*, 249, 318.

CHAPTER IV: JULY

1. U. S. Congress. 50th. 1st sess. Senate executive document 33, 16.

2. Murphy, 385.

3. *Ibid.*

4. M. Carrington, 25–26.

5. Bisbee, *Through Four American Wars*, 168.

6. J. B. Carrington, 70.

7. M. Carrington, 101.

8. U. S. Congress. 50th. 1st sess. Senate executive document 33, 9.

9. M. Carrington, 101.

10. U. S. Congress. 50th. 1st sess. Senate executive document 33, 13.

11. *Ibid.*, 9.

12. *Ibid.*

13. Murphy, 386.

14. U. S. Congress. 50th. 1st sess. Senate executive document 33, 14.

15. M. Carrington 29, 107.

16. H. B. Carrington, 9.

17. M. Carrington, 112–15.

18. *Ibid.*, 115.

19. U. S. Congress. 50th. 1st sess. Senate executive document 33, 10.

20. Hebard and Brininstool, I, 264.

21. U. S. Congress. 50th. 1st sess. Senate executive document 33, 12.

22. Murphy, 386.

23. Bisbee, "Items of Indian Service," 27.

24. Murphy, 386.

25. Gatchell, "Life of John Ryan," 49.

26. Bisbee, 27.

27. M. Carrington, 184–85.

28. Murphy, 386.

29. Ostrander, 149.

30. Murphy, 387.

31. U. S. Congress. 50th. 1st sess. Senate executive document 33, 11.

32. Hebard and Brininstool, II, 90.

33. Glover, 339.

34. F. Carrington, 74–75.

35. *Ibid.*, 76.

36. *Ibid.*

37. *Ibid.*, 77–78.

38. Glover, 339.

39. F. Carrington, 78.

40. Hebard and Brininstool, II, 91.

41. F. Carrington, 79–80.

42. *Ibid.*, 80.

43. Hebard and Brininstool, II, 92.

44. U. S. Congress. 50th. 1st sess. Senate executive document 33, 13.

45. Glover, 339.

46. Hebard and Brininstool, II, 94.

47. U. S. Congress. 50th. 1st sess. Senate executive document 33, 55.

48. Hebard and Brininstool, II, 93.

49. U. S. Congress. 50th. 1st sess. Senate executive document 33, 12–13.

50. *Ibid.*, 13, 16.

Other sources used for background material: *Army and Navy Journal*, Vol. 4, 215, 642; Brady, 215; Brown, 112–16; Bryant, 166, 173; Burt, 120, 123; David, 121; De Land, 65, 77; Dunn, 480, 486; Fox, 589; Palmer, 209; Schreibeis, "The Old Saw Mill," 10–11, 20; U. S. War Dept., 18th Infantry Regiment, Muster Rolls and Record of Events, July 1866; U. S. War Dept., Fort Philip Kearny, Dakota Territory, Post Returns, July 1866; U. S. War Dept., Dept. of the Platte, Letter Book No. 1, 1866; Vestal, *Jim Bridger*, 252, 259, 261–68.

CHAPTER V: AUGUST

1. U. S. Congress. 50th. 1st sess. Senate executive document 33, 18.

2. U. S. War Dept., 18th Infantry Regiment. Muster Rolls and Record of Events, August 1866.

3. U. S. Congress. 50th. 1st sess. Senate executive document 33, 20.

4. Hebard, "James Bridger," 145–48.

5. *Army and Navy Journal*, December 29, 1866, Vol. 4, 294.

6. Fox, 594.

7. F. Carrington, 97.

8. *Army and Navy Journal*, November 3, 1866, Vol. 4, 169.

9. M. Carrington, 141–42.

10. U. S. War Dept., 18th Infantry Regiment. Muster Rolls and Record of Events, August 1866.

11. U. S. Congress. 50th. 1st sess. Senate executive document 33, 44.

12. Boehmer, George A., Unpublished notebook. Bureau of American Ethnology, Smithsonian Institution.

13. U. S. Congress. 40th. 1st sess. Senate executive document 13, 36.

14. U. S. Congress. 50th. 1st sess. Senate executive document 33, 17.

15. *Ibid.*, 17–18.

16. *Army and Navy Journal*, November 17, 1866, Vol. 4, 198.

17. Hebard and Brininstool, I, 286.

18. Glover, 367–69.

19. U. S. Congress. 50th. 1st sess. Senate executive document 33, 18, 48.

Other sources used for background material: Dunn, 487, 503; Shockley, "Fort Phil Kearny," 28; U. S. War Dept., Fort Philip Kearny, Post Returns, August 1866.

CHAPTER VI: SEPTEMBER

1. U. S. Congress. 50th. 1st sess. Senate executive document 33, 23.

2. U. S. War Dept., Fort Phil Kearny, Dakota Territory. Board of Survey Orders, September 1866.

3. U. S. Congress. 50th. 1st sess. Senate executive document 33, 22.

4. *Ibid.*, 23.

5. U. S. War Dept., Fort Phil Kearny, Dakota Territory. Post Returns, December 1866; Hebard and Brininstool, II, 98.

6. Bratt, 87–94.

7. U. S. Congress. 50th. 1st sess. Senate executive document 33, 24.

8. *Ibid.*, 28.

9. *Ibid.*, 22.

10. Gatchell, "Life of John Ryan," 50.

11. Hebard and Brininstool, II, 96–97.

12. Bisbee, *Through Four American Wars*, 170.

13. Gatchell, 50.

14. U. S. Congress. 50th. 1st sess. Senate executive document 33, 24.

15. F. Carrington, 85–86.

16. U. S. Congress. 50th. 1st sess. Senate executive document 33, 30.

17. *Ibid.*, 23–25.

18. F. Carrington, 90.

19. U. S. War Dept., Dept. of the Platte. Letter Book No. 1, 1866.

20. F. Carrington, 121.

21. U. S. Congress. 50th. 1st sess. Senate executive document 33, 25.

22. U. S. War Dept., 18th Infantry Regiment. Muster Rolls and Record of Events, September 1866.

23. U. S. Congress. 50th. 1st sess. Senate executive document 33, 28–29.

24. Hebard and Brininstool, I, 99.

25. U. S. Congress. 50th. 1st sess. Senate executive document 33, 25.

26. *Ibid.*, 25–27.

27. M. Carrington, 159–60.

28. U. S. Congress. 50th. 1st sess. Senate executive document 33, 29.

Other sources used for background material: Bisbee, "Items," 28; David, 123–124; Dunn, 487; Ostrander, 255; Schreibeis, "Tragedy of Fort Phil Kearny," *Old Travois Trails*, 6; Shockley, "Fort Phil Kearny," 28; Vestal, *Jim Bridger*, 266–67.

CHAPTER VII: OCTOBER

1. U. S. Congress. 50th. 1st sess. Senate executive document 33, 32.

2. U. S. War Dept., Fort Philip Kearny, Dakota Territory. Board of Survey Orders, October 1866.

3. U. S. Congress. 50th. 1st sess. Senate executive document 33, 32.

4. *Ibid.*, 31.

5. *Ibid.*, 46.

6. U. S. Congress. 40th. 1st sess. Senate executive document 13, 31.

7. U. S. Congress. 50th. 1st sess. Senate executive document 33, 32.

8. Story, 6–7.

9. Wellman, 95–100; Brown and Schmitt, 179–181.

10. U. S. Congress. 50th. 1st sess. Senate executive document 33, 32–33.

11. *Ibid.*, 32.

12. M. Carrington, 172.

13. Murphy, 386.

14. M. Carrington, 151.

15. *Ibid.*, 152–56.

16. F. Carrington, 116–17.

17. U. S. War Dept., 18th Infantry Regiment. Muster Rolls and Record of Events, October 1866.

18. M. Carrington, 156.

Other sources used for background material: *Army and Navy Journal*, Vol. 4, 214, 236; Brady, 217; Burt, 120; Hebard and Brininstool, I, 289, 293; II, 94; Ostrander, 255; Shockley, "Fort Phil Kearny," 27–32; U. S. War Dept., Fort Philip Kearny, Dakota Territory, Post Returns, October 1866; Young, 345–49.

CHAPTER VIII: NOVEMBER

1. U. S. Congress. 50th. 1st sess. Senate executive document 33, 47.

2. Bratt, 96–98.

3. U. S. War Dept. *The War of the Rebellion ... Official Records*, Ser. I, Vol. 38, Pt. I, 94, 527, 558, 560, 577–78, 586–88.

4. U. S. Congress. 50th. 1st sess. Senate executive document 33, 34.

5. *Ibid.*, 20–21.

6. *Ibid.*, 21.

7. M. Carrington, 171; Hebard and Brininstool, I, 305.

8. F. Carrington, 120.

9. *Ibid.*, 96.

10. U. S. Congress. 50th. 1st sess. Senate executive document 33, 33; F. Carrington, 111.

11. *Army and Navy Journal*, November 3, 1866, Vol. 4, 169.

12. U. S. Congress. 50th. 1st sess. Senate executive document, 33, 34.

13. Murphy, 391.

14. Bisbee, *Through Four American Wars*, 172–73.

15. F. Carrington, 122.

16. U. S. Congress. 50th. 1st sess. Senate executive document 33, 34–35.

17. *Ibid.*, 36.

Other sources used for background material: Bisbee, "Items," 29–30; "Bradley Manuscript," 223–24; Burt, 127; Gatchell, "Life of John Ryan," 51; Ostrander 137, 191–95, 260; U. S. Congress, 40th, 1st sess., Senate executive document 13, 41–42, 63; U. S. War Dept., Dept. of the Platte, Letter Book No. 1, 1866; U. S. War Dept., 18th Infantry Regiment, Muster Rolls and Record of Events, November 1866; U. S. War Dept., Fort Philip Kearny, Dakota Territory, Post Returns, November 1866; Vestal, *Jim Bridger*, 273.

CHAPTER IX: DECEMBER

1. U. S. Congress. 50th. 1st sess. Senate executive document 33, 49.

2. *Ibid.*, 47.

3. U. S. Congress. 39th. 2nd sess. House. *Message of the President* (Executive document 1) Washington, D. C., 1867.

4. U. S. Congress. 50th. 1st sess. Senate executive document 33, 37.

5. *Ibid.*

6. *Ibid.*, 38.

7. Bisbee, "Items," 29.

8. U. S. Congress. 40th. 1st sess. Senate executive document 13, 37–38.

9. *Ibid.*, 14.

10. Guthrie, 718.

11. *Ibid.*

12. Murphy, 389; Hebard and Brininstool, II, 99.

13. F. Carrington, 134.

14. M. Carrington, 194.

15. Vestal, *Jim Bridger*, 270.

16. *Old Travois Trails*, Vol. 3, No. 3, 1942, 65.

17. Bisbee, *Through Four American Wars*, 176.

18. U. S. Congress. 50th. 1st sess. Senate executive document 33, 36–38.

19. *Ibid.*, 39; F. Carrington, 135.

20. U. S. Congress. 40th. 1st sess. Senate executive document 13, 38; U. S. Congress. 50th. 1st sess. Senate executive document 33, 39.

21. U. S. Congress. 50th. 1st sess. Senate executive document 33, 39.

22. Vestal, *Jim Bridger*, 273; M. Carrington, 202.

23. U. S. Congress. 50th. 1st sess. Senate executive document 33, 40.

24. F. Carrington, 143.

25. *Ibid.*, 143–44.

26. U. S. Congress. 50th. 1st sess. Senate executive document 33, 44.

27. Grinnell, 243–44.

28. U. S. Congress. 50th. 1st sess. Senate executive document 33, 45.

29. U. S. Congress. 40th. 1st sess. Senate executive document 13, 64.

30. Murphy, 389–90.

31. U. S. Congress. 40th. 1st sess. Senate executive document 13, 15.

32. U. S. Congress. 50th. 1st sess. Senate executive document 33, 45.

33. F. Carrington, 146.

34. U. S. Congress. 50th. 1st sess. Senate executive document 33, 46.

35. *Ibid.*

36. Murphy, 390.

37. U. S. Congress. 40th. 1st sess. Senate executive document 13, 15.

38. Murphy, 390–91.

39. U. S. Congress. 50th. 1st sess. Senate executive document 33, 41.

40. Guthrie, 717.

41. U. S. Congress. 40th. 1st sess. Senate executive document 13, 15.

42. U. S. Congress. 50th. 1st sess. Senate executive document 33, 45.

43. F. Carrington, 146–47.

44. Hebard and Brininstool, II, 101–102.

45. J. Carrington, 71.

46. Hebard and Brininstool, II, 101–102.

47. F. Carrington, 149.

48. U. S. Congress. 50th. 1st sess. Senate executive document 33, 49–50.

49. U. S. Congress. 40th. 1st sess. Senate executive document 13, 35.

50. Hunton, John, Letter to Grace R. Hebard. *The Frontier*, Vol. II, 1931, 376.

51. U. S. Congress. 50th. 1st sess. Senate executive document 33, 44.

52. Shockley, "A Forgotten Hero," 17–20; Burt, 128–30; Ostrander, 168.

53. Ostrander, 169.

54. H. B. Carrington, 8.

55. F. Carrington, 151.

56. *Ibid.*, 152.

57. *Ibid.*, 153–54.

58. David, 129.

59. Guthrie, 717.

60. H. B. Carrington, 16.

61. David, 127.

62. *Army and Navy Journal*, April 13, 1867, Vol. 4, 546.

63. U. S. Congress. 40th. 1st sess. Senate executive document 13, 65.

64. Guthrie, 717.

65. F. Carrington, 155.

66. David, 129.

67. F. Carrington, 155, 158.

68. U. S. Congress. 40th. 1st sess. Senate executive document 13, 35.

69. *Ibid.*, 24–25.

70. Gordon, 281.

Other sources used for background material: "Bradley Manuscript," 223; Brady, 219–22; Cook, 229; Dunn, 492–99; Ellison, 5–15; "Peno Creek," 317–18; Richardson, 185–86; Robinson, 360, 363; U. S. War Dept., 18th Infantry Regiment, Muster Rolls and Record of Events, December 1866; U. S. War Dept., Fort Philip Kearny, Dakota Territory, Post Returns, December 1866; Vestal, *Warpath, the True Story of the Fighting Sioux*, 51–68.

CHAPTER X: JANUARY

1. U. S. Congress. 50th. 1st sess. Senate executive document 33, 49.

2. U. S. Congress. 40th. 1st sess. Senate executive document 13, 36.

3. U. S. Congress. 50th. 1st sess. Senate executive document 33, 42–43.

4. *Ibid.*, 39–41.

5. F. Carrington, 164.

6. U. S. Congress. 40th. 1st sess. Senate executive document 13, 28.

7. *Ibid.*, 29.

8. *Ibid.*

9. Gordon, 281–84.

10. *Ibid.*

11. U. S. Congress. 50th. 1st sess. Senate executive document 33, 44.

12. *Ibid.*, 49.

13. F. Carrington, 187–89.

Other sources used for background material: *Army and Navy Journal*, Vol. 4, 411, 413; "Bradley Manuscript," 223–24; Brady, 217; M. Carrington, 211–43; Hafen and Young, 353; Hebard and Brininstool, I, 330; Robinson, 371; Shockley, "Fort Phil Kearny," 28; U. S. War Dept., 18th Infantry Regiment, Muster Rolls and Record of Events, December 1866–January 1867.

CHAPTER XI: AFTERMATH

1. M. Carrington, 220–21.
2. U. S. Congress. 40th. 1st sess. Senate executive document 13, 8–9.
3. *Ibid.,* 16.
4. *Army and Navy Journal,* January 5, 1867, Vol. 4, 317.
5. U. S. Congress. 40th. 1st sess. Senate executive document 13, 40.
6. *Army and Navy Journal,* February 9, 1867, Vol. 4, 397.
7. U. S. Congress. 40th. 1st sess. Senate executive document 13, 7.
8. *Ibid.,* 55.
9. U. S. Congress. 50th. 1st sess. Senate executive document 33, 50.
10. *Ibid.,* 50.
11. *Army and Navy Journal,* June 29, 1867, Vol. 4, 714–15.
12. U. S. Congress. 40th. 1st sess. Senate executive document 13, 61–66.
13. *Army and Navy Journal,* February 16, 1867, Vol. 4, 406.
14. Shockley, "Fort Phil Kearny," 32.
15. Murphy, 392.
16. Gordon, 283.
17. David, 135.
18. Shockley, 32.
19. Hebard and Brininstool, II, 105.
20. Murphy, 392.
21. *Ibid.*
22. Shockley, 32.
23. *Ibid.*
24. Gordon, 283.
25. U. S. War Dept., Fort Philip Kearny, Dakota Territory. Post Returns, March 1867.
26. *Ibid.,* May 1867.
27. *Army and Navy Journal,* February 16, 1867, Vol. 4, 406.
28. Murphy, 392.
29. *Army and Navy Journal,* May 2, 1868, Vol. 5, 582.
30. Hebard and Brininstool, II, 54.
31. *Ibid.,* 66–67.
32. *Army and Navy Journal,* May 30, 1868, Vol. 5, 646.
33. Carrington, H. B., Letter to George Coutant, June 6, 1902. (Hebard and Brininstool, I, 340–41.)

Other sources used for background material: Bisbee, "Items," 31–32; Bisbee, *Through Four American Wars,* 175; Brady, 382; Burt, 139; F. Carrington, 217; De Land, 203; Dunn, 500–04; Frackelton, 24; Grinnell, 244; Guthrie, 718; U. S. Interior Department, *Annual Report on Indian Affairs,* 1867, 231; U. S. War Dept., 18th Infantry Regiment, Muster Rolls and Record of Events, February–July 1867; Vestal, *Jim Bridger,* 292–94.

Index